GUBU
NATION

Grotesque Unbelievable Bizarre Unprecedented Happenings in Ireland

GUBU (gu-bu) acronym for Grotesque Unbelievable Bizarre Unprecedented. Conveying amused disbelief. [C20 Hiberno-English] See also 'Bloody Hell!' and 'Crikey!'.

GUBU
NATION

**Grotesque Unbelievable
Bizarre Unprecedented
Happenings in Ireland**

Damian Corless

MERLIN
PUBLISHING

First published in 2004 by
Merlin Publishing
16 Upper Pembroke Street
Dublin 2, Ireland
Tel: +353 1 676 4373
Fax: +353 1 676 4368
publishing@merlin.ie

ISBN 1-903582-57-1

A CIP catalogue record for this book is available from the British Library.

5 4 3 2 1

Typeset by Carrigboy Typesetting Services
Cover Design by Faye Keegan Design
Printed and Bound in Denmark by AIT Nørhaven A/S

CONTENTS

Acknowledgements vii

It Is Important to Reassure People 1

Did You Ever Go Over a Hill in a Car Real Quick? 7

He Kept Smiling and Wanking at Us 13

The Family Tried to Stop Him Watching 18

The Common Market Applied to Light Music 22

Happy As a Pig in Muck 28

You'd Be Barred from Making Love in the
        Underwater City 33

You'd Think We Were in Fucking Casablanca 39

The Bishop Requests You Do Not Attend 43

A Row in the House 47

He Believed He Was Going to Be the Next Jeffrey Archer 51

The Screws Were All Astounded 59

If My Wife Only Had One of Yours I'd Die Happy 64

We'd Never Have Gotten to the Bottom of It 67

Moral Depravity, My Lord 75

Only Messing . . . 79

I Don't Know Anything About These Singing Groups 83

Obviously There's Been a Lot of Atrocities Off the Pitch 87

Shrubs Were Also Pulled Up 94

Boogie Mama Boogie, You Wild Bitch 99

This Kind of Near the Borderline Activity Won't Do 103

They'll Go Wild For This in America 107

People Will Get Drunk . . . 117

Radio Downtown Fucking Burbank 120

I Will Have You Shot 129

A Fairly Average Reputation For Religious Tolerance 133

They Said It Couldn't Be Done 139

It Is an Unpleasant Duty to Criticise Foul Play   143
There Are Certain Things in Life That Certain
    Other Things Just Don't Apply To   149
Coup D'État of the Yahoos   153
The Third Most Famous Woman in Britain   158
Armchair Liberals Who Sit at Home Condemning
    Apartheid   161
A Midnight Swoop on a Congested Area   165
When Irish Teeth Are Smiling   171
An Incitement to Crime   177
This Is National Mood Day   181
They're a Pack of Foreigners   186
The Murderers of the Children of Dublin   191
A Lot Better Than Shovelling Gravel For a Living   195
No Man of Spirit Would Have Done Otherwise   205
Only a Shower of Wife-Swopping Sodomites   211
Van Morrison, I Take It, Are a Group   215
We Have Been Committing National Hari-Kiri For
    Generations   222
Every Name Under the Sun   230
Who Will Mind Their Children If They Are Elected?   235
God Save Ireland from Intellectuals   242
White Shoes, Wind Jammers, the Hair All Fixed   249
Fluky Weather in Dublin Bay   253
Ask the Medical Men to Sleep with a Girl
    Who Has AIDS   258
Catholics Interfering in Ulster Since 1641   262
Who Does That Fucking Nigger Think He Is!?!   269
We Have Our Own People Going to America   273
'The Greatest Bleeding Heart Racket in the World'   277
Her Shapely Little Bottom on a Chair in Stephen's
    Green   299
This Could Be of Major World Importance   304
There's a Big Fellow Called Salvador   308

ACKNOWLEDGEMENTS

To Martin & Kathleen. Mary, Ivan, Anne Marie, Ashlinn, Helen, Toon, Sophie, Oliver Nanook Norp and an assortment of O'Rourkes. I'm indebted to Kevin Hamilton & John Ryan for their work on the prototype. For their help with the present volume I'd like to thank Ian O'Doherty, Artie Mathews, Paul Woodfull, Graham Linehan, Brian Hanley & Emmett O'Reilly. At Merlin, Aoife Barrett, Chenile Keogh & Julie Dobson were wizard! Thanks to Joan Fitzpatrick, Peter Carvosso, Peter Reilly & Alan O'Brien. Finally, I'd just like to register my admiration for the talent and integrity of ace journalists Brian Boyd, Ken Sweeney, Jonathan O'Brien, Nick Kelly and Aiden Lambert, and to thank them in advance for their continued support.

For source materials, I plundered the vaults of the Gilbert Library in Pearse Street, the National Library and the National Archive. Individual writers I've drawn upon include Tim Pat Coogan, Sam Smyth, Eoin Dillon, Kate Shanahan, Declan Lynch, Eoin Hennigan, Fearghal O'Connor, Pat Brennan, Tim Ryan and Michael Nugent.

IT IS IMPORTANT TO REASSURE PEOPLE

Joe Jacob TD Vs Nuclear Hysteria.

Who? The Junior Minister for nuclear emergencies.
When? Late September 2001, two weeks after 9/11.
What? A jittery Irish public needed its nerves soothed.
Where? Marian Finucane's underground bunker studio.
Why? Fears were rife that Sellafield might be destroyed.

It was late September, 2001. The world had changed. With the charred remains of the Twin Towers still smouldering, US forces began landing at Shannon Airport on their way to take out the Taliban. This stealthy act of Irish hospitality took on a less cosy hue when the World Health Organisation put all Western states on red alert against chemical or biological attack by the agents of Osama bin Laden.

On behalf of a jittery public, the *Marian Finucane Show* attempted to find out what measures were in place to cope with a worst case scenario. After being shunted around six or seven government departments, the show's researchers drew a blank. An unimpressed Marian let her listeners know about the wild goose chase.

The following morning, Joe Jacob, Junior Minister at the Department of Public Enterprise, stepped forward as the man with the plan. He told Marian: 'Immediately I heard about it I had my officials contact you and yours to explain the situation and offer myself this morning to come in to you and talk to your readers.' It was a minor slip, confusing 'readers' for 'listeners', but it began an enthralling banana skin slalom.

Joe Jacob had moved promptly to address the nation because, he explained: 'It is important to reassure people and know that there is in place a national emergency plan for nuclear accidents.'

His reassurances were grounded in hard work and foresight. He'd been working on the national emergency plan with 'the committee' for fully two and a half years. Together, they had devised 'a new plan, an updated plan, a state of the art plan'. Perhaps most reassuring of all, he told the listeners: 'It is in place.'

A dry-run, which would 'assimilate' real emergency conditions, would happen within four weeks. Shortly after that, every home in Ireland would receive 'a fact sheet that has been planned for two years'. The minister had come into the studio, he added, 'very qualified to talk to you about nuclear issues'.

The government had a plan, but when Marian sprung her own simulated emergency on Joe Jacob she uncorked the devil in the detail. 'Let's pretend,' she said, 'that Ireland had come under attack eight minutes ago, just as the show had gone on air. What instructions should the listeners be hearing?'

'Erm,' said the minister. 'Well, that information will be issued, based on the technical expertise that will assess the situation when it happens, the scale of the incident, the, the, the potential of the, the incident deteriorating or whatever.'

His host hit him with a for instance: 'Say it's a bad situation, say a plane crashed into Sellafield, say the wind was blowing this way and it happened eight minutes ago, what advice do we give our citizens and what happens?'

'I'm telling you that, if a plane crashed into Sellafield, we're talking about a very major accident there, something like a great power like the United States aren't geared to cope with last week. So we would tell people the situation and they would know from again this famous fact sheet that I'm talking about.'

Sounding somewhat less than fully assured, the presenter pressed him: 'But tell me what to do!'

'But I'm telling you what, what, that . . .'

Marian persisted: 'You are going to give me the fact sheet in a couple of weeks time and I'll read it, but I'm talking now and it happened nine minutes ago.'

'Nine minutes ago, and I'm telling you first of all information, emergency, through all means of communication such as I have issued, itemised . . . '

And so the clock ticked on. After hitting several more dead ends, Marian wanted to know what the plan had to say to those who found themselves in a car or bus when the hard rain began to fall.

'All right Marian, I'll tell you what to do and that's the first thing you would do and it's called sheltering.'

When the minister had outlined the procedure in question, Finucane wanted clarification on one point: 'What do you mean shelter?'

'Sheltering is the terminology we use for, what you say, remaining indoors, so that's communications.'

The mock emergency reached eleven minutes old. 'I hope we are making good ground,' ventured the minister. The presenter let that pass, but with fifteen minutes on the clock the plain people of Ireland were clamouring to give him their answer. 'The phones upstairs are going bananas,' said Marian.

By now, the listening nation had just found out from the minister that iodine tablets might come in handy for preventing death. Marian asked, on behalf of her audience, 'where and when these items might be had'.

'That will be in the fact sheet when it gets to your home,' the minister assured her. Marian wondered whether Joe Jacob himself actually knew what was in his famous fact sheet. He assured her: 'I have it in my hand, so I know exactly what's in the fact sheet.'

As the item wound to a finish, the switchboard was close to meltdown. The show's producer told Finucane through her headset to tell the multitude of callers that, no, they were not listening to a comedy hoax. The producer, Eamon Keane, revealed afterwards: 'One man rang up and said he had to stop his car because he was crying with laughter. It was only when he met somebody at a petrol station that he was told it was for real. His laughter then turned to anger.'

One caller remarked: 'I am reminded of a phrase – "stick your head between your legs and kiss your arse goodbye" – that's basically what we're being told to do.' Another said: 'I would feel safer with Captain Mainwaring of *Dad's Army* in charge.' One mother phoned in to complain that her little ones were in tears, having some-how gleaned from the minister's interview that the government planned to distribute suicide pills to every home, to be taken in the event of an emergency.

The howls of public outcry bore echoes of the panic generated by Orson Welles in 1938 when he spooked radio listeners with his wickedly realistic *War Of The Worlds*. Health Minister Micheál Martin was bounced onto the main evening news to repair the dent in public morale caused by his colleague's reassurances.

Minister Martin told the Irish people there was no need to panic over iodine tablets. 'We have sufficient stock in all health board areas,' he said. This worked for just as long as it took for health boards to reveal that their stocks were either out of date, or had been destroyed because they were out of date. Minister Martin apologised and said he'd given his assurance 'in good faith'. A spokesman for the Taoiseach then hit out at the media for 'creating hysteria'. Another warned the same media to leave off Joe Jacob. 'He is doing a great job,' said the official.

Six weeks after telling Marian Finucane that he would be staging an emergency dry-run in four weeks' time, Joe Jacob invited the media to witness the exercise. It began with a simulated earthquake at the Wylfa nuclear plant in Wales, one of the Earth's most earthquake-free zones. The exercise, minister Jacob pointed out, was part of an ongoing emergency response plan. It was *not*, he stressed, being staged as 'a reaction to anything'. In particular, it was definitely 'not a reaction to the events of the eleventh of September'.

Once again the clock was running on the minister, but this time he was in full control. He'd had six weeks to prepare a set piece that would achieve one of his stated aims of the day: to restore confidence in the country's 'total state of readiness' for a nuclear crisis.

Seven hours after his improbable earthquake hit Wylfa, Joe Jacob was asked what advice the public would be receiving around now? 'Stay indoors,' he said, declining to give further instructions on the grounds that these would be dictated by the circumstances of the incident.

But, grumbled the media who'd been summoned to the showpiece, Joe Jacob was the one in charge of the circumstances of the incident! He had picked Wylfa as the disaster scene, he'd selected an earthquake as the cause, and he'd decided on the time-scale of the emergency.

What was the point of the exercise if all he was going to say was 'stay indoors'?

One questioner persisted. 'What, seven hours into an emergency, should the Irish public be doing about food consumption? Should they be popping their iodine pills?'

'Ah,' said the Minister, 'we are talking hypothetically at this point.'

Joe Jacob wasn't going to be lured onto that slippery slope again.

DID YOU EVER GO OVER A HILL IN A CAR REAL QUICK?

'I've Cured AIDS' Says Finglas Man.

Who? Former security guard, Fred Bradley.
When? 1992.
What? A spill on the road to Damascus changed his life.
Where? On a narrow rural stretch on the outskirts of Dublin.
Why? God grabbed the steering, the Virgin told him to heal.

On November 20th, 1992, the *Finglas Forum* freesheet ran an eye-catching front page headline. 'I'VE CURED AIDS' said the block type framing a photo of smiling local man Fred Bradley. According to the report, the moustachioed ex-security guard from Finglas South had stolen a spectacular march on medical science.

Revelling in the attention that followed the coverage, Bradley staked his claim as not just a good faith healer, but a great one. He explained: 'Finbar Nolan and them, the most I ever heard of them curing was bronchitis or a skin allergy or something like that. Faith healers have actually been with me here and they reckon that I am the best faith healer. They look at me as the divine faith healer, King of all the faith healers. The likes of Finbar Nolan and all these other boys – they wouldn't have the power to take a person out of a wheelchair, or to cure a person of a brain tumour, or take a child out of a coma.'

But, according to himself, Fred Bradley had all those powers and then some. The long list of afflictions he'd cured included deafness, paralysis, Parkinson's Disease and even the most dreaded and incurable of them all, AIDS.

Anyone inclined to laugh out loud at Bradley's claims would have found themselves struck dumb by a visit to his weekly Sunday roadside clinic. Held on a narrow byway between Mulhuddard and Blanchardstown in rural north Dublin, the healing session drew the distressed, the desperate and the dying in their scores, in the hope that Fred Bradley could help where medicine couldn't.

They began arriving on the scene a whole hour before the session started, in their family cars and their Hiace vans, parking alongside a holy place known as Our Lady's Well. A casual passer-by would never recognise the low concrete bunker on the grassy verge as a Marian shrine. Its coating of blue and white paint – the colours of the Virgin – was weathered and faint. On closer inspection there were two slogans roughly scrawled in black on the surface. These said 'Holy Mary Pray For Us' and 'Vouchsafe That I May Praise Thee Sacred Virgin, Obtain'.

Shortly before four in the afternoon, Fred Bradley turned up wearing a crucifix around his neck and cradling a statuette of Our Lady wrapped in plastic. The thirty or so vehicles poured out their occupants who made a dash in the drizzle towards the shrine. As the crowd formed a line along the side of the road, Fred Bradley stepped barefoot into the freezing muddy moat around the shrine. Many of those waiting to have their face and hands washed by the healer had to be carried or steadied. A garda patrol car glided by this hushed, heartbreaking procession.

Two days later, amid the clutter of toys in his compact living-room, Fred Bradley explained how he'd found his personal road to Damascus on a quiet stretch near Mulhuddard. It all came about through an act of divine intervention as he steered his motorbike past the by-now famous shrine. The letters L*O*V*E* tattooed between his knuckles melted into a blur of movement as he demonstrated how the handlebars of his motorbike were yanked from his control by an unseen force.

Picking himself off the ground and finding himself unharmed, apart from sore knees, he noticed Our Lady's Well and offered up a short prayer. Next thing, he recalled: 'I felt a deep heat coming down the back of my neck and when I turned around Our Lady was floating about three feet off the ground. A shining beam of light came out of her and she didn't say anything, but I knew she gave me the power to do something.'

Fred Bradley admitted that he had been no paragon of piety before that epiphany, but: 'From that day I've lost track of the people that's after been cured. People with cancer, with brain tumours. I couldn't count how many people I've taken out of wheelchairs.' To back this up he could cite the hundreds of letters of thanks sent to him by those cured, plus video footage showing him actually 'taking a person out of a wheelchair'. A request to see this video had to be turned down because 'one of the mates has it'.

Fred Bradley was adamant that he'd cured a number of AIDS cases. He added: 'AIDS is not a disease that was brought across the water – it's God. It's like cancer. It's like, there's diseases put out to keep the races down.'

He was anxious to point out that – unlike some religious fundamentalists – this didn't mean he regarded AIDS as a punishment from God on wrong-doers. It was simply a means of culling the population. Which raised the question – what was he at, going around curing people of God's cull? But instead of asking this, a different question was put to him.

How could he be sure that he'd cured anybody, especially since the symptoms of AIDS are known to blow-up
and subside?

He answered: 'The young lad that came to me, he'd lost
about seven stone in weight. His face was gone in, it was
dreadful. He'd sores all over his face. I remember washing
him down and praying. Before he left, he said: "I see a
cross on your chest." This day I hadn't got the cross, yet he
saw the cross. I thought maybe he was on drugs for
medication, but obviously he wasn't, he *did* see it!'

Ask a silly question . . .

Did Fred Bradley harbour any concerns that his claims
of miracle cures might raise false hopes in those infected
with HIV?

'Every race comes to me,' was his surprise response.
'Japanese come to me. You've Protestant people come to
me . . .'

As the interview progressed, the disjointed replies and
ambitious leaps of logic became, if anything, more
pronounced. Fred Bradley had been invited onto the youth
TV show, *Jo Maxi*. On the programme he'd been con-
fronted by a young woman 'who believed in nothing'. He
related how: 'She says to me would it not be like the
moving statue – my imagination? But what they didn't
know was, at that dome (Our Lady's Well), *there is no statues
there*. Anyone who ever put a statue there, it was smashed.'

Because of the threat of desecration by vandals, Fred
Bradley's weekly Sunday meets were bring-your-own
affairs, explaining why the Virgin had arrived wrapped in
plastic. He and his assistants would also bring along a
donation box. Any cash offerings collected were to go
towards erecting an iron, vandal-proof, statue of Our
Lady, and towards installing ramps to allow wheelchair

access to the Virgin on the verge. The ramps were badly
needed because two of those seeking a cure had already
been seriously injured in tumbles. He complained bitterly
that £1,800 collected for the purpose of doing-up the
shrine had been entrusted into what proved to be the
wrong hands and could not be put to its intended use.

Returning to more spiritual themes, Fred Bradley
volunteered his own personal meditation on death. 'I'd
welcome death with me open arms,' he declared. 'There's
no fear because I know what's on the other side. I'll tell
you what it's like. Did you ever go over a hill in a car real
quick and your stomach goes up? It's a thousand times
worse than that. And you can feel yourself floating. I'm
telling you, if death is like that I'd welcome death
anytime.'

Which begged the question – if death isn't such a bad
thing after all, why was Fred Bradley expending so much
of his time and energy saving people from it?

He answered: 'An awful lot of people who come to me
are only young people. There's people coming to me with
cancer from seven years upwards. You've skin rashes,
deafness – I've cured young lads who were born deaf. And,
like, I could be a millionaire if I wanted to be.'

But, despite this earning potential, he didn't accept
money for himself?

'No. I was going to take up donations to do up the well,
'cos I have seven kids here myself . . . If people are in pain
they'll pay any amount of money. I refuse an awful lot of
money . . .'

He recalled talking to an American priest who told him:
'Fred, if you were over in America you'd have cars, you'd
have bodyguards. People who can heal over there – it's big
time.'

But he wasn't in it for the money. The most he'd ever accepted for himself was 'a bag of spuds' for fear of upsetting the grateful donor. 'If I was taking money,' he mused, 'within the first month I'd have been a multi-millionaire.'

Initially, he did have his doubters. He recalled: 'At first people were saying, "He's doing it for the money." But when they went out to the well and saw it – no money would pay you to stand out there for five or six hours in your bare feet and be in and out of that water. Three or four other faith healers went to that well and none stayed, because they wanted big money.'

Ah, so traditionally there had been other faith healers at Our Lady's Well?

'No. They came when I was there and they went to one side trying to get to cure people, and there were men there that I do have there, minding me and that, and I told them: "No, I don't want *them* there."'

This might have opened an interesting avenue of discussion, but time had run out and Fred Bradley was in full flight again.

'There were men that tried to open up stalls and I wouldn't have that, 'cos I was in Knock and I've seen what Knock is. It's a big money racket – it's a rip off from start to finish.'

HE KEPT SMILING AND WANKING AT US

Covering a paper trail.

Who? Eamon De Valera, the FF faithful, low-paid journalists.
When? From 1931 to 1995.
What? The *Irish Press*, a community chest covertly privatised.
Where? Ownership was quietly switched to the US.
Why? Dev: 'The money was just resting in my account.'

From the time of its birth in 1931 up to its messy death in 1995, the *Irish Press* nurtured many fine writers – generally until they were able to find something that paid better. In its youth, the in-house organ of Fianna Fáil was like a demented national teacher in the mould of Pádraig Pearse, determined to inflict maximum Irishness on a nation that wasn't nearly Irish enough. In its middle years it became a pillar of the Establishment, but improved circumstances didn't mellow its Scrooge-like parsimony towards its employees. In its dotage it was creaky, incoherent and dispirited, keeping track of its readership trends mostly through the obituary columns.

The story of the *Press* nails the lie that financial sharp practice by politicians is a recent aberration. The money which founded the *Press* was originally given to secure Irish freedom, not to start a newspaper. Later on, the Fianna Fáil faithful dug deep to invest in a common cause, a community chest. But behind the scenes the organ's founder, Eamon de Valera, was pulling strokes to make the *Press* his private property.

In the years 1919–1921, during the struggle for Independence, Irish Americans had contributed large sums in bonds to bankroll a Republican government in Dublin. After Independence was won, a chunk of that money, worth a small fortune, remained clogged up in United States vaults. The Free State government claimed rightful control of the outstanding funds but, through shrewd manoeuvring, de Valera got his hands on the bonds and used them as seed-capital to start the *Press*.

Irish Press Limited was formally incorporated in Dublin in September, 1928. Immediately, 200,000 ordinary shares in the new company were advertised nationally at £1 each. Buried in the small print of the newspaper adverts was mention of a Controlling Director. Those who bothered to read that far down the column learned that: 'The powers of the Controlling Director are set out in Articles 76 to 78 inclusive, of the Articles of Association.' So any investor in Donegal or Kerry or Cork would have to trek to the Companies Office in Dublin Castle to find out what these powers, mentioned in passing, actually might be.

Lodged there was the information that the Controlling Director – one Eamon de Valera – had 'sole and absolute control of the public and political policy of the company'. It went on: 'The Controlling Director can appoint, and at his discretion remove or suspend all editors, sub-editors, reporters, writers, contributors . . . and all such other persons as may be employed in or connected with the editorial department and may determine their duties and fix their salaries and or emoluments.'

In other words, de Valera could hire and fire anyone, he could decide who got paid what, he could dictate every word in the newspaper, he could do the cartoons if the fancy took him.

Having sold the 200,000 shares mostly to his own supporters, Dev set up a shadow company in the States, the Irish Press Corporation, for the purpose of hoovering up those shares and taking covert control of the *Press*. He then sold thousands of 'A' shares in the second company to Irish Americans and recently arrived Irish emigrants. He took the money for the 'A' shares, but the only shares that really mattered were 200 publicity-shy 'B' shares which carried the voting rights and which he kept all to himself.

By trading on his own saintliness, Dev managed to keep the lid on the shares scandal until 1958 when sworn enemy Noel Browne – after many frustrated attempts to have the matter tabled for debate – confronted him with the sordid facts in Dáil Éireann. Browne charged de Valera with lying about the amount of *Press* shares he and his family owned, and with swindling the shareholders out of money by buying shares back from them at an artificially low price set by him.

Dev's response in the chamber foreshadowed Father Ted Crilly's mantra: 'The money was just resting in my account.' (These weren't De Valera's exact words, but they give the gist of his flimsy defence.) Dev then handed over to another Fianna Fáil deputy who condemned Browne's 'slimy private member's motion'. Fianna Fáil's voting strength easily defeated the motion and then, to minimise the damage in the following day's papers, de Valera made the shock announcement that he was going to retire as Taoiseach and stand in the next year's Presidential election. The ploy worked and the retirement story dominated the following day's news.

Dev's claim that he wasn't in it for the money would have had a greater ring of truth coming from his staff at the *Press*. The paper's first editor, Frank Gallagher, worked 13-hour days for yellowpack rates. Gallagher resigned after four years. He'd threatened to go sooner, when one of Dev's downsizers insisted on sacking the women's editor for using agency bumph instead of writing her own. In fact, she'd prepared a fortnight's worth of material before going on holidays to save the company the expense of replacing her. Incredibly, the publication's Irish language editor was paid just half of what his counterparts got, on the grounds that he was privileged to hold the most exalted post in the organisation.

Issue 1 of the *Irish Press*, in 1931, carried a front page plug for the All-Ireland Hurling Final. 'Kick-off 3pm' it said. Embarrassingly, for a paper pledged to champion Gaelic Games, hurling kicks-off with a throw-in.

In its sickly final years, the *Press* stable was an Aladdin's Cave for connoisseurs of the *sic* joke. Either demoralised staff had given up trying or, as some suspected, there were fifth columnists at work actively sabotaging the pages in the name of gallows humour.

The following really appeared . . .

On spelling errors: 'Repeated spelling errors, often involving phonetic mistakes, ('sity' for 'city'). Just wyh a child scrambles letters and words consistenely while learning to read is not known. Studies of minute electrical impulses in the brains of dyslectic children have turned up no identifiable abnormalities so far. Still, neurologisst have operated under the assumption that subtle problems with the brains circuitry could account for the misprocessing of iformation."

From Anne Nolan of The Nolan Sisters: 'Frank Sinatra was difficult to get near because of the enormous entourage. I remember after one show we did there were no seats for us in the auditorium and he insisted that we were allowed to sit on the steps behind the orchestra. All through the show he kept smiling and wanking at us.'

On a ballet school: 'Nina Tully, now grey haired and not as supple as she used to be, has run her ballot school since it opened in 1936 . . . Whether your little darling is graceful and lithe or bow-legged with a sticky-output bottom, she or he may learn to be a ballet dancer ... Today just four of the;m turn up ans with two minutes to go hey come leapingn into the dance room, four of the friekiest, larkiest little you've ever seen. Nina Tully wanks in . . .'

Reporting a tragedy: 'A 55-year-old Derryman was killed while felling trees at a farm on the outskirts of Derry yesterday . . . Mr Magee was felling trees at a farm at Ardmore when part of a tree struck him on arrival at Altnaglen Hospital.'

On inappropriate peering: 'Hamilton Jordan became the centre of controversy recently when news reports alleged he tried to pee down the bodice of the Egyptian ambassador's wife at dinner, quipping: "I've always wanted to see the pyramids."'

The *Presh* finally shat, er shut, in 1995.

THE FAMILY TRIED TO STOP HIM WATCHING

The League Of Decency Vs *The Spike*.

Who? JB Murray, founder of the League Of Decency.
When? 1978.
What? A heart attack brought on by an RTÉ TV show.
Where? In his Dublin living room.
Why? A woman cured of shyness took her clothes off.

It was yet another cowardly capitulation on the part of the national broadcaster but, for once, the Dublin 4 set and the Backwoods Brigade found themselves in full agreement – the sudden demise of *The Spike* had been a mercy killing. The school-based drama series had taken Irish television down corridors which needed to be bricked off forever.

It was early 1978 when RTÉ took a much hyped plunge into gritty contemporary drama. Scripted by a forty-year-old teacher, Patrick Gilligan, *The Spike* was trumpeted as a warts'n'all examination of urban life as it manifested itself in a Dublin technical school.

The first few episodes passed by uneventfully enough – there were some complaints about crude language, but nothing to fuse the switchboards. On the contrary, the viewing public warmed to the series in sufficient numbers to put the show at No 3 in the TAM ratings behind perennial favourites *Hall's Pictorial Weekly* and *Quicksilver*.

The critics, however, hadn't a good word to say about this mutant offspring of *Please Sir!* and *Colditz*. *The Spike*, they concurred, was fabulously bad. One writer deemed it 'ill-judged, badly-written, wildly exaggerated, tasteless, naive and so embarrassing in its infantile approach to serious matters'. Another described the early episodes as 'hamfisted, lurid melodrama'. In addition, several teachers groups tut-tutted that it was dragging their profession into disrepute.

They had a point. In one bedroom scene the school's pensive headmaster is asked by his wife what he's thinking about. 'Hoors,' he replies.

By Episode Four there were mutterings that the show was also calling the acting profession into disrepute. In this instalment the principal reluctantly enrolls his own daughter in the Spike after she's been expelled from her convent school. The young girl isn't settled in a wet day when one of the teachers plies her with gin in an effort to seduce her. Another teacher, who eavesdrops on the attempted seduction, is literally driven mad by the scene. And so the corridors of a tough Dublin comprehensive resonate with the poesy of dementia: 'Light came from my fingernails. Deep in honeyed flesh sweet buds catch fire . . . Birthwards there is such pain, such pangs, such joy.' Such utter drivel was a sure sign that *The Spike* had come off its hinges.

Hibernia magazine's television critic could only applaud. 'I vowed a couple of weeks ago that I would write nothing more on this blackboard bungle,' he wrote, 'but the series is now becoming cherishable . . . RTÉ seems to have found the magic formula for successful comedy.' Others were not so amused. The knives were out for *The Spike*, but nobody could quite believe it when the intended victim gleefully impaled itself in a pre-meditated act of hari-kiri. It was Episode Five. The plot of that landmark instalment is worth recounting.

The school is hosting a series of evening classes in subjects which include Fur Appreciation, Overcoming Shyness and Floor Scrubbing (honest!). In a not untypical line of dialogue, the Fur Appreciation teacher advises: 'Having got your skin soft and pliable you will be ready for formication.' *Fwoooarr, missus!* Meanwhile, the man giving the class in Overcoming Shyness is so painfully bashful that he downs large measures of Dutch courage before facing his audience. This paves the way for an hilarious scenario where the tanked-up teacher demonstrates the techniques of 'bottom pinching' and 'the friendly crotch grab'. The episode reaches its surreal climax when the shyest girl in the class is miraculously cured. Quick as a flash she's next door whipping her kit off for the still life art group, and the viewing nation.

Strange but true: sown into the fabric of Episode Five was an offhand disparaging reference by one of the teachers to the League of Decency. Slump forward Mr J B Murray, founder and Chairman of an organisation by the same name. Sitting at home that evening maintaining his customary vigil against filth, Mr Murray was seized with apoplexy. His wife told the press: 'He got a pain in his chest while telephoning the newspapers to complain.' According to the *Irish Times*: 'The family tried to stop him watching it . . . but he insisted and he got very worked up by the nude scene.'

Meanwhile, back in the real world, even the most fervent champions of freedom of expression were making heavy going of defending the indefensible. The show's series producer, Noel O'Brien, discharged a round into his own foot by arguing that the programme 'was trying to examine attitudes of pupils and staff in a school to nudity'.

The countdown to Episode Six was underway and RTÉ's Director General, Oliver Moloney, had a crisis on his hands. JB Murray was on the mend and spoiling for a fight. Several Limerick County Councillors were up in arms and Fine Gael's Education spokesman, Eddie Collins, had drafted a stiff letter. Clearly there was no alternative – Moloney 'deferred' the show just hours before the next instalment was due to screen.

'THE SPIKE GETS AXED' proclaimed the *Evening Press* from its front page, although the shock news hadn't reached the rear of the newspaper where readers were promised an episode called 'Requiem For A Head', an everyday tale of suburban schoolgoing tomfoolery. The teaser read: 'When young Tommy Greene dies transporting explosives, one of Headmaster O'Mahony's best teachers comes under suspicion.' When 9.20 arrived that night the station substituted *Love Is The Answer*, the altogether more edifying story of life in an Italian boys' town founded by a Dublin priest.

The 'deferral' came too late for one of the actors in the series who required medical treatment after he was, as the *Evening Press* elegantly put it, 'thumped by a fat elderly lady'. A few days after the axing the nation awoke to the headline 'JP MURRAY IS BACK IN HOSPITAL'. The unfortunate moralist was not much longer for this world. *The Spike* itself was bundled away like a demented auntie locked in the attic for the greater good.

There it has stayed.

THE COMMON MARKET APPLIED TO LIGHT MUSIC

Everyone Vs The Eurovision Song Contest.

Who? Sinn Féin. Cyclists. Gaelic League. Animal Rights. Etc.
When? April, 1971.
What? They were against hosting Eurovision for the 1st time.
Where? It took place at the Gaiety Theatre, Dublin.
Why? Eurovision represented a Pandora's Box of wrongs.

Dreary Dublin hadn't seen such a fashion parade since the exile of Castle society with the gaining of independence. The tinted glasses of the conductor from Germany set tongues wagging, as did the venus flytrap eyelashes of the exotic dollybirds from all points east. In Stephen's Green the UK entrant set pulses racing with hot pants that could 'hardly have been more than about nine inches from top to bottom'. Europe's beautiful people were in town for the staging of Ireland's first ever Eurovision Song Contest in April 1971. They weren't entirely bowled over by the capital city. One member of the French delegation took a dim view of Dublin's restaurant culture. 'Either it is very expensive,' she observed, 'or it is very dreadful.'

When it came to organising protests, though, the host nation dazzled its guests with the colour and variety of its Eurovision pageant. The tidal wave of national pride which had greeted Dana's victory a year earlier had gone into a distinct ebb. If its army of critics were to be

believed, the Eurovision Song Contest was at fault for all
kinds of everything.

A week of rehearsals preceded Contest night, the
Gaiety Theatre having been 'disembowelled' to accommodate the summit meeting of song. The coming year
would bring a referendum on Ireland's entry into the
EEC. For those opposed to Irish membership, the Gaiety
would serve as a surrogate European Parliament, ripe for
the storming.

Sinn Féin's protest was strictly political. Spokesperson
Máirín De Burca made clear: 'We want to get across to all
these countries that everybody in Ireland is not for our
entry into the Common Market.' Conradh Na Gaeilge
attacked on the cultural front, objecting to RTÉ devoting
scarce resources to 'a pop contest'. The Irish branch of the
Celtic League, meanwhile, berated the organisers' failure
to choose an Irish-language entry. The Gaelic League – no
relation – announced a march from the GPO to RTÉ's
Montrose HQ on the afternoon of the show to protest
about the time and money being wasted on 'this type of
thing'.

The Irish Council Against Blood Sports vowed to take
'a secret course of action' if RTÉ went ahead with its
proposed interval film showcasing a drag hunt. The station
responded that the intermission sequence was 'in good
taste'. The anti-blood sports group countered that RTÉ
was being 'irresponsible' and showing Ireland in a
barbaric light. However, when push came to shove, the
Council cried off its planned disruption in the cause of
'national interest and prestige'.

The National Athletic & Cycling Association came out
strongly against Eurovision in protest at RTÉ's paucity of
bicycle-related programming. The disgruntled cyclists

didn't want to risk disrupting the actual contest, so they
staged a protest bicycle race around Donnybrook the
afternoon *before* the extravaganza. Not all the protesters
would be so obliging. Newspapers warned guests, delegates
and journalists to expect a thicket of pickets outside the
Gaiety. One report also raised the unsettling spectre of 'a
militant Women's Lib wing who will chant "*Rhythm and
babes means rhythm and blues*" at passers-by'.

The most concerted assault on Eurovision came from
within the national broadcasting service. The RTÉ
Workers' Anti-Redundancy Committee came up with
sufficient cribs to stock a good-sized diocese in Christmas
week. For starters, the Committee likened the song contest
to 'the Common Market applied to light music'. This,
evidently, was a bad thing.

Furthermore, they insisted: 'The song contest, like the
Common Market, brings redundancy. In order to take
part, RTÉ rushed into colour expense before it was ready.
They spent nearly £200,000 they had not got. On Sunday
morning RTÉ workers will have to face a black and white
world as their managers attempt to get this money back by
traditional means – cut-backs, bad home programmes and
redundancies.'

Other gripes included a lack of consultation with staff,
'the vulgarity of that musical non-event' and 'that the
contest was creating a new kind of apartheid, the colour
bar'. This referred to the fact that there were only 3,000
colour televisions in Ireland. So, by broadcasting in colour,
RTÉ had elected to pander to a tiny well-off minority. The
Workers' Committee additionally charged that the station
was 'staging the contest because colour broadcasting
justifies the employment of a small number of senior
managers'. It was jobs for the big boys, they fumed. The

workers' charge-sheet was made available in English, Irish, French and German.

The Eurovision circus had never seen anything like the hostility that enveloped it in Dublin. Some foreign TV crews completely ignored the sideshow outside the Gaiety. Others, such as the Swedes, built it into their coverage as an Irish running joke. At least one unprepared foreign team tried to borrow an extra camera to capture the placard-wavers. Predictably, RTÉ hadn't one to spare. The Dutch were better resourced. They filmed the chanting Women's Libbers for a special report on the plight of the downtrodden Irish female. The programme was broadcast in the Netherlands as a prelude to the song contest.

Adrian Cronin, the contest's Director of Operations, stressed the 'non-political' nature of Eurovision. He stoically accepted that it was in the nature of 'left-wing groups' to whinge. 'This is an age of protests,' he reflected. It was also an age of bomb threats. The Monday after the Contest, the *Irish Press* carried a curious story. The paper claimed that Friday's dress rehearsal had been taped and delivered into the hands of the BBC in London. According to the report, in the event of terrorist disruption, the pre-recorded dry run would have been transmitted from London. 'How the voting system would have worked out is another question,' the writer concluded, somewhat undermining his own story.

Nobody was particularly surprised when an anonymous phone caller threatened to kidnap the UK contestant, Clodagh Rodgers. Security was upped a notch, and attention quickly returned to what the singer of *Jack In The Box* would be wearing on the night. One female reporter carped: 'The well publicised "best legs in show business" – said to be insured for an astronomical sum – proved slightly knock-kneed when revealed in toto.' Clodagh's own thoughts: 'Well, they're getting a bit fat.' She'd be wearing a maxi dress.

The jury were warned to pay no heed to the fat content or otherwise of the contestants. The songs were to be the sole criteria for success. The hopes and expectations of Ireland were riding on Angela Farrell and the instantly forgettable *One Day Love*. The whole country was rooting for a respectable mid-table finish. One columnist predicted that, in the unlikely event of an Irish win: 'RTÉ will express immense delight while it diplomatically offers the holding of next year's contest to the runner-up.'

Not that Ireland seemed to be the only country that wasn't really trying. Yugoslavia's determination not to squander its GNP on hosting the schmaltzfest was evident in a dirge that might have been lifted from a horticultural handbook: '*In some other garden you are now a rose / Your boy dreams of you / Your boy is sad.*' When the votes were totted, wealthy little Monaco had taken the dubious honours with a pretty singer, Severine, a memorable tune and another outdoor existentialist dilemma. The dreamy blonde sang: '*We all have a bench, a tree or a street / Where we nursed our dreams / We all have a bench, a tree or a street / Too short a childhood.*'

The other big winner of Eurovision 1971 was its hostess, Bernadette Ní Ghallchoir. Everyone agreed that the twenty-three-year-old model, teacher and linguist from Monaghan had done the country proud. Bernadette announced that during rehearsals she'd been offered a role in an Italian gangster movie. Her big screen debut would climax with her pretty face destroyed by pretend acid. She was looking forward to it immensely.

The most conspicuous loser of Eurovision 1971 was Mrs Mary Weston. Mrs Weston had mounted a one

woman demonstration outside the Gaiety in support of
'poor widows' scraping by on £4 a week. She was
dismayed that TDs had just awarded themselves another
juicy pay hike taking them up to the £50 mark. Mrs
Weston's protest came to an undignified end when she was
set upon by an unidentified ruffian who made off with her
placard.

Ireland had staged Eurovision without a hitch, apart
from the few moments towards the start of the show when
a section of the audience *shushed* some hecklers who'd
managed to infiltrate The Gaiety. The trouble subsided
when it turned out that the heckles were not heckles at all,
but the peculiar babble of our continental neighbours
leaking out from the commentary booths.

The country exhaled audibly and basked in a mood of
relieved self-congratulation. Hopefully we'd never have to
go through *that* again.

HAPPY AS A PIG IN MUCK

Big Jack Vs The English Language.

Who? Irish football manager and saint, Jack Charlton.
When? 1986–1995.
What? Charlton inflicted his own system on his native tongue.
Where? Lansdowne Road, Euro '88, Italia '90, USA '94.
Why? Because everything bows to success, even grammar.

Jack Charlton was a graduate of the Humpty Dumpty school of linguistics. 'When I use a word,' declared Lewis Carrol's precocious egghead, 'it means just what I choose it to mean – neither more nor less.' So it was with the gruff Geordie. The system Big Jack brought to Ireland dismayed the purists. Time and again he'd punt his syntax hopefully down the channels, relying on bluster and aggression to grind out a result.

The cracks in Charlton's verbal game-plan were apparent from early in his ten year reign. After defeat by Bulgaria in 1987, Jack reflected: 'The game in Romania was a game we should have won. We lost it because we thought we were going to win it. But then again, I thought there was no way we were going to get a result there.' Minds boggled, but a run of good results, culminating in qualification for Euro '88, gave him *carte blanche* to run roughshod over the niceties of linguistic precision. Jack rechristened several of the household names he'd inherited. Paul McGrath became 'John' McGrath, Dennis Irwin became 'David' Irwin and Liam Brady was renamed 'Liam O'Brady'. Jack wasn't one to mince words, he pulverised them.

By leading the Republic to the 1990 World Cup finals, Charlton achieved infallibility. As the Republic's footballing stock went through the roof, Big Jack became a living embodiment of Victor Hugo's dictum that everything bows to success, even grammar. A grudging admiration took root across the water, with the semantic spin-off that the team were adopted as 'Jack Charlton's Republic Of Ireland' (although one ITV commentator preferred 'Jack Charlton's Team Of International Misfits').

Charlton was in full swash and the English language was buckling. He contended, for example, that: 'If, in winning the game we only finish with a draw, that would be fine.' On another occasion he confounded geographers everywhere by observing that the English people 'fought two wars against the Germans. We probably got on better with the smaller nations like the Dutch, the Belgians, the Norwegians and the Swedes, some of whom are not even in Europe'. Then there was the admission that: 'It is true that I don't write letters to people or call them on the phone to tell them they are finished. That, for me, has an air of finality about it.'

Eventually, though, Big Jack's linguistic sloppiness embroiled him in a bitter war of words with a journalist named Paul Rowan. Rowan originally set out to write a history of the Football Association of Ireland. In its intended form, the project might have been less than riveting. But when Rowan cadged a lift in Jack's car for a round trip from Dublin to Sligo, he got the scoop of his young career.

Over the course of a five-hour exchange, Charlton ransacked the reputations of several Irish soccer heroes. Striker Frank Stapleton was 'a begrudger'. Jack elaborated: 'Instead of Frank thanking me for stretching out his career and making something of it, he fuckin' always burns his boat.' He regretted taking Stapleton to Italia '90: 'I don't need Frank but I took him. Biggest fuckin' mistake I ever made. I should have sent him home in Malta 'cos he was a miserable . . . He didn't help for one minute, he never stopped moaning and grousing. Knowing he wasn't going to fuckin' play he could have helped and joined in with the training, instead of which he carried on like a spoiled brat.'

Jack revealed to Rowan the thinking behind Liam Brady's humiliating first half substitution in his testimonial game against Germany at Lansdowne Road. The Irish fans, complained Charlton, 'would expect me to call him up for every international match in spite of the fact that he's not quick and not playing. So I put him on display'. Brady was paraded and swiftly, some would say callously, withdrawn to drive home the point that Jack picked the team, not the fans. 'The Irish don't give up their fuckin' heroes easily,' he remarked, 'so you've really got to show 'em.' It was Brady's big day but he was surplus to requirements for the friendly. 'I'm not going to give up a result against the Germans for Liam or anybody,' he stated bluntly.

Shortly after Charlton's arrival as Irish coach his youth team auxiliary, Liam Tuohy, tendered his resignation. Some said Tuohy jumped, others maintained he was shoved by the bullish new man. Charlton had no doubts. He told Rowan that: 'Tuohy just dropped me on my head. Now, with everything I've achieved, the one thing that gives me great pleasure is that I stuffed it up his arse.'

When Rowan released extracts of his book to the media in late 1994, Charlton barked indignantly that he hadn't known that his conversation was being taped. Rowan responded that Jack knew full well that he was on tape, adding that out of sixty people interviewed for his book Charlton was the only one who'd looked for a fee.

The controversy abated over the following weeks until Jack rekindled it on *The Late Late Show*. On the programme, he claimed he'd been duped into believing that the bulk of the conversation was off-the-record. As far as he was concerned, only the first twenty minutes of dialogue was for public consumption. When he realised the truth of the matter he'd tried to confiscate the tapes.

Rowan's response was some time in coming. He searched through his recordings and released an extract taped on the home leg of the Sligo trip. This, he insisted, proved that Jack knew he was being taped at an advanced stage of their conversation. He said he took this course of action 'reluctantly' having being called a 'liar' and a 'cheat' by Jack on the television almost a month before. Incidentally, there were now just fourteen shopping days left to Christmas.

The extract featured Rowan asking Jack about his relationship with club managers. Jack replies that they've already discussed the topic. Rowan explains: 'We talked about it just on that little ride around the centre (of Sligo). But I didn't have my tape on at the time.' So Jack must have known he was being taped several hours into the conversation.

The following day Jack set the record straight. 'Of *course* I knew it was being recorded,' he said. 'I've never denied that.' Having now clarified his position, Jack was 'no longer interested' in discussing the matter. Rowan considered Jack's final words on the subject 'unbelievable and bizarre'.

Things were never quite the same for Big Jack after the Rowan affair. The people's deity had been shown to have feet of clay and his players reciprocated with performances that suggested boots of lead to match. Comprehensive defeats by Austria and Portugal, and a humiliating draw against Liechtenstein – more a tax loophole than a footballing power – left Charlton gawping for excuses on the wilder outskirts of his imagination. He blamed defeat by Austria on the proposition that 'there was some legs missing'. A sloppy home draw against Northern Ireland brought forth the novel contention that: 'March is probably the one month when you cannot predict a result.'

This manner of mumbo-jumbo only washed while the team were winning. The red card from his employers came just weeks short of the 10th anniversary of his appointment. By way of consolation, Jack and his missus were showered with civic honours. 'I'm happy as a pig in muck,' he said, accepting honorary Irish citizenship. He warmed to the farmyard theme when he was conferred with the Freedom of the City of Dublin. His memorable comment on that occasion: 'I think it means I can now drive my sheep over the bridge.'

YOU'D BE BARRED FROM MAKING LOVE IN THE UNDERWATER CITY

The Life Story Of Aidan Walsh's Life.

Who? Cork-born Master of the Universe, Aidan Walsh.
When? For the next forty million years, at least.
What? With the Earth gone, humans endure as 'happy slaves'.
Where? On a spaceship constructed beneath the Liffey.
Why? So Aidan can speculate on space currency.

'Elvis is dead – now I take over.' With those immortal words, Aidan Walsh introduced himself to the Irish public in 1987, unveiling his extraordinary debut album 'Aidan And The Masterplan: The Life Story Of A Life'. Aidan didn't quite take over where Elvis left off, but he never stopped thinking big. From an early age, his overriding ambition in life was to become Master of the Universe.

Only Aidan himself knows how close he has come to realising that ambition, but in the year 2000, after attending the big-screen premiere of his life's story, he could state with justifiable pride: 'A lot of people couldn't believe I did so much in my time. And at the film last night I said, there it is – there it is in black and white.'

Born in the 1950s in Cork and placed immediately into care, Aidan Walsh never knew his parents. Brought up in a harsh religious-run institution, he ran away several times before he was finally released to make his own way in the

world. Aidan quickly learned that freedom has its perils. At
the age of sixteen, while he was working in a Cork hotel,
someone doctored his cornflakes with 'sugar' that was
really poison. Luckily for him, he picked that very day to
take up drinking.

'There was a big wedding do,' he later recalled. 'I
started drinking everything – whiskey, scotch, porter,
Babycham – I drank the lot. I had to drink very fast or I'd
be caught. That night I bought a pipe and started smoking
it in front of everyone.' At that point he received an
extraterrestrial message. 'All the Masters from all the other
galaxies were giving out to me but I was only a young
kangaroo growing up. I got so sick there was a load of
eagles coming out of my stomach through my mouth
giving me the message don't you drink anymore.'

The episode had a happy ending: 'I went back into work
the next day and they said, "How come you're not dead?
There was poison in your cornflakes." I nearly had a heart
attack. But the drinks I had that day killed the poison. I never
drank or smoked since.' The poison scare didn't put him off
sugar, but he resolved never to consume it at home, only
when he was out and in company.

Hitching onto the can-do spirit of the entrepreneurial
Eighties, Aidan cashed in his collection of prize bonds and
set himself up as a professional video-maker. 'I used to get
£150 for weddings,' he told one interviewer. 'I had to pay
tax on that – just in case the tax people might be reading
this.' A video shoot in Dublin's Belvedere College brought
him into contact with Joe Connolly, the chief organiser of
the Community Games. Connolly took Aidan under his
wing: 'He taught me a lot about books, writing and
trademarks.' As a way of saying thanks, Aidan recorded
a song called *The Community Games* in which he praised

such activities as: '*basketball, hockey, swimming and drink*' and '*throwing a bone arrow*'.

Business was good in the wedding video game, and Aidan eventually had spare funds to divert into his real passion – the establishment of a music centre for young bands in the then derelict Temple Bar area of Dublin. Disagreements with business partners ended his involvement with the Temple Lane studio complex. Aidan went solo and set up his own Eagle Studios in nearby Parliament Street. Unfortunately, the strict security procedures which Aidan imposed on his clients tended to jar with their laid-back rock'n'roll ways.

The musicians were issued with identity documents, and warned that anyone who failed to produce the correct papers could face a fine or some other punishment. Tightening the controversial security measures did nothing to improve strained customer relationships. At one point, Aidan introduced a system whereby two halves of a torn photograph would have to be matched up before patrons could gain admittance to their rehearsal space.

When the British tycoon Richard Branson began looking for a site on which to build a Virgin Megastore in Dublin, he found that he had a rival in Aidan Walsh. Well before Branson began eyeing-up the old McBirney's building on the quays, Aidan had opened talks with its owners. He had drawn up detailed architectural plans for a one stop shop for rock's royalty.

He explained: 'On the top floor, there would be rooms for rock bands – private rooms where rock stars could live and sleep. On the second floor there's a canteen, foodstore, toilet, and restaurants for the bands from upstairs. Underneath that you'd have rehearsal rooms and so on. There was one floor we didn't have anything on. Pity.'

Aidan reckoned he could get his scheme off the ground
with £500,000. The only fly in the ointment was his bank
manager: 'He turned me down flat. Said I'd have to have
£200,000 already before he'd give me a loan. But the only
reason I went there in the first place was because I had no
money.'

Aidan's own singing career took off when the British indie
label, Kaleidoscope, signed him after seeing him just once.
His debut album contained the classic tracks *Kissing And
Eating With Women* and *Have You Ever Given Money Away?*. The
latter advised against giving any money to the government
'*because they only give it back to their pals*'. Elsewhere, the line '*I
spent four grand*' was followed by '*not all in one go*'. The add-on
was in case the Revenue might think he had piles of cash
worth investigating.

He followed up his debut with the surreal *Christmas In 4
Dimension*, but Aidan Walsh's music ultimately proved too far
ahead of its time to woo the Elvis market. As his recording
career stalled, the hiatus gave him space to return his
attentions to matters of a deeply personal nature.

His family tree, as he sketched it, was extremely
cosmopolitan: 'My grandfather came from Bermuda. My
grandmother came from Swinford. My aunts live in
Australia. I arrived on the planet Earth. I came out of a
kangaroo.' The first family member Aidan had tracked
down was his half-brother, Willie. Aidan was in his late
teens at the time, Willie was two years his senior.

A few years before Willie's untimely death in the 1990s,
the two brothers went on to *The Gerry Ryan Show* to appeal
for information about an auntie they hoped to trace. It was
a longshot, but it paid off handsomely when the aunt's
former best friend phoned in saying she had a contact
address in Australia. In due course, Aidan and Willie

arrived at Melbourne Airport. A television crew was on hand to film the reunion.

The clip of the encounter was never screened. Aidan maintained that it was dropped in favour of a pressing news item. At the same time he conceded that some family members had taken a bad reaction to the encounter. Instead of the tearful embrace the camera crew had expected, they saw Aidan step off the plane and burst into a raucous rendition of *The Hokey-Cokey*. He reflected: 'When you find your aunt for the first time you should be sad and crying, but I wasn't. I was happy as Larry.'

Aidan Walsh is fully aware that a lot of people think he lives on another planet. That doesn't bother him because he has a reputation as a leg puller, and, besides, he is *from* another planet. While his career appears to have taken a varied and winding path, Aidan maintains that he has never veered from the course of universal domination. To this end, he has been willing to stop at nothing, including mass hypnotism, space travel and exploiting an advantageous interplanetary currency exchange rate. To further his single-minded plot he's even taken menial jobs. His first weekly pay-packet, for example, was just £4.50 back in the Seventies, washing pots and pans in a hotel. He reasoned: 'I had to work for that much money 'cos if people discovered who I was they would have taken me back to my planet 'cos I was taking over this planet. They didn't realise that I was conquering the whole universe.'

Walsh's scheme for eventual mastery of everything rests on enslaving immature minds. He once confided: 'When all young people are making love to their girlfriends I control all their babies. They're doing it for *me*. They think they doing it for themselves but they're not. But when the babies are eighteen or nineteen they see me on TV and I

brainwash all the babies by singing "*Rock your brainy head*".
And suddenly all babies all over the world stop everything
and leave their mammies and daddies and come to my
planet and they're all happy slaves and I am The Master.
That's how I control the whole Earth. Without killing
anyone.'

In return for gainful employment and not being killed,
Aidan's slaves will hand over their wage packets which The
Master will then use to engage in currency speculation
between the Earth and an unnamed planet. The happy
slaves will actually make a tidy profit on the deal, but
nothing compared to Aidan's earnings. 'They don't realise
what I'm up to,' he chuckles.

As for the travel arrangements between planets: 'After
twelve o'clock my brain opens up every night. Then all
eagles coming out of me and go into my other world and
get there in two minutes. I leave TV on every night to
recharge my eyes.'

A priority task for Aidan's happy slaves will be the
construction of an Underwater City somewhere beneath the
Liffey. He once outlined some of the house rules: 'You'd be
barred from making love in the Underwater City. We'd be
very strict on that to keep the numbers down. If you come to
the city you never die. You'd be 2,000 years old and you
wouldn't know it. When the world blows up, the Underwater
City becomes a flying saucer and leaves the Earth. We'd be
able to float around for forty million years.

'There'd be about three million people in the flying
saucer – it would be a big one. There'd be two of
everything – two guards, two priests, two doctors.
Animals? We might have one or two. And I'd be the
master of it. Master of the Universe.'

YOU'D THINK WE WERE IN FUCKING CASABLANCA

Taming The Left-Wing Political Queers.

Who? Micheál O'Móráin, Minister for Justice.
When? November, 1969.
What? He sparked a tribunal into illegal moneylending.
Where? The inquiry focused on Bill O'Herlihy and RTÉ.
Why? To root out exaggeration and general uppityness.

On November 11, 1999, Dublin's Point Theatre hosted Ireland's biggest ever televisual event, with the organisers of the *MTV Europe Music Awards* claiming one billion viewers. Thirty years earlier to the day, on November 11, 1969, one of the most ignominious chapters in Irish broadcasting history opened when the *7 Days* current affairs programme aired a report on illegal money-lending in Dublin.

Reporter Bill O'Herlihy told viewers that loan-sharking was widespread in poor areas, that failure to meet repayments could have health implications, and that the gardaí didn't seem overly pushed about tackling the problem. Fianna Fáil Justice Minister Micheál O'Móráin responded by shooting the messenger. He accused the *7 Days* team of gross exaggeration, of paying people to tell lies and of plying contributors with drink. O'Móráin immediately dispatched gardaí to question the programme makers but, he told the Dáil, they'd given 'no co-operation'.

It was not the first time the Castlebar solicitor had pulled ministerial rank to set the guards on someone. In

1968, O'Móráin locked horns with Fine Gael's Patrick
Reynolds over voting irregularities in a Leitrim polling
booth. During that year's local elections, the FG personation officer had nipped out to powder his nose. He
arrived back a couple of minutes later to find he'd missed
a stampede of voters including, it later emerged, a man in
America, a missing man, a bed-ridden woman, a hospi-
talised woman and a mental home inmate.

O'Móráin accepted there had been personation but he
maintained that there was no way of tracing the culprits.
Under Dáil privilege, Reynolds named the wrongdoers as
none other than the presiding officer and his polling clerk
wife. Worse, he accused the minister of spiking the garda
investigation. The next day Reynolds was livid as he
addressed the Dáil. O'Móráin had sent the cops around to
his home the previous evening to question him. As the
Dáil erupted, the minister taunted him with cries of: 'You
ran away!' (from the gardaí).

When it came to political cut and thrust, O'Móráin
favoured the broadsword over the rapier. He habitually
referred to one constituency opponent as 'The Maggot
Durkan' and branded the Labour Party as: 'Left-wing
political queers from Trinity College and Telefís Éireann.'

The government's considered response to the *7 Days*
report into illegal moneylending was to order a sworn
public inquiry, not into the moneylenders themselves, but
into the TV programme. Fianna Fáil's patience with RTÉ
had been fraying for some time. In 1966, a dispute blew up
between the Department of Agriculture and the National
Farmers' Association (NFA) over cattle prices. Agriculture
Minister Charles Haughey issued a statement saying
farmers shouldn't sell just now – the NFA issued a response
urging the opposite. The RTÉ early evening news carried

both statements. A furious Haughey rang the station and the NFA's statement was axed from later bulletins. Taoiseach Seán Lemass stepped in to remind RTÉ that it was 'an instrument of public policy'.

Shortly after the moneylending programme, planned field-trips by *7 Days* to North Vietnam and Biafra were cancelled. The Fianna Fáil Chairman of the Authority, CS 'Todd' Andrews, explained that reporting from Biafra might be seen as 'hobnobbing with rebels'. Just before the Biafran no-go the government had launched a referendum campaign to replace PR with a first-past-the-post system. A *7 Days* report demonstrated how the change would give Fianna Fáil an everlasting grip on power. Between the report and the referendum, *7 Days* was transferred to the news department, a place where straight reporting with no editorialising was the strict rule.

The moneylending tribunal found *7 Days* guilty as charged by Minister O'Móráin. The fact that the programme had undoubtedly exaggerated a tad here and embellished a mite there was used as evidence that no real moneylending problem existed, and as a rod to beat RTÉ's 'left-wing political queers' back into their closet for years to come.

Micheál O'Móráin's reign came to an unseemly end in 1970 during the shambles which led to the Arms Trial. As Minister for Justice, his brief encompassed breaking up plots to import illegal firearms into the country. However, a potent mixture of old school Republicanism and strong liquor blunted his effectiveness.

Peter Berry, O'Móráin's Secretary at the Justice Department, was kept posted on the gun-running conspiracy by the Special Branch. Berry in turn reported these developments to his Minister who was generally as drunk as several skunks. When Berry informed his minister that a security cordon had been mounted around Dublin Airport, O'Móráin's enigmatic response was: 'You'd think we were in fucking Casablanca or somewhere!' When Berry became convinced that O'Móráin hadn't bothered to tell Taoiseach Jack Lynch about the plot, he went to President de Valera who referred him to the Taoiseach. From here on, O'Móráin was effectively out of the loop.

Days after the arms landing was thwarted, Micheál O'Móráin was summoned to a meeting with Lynch to discuss his role in the farrago. The prognosis for the Justice Minister was terminal, though not serious. One commentator later noted: 'When able to focus, he seemed to be treating the whole matter as an entertaining drama.'

The night before he was to be officially carpeted out of his post, the minister carpeted himself at a public function. He was taken to hospital. The next day a government statement said he'd be indisposed for 'some weeks' and that 'under medical direction he is not to receive any visitors or to enter into any communication with anybody'. After two weeks of this solitary confinement, the minister quietly resigned.

THE BISHOP REQUESTS YOU DO NOT ATTEND

The Bishop of Kerry Vs Jayne Mansfield.

Who? Hollywood's most buxom Catholic mother-of-five.
When? April 1967.
What? Churchmen urged the faithful to boycott a show.
Where? The Mount Brandon Hotel, Tralee.
Why? A Bishop doesn't have to explain.

There was only one contender for Kerry Joke Of The Year, 1967. It was the one about the bishop and the actress.

Jayne Mansfield's Hollywood career had been on the skids for some time when she signed up for a one night stand in Tralee's Mount Brandon Hotel. The booking immediately divided the town's Urban Council. Councillor Michael O'Regan sounded a dire warning. 'This is not the proper person we should have entertaining here,' he thundered. 'The lady says she cannot sing or dance, but is a sex symbol.'

By the time the great day arrived, the issue of whether Ms Mansfield's celebrated sexiness was appropriate to Tralee had escalated into a heated national debate. The promoters were confident that 3,000 paying punters would settle the matter in their favour. Their optimism was punctured by a twin-pronged jab of divine intervention. The Bishop of Kerry asked only one thing of his flock:

unquestioning obedience. His pithy message to massgoers
on the morning of the planned show was polite but firm:
'Our attention has been drawn to an entertainment in
Tralee tonight. The Bishop requests you do not attend.'

If persuasion was needed, the Dean of Kerry weighed
in with the hard evidence. He quoted the siren's own
words. 'I am a sexy entertainer,' she had said. The Dean
continued: 'I appeal to the men and girls of Tralee to
disassociate themselves from this attempt to besmirch the
name of our town for the sake of filthy gain. I ask all our
people to ignore the presence of this woman and her
associates. They are attempting something that is contrary
to the moral teaching of our faith, that is against our
traditions and against the ordinary decencies of life,
something that is against everything we hold dear.'

Worse still, according to the Dean, the very presence
of this particular Catholic mother of five in the town
would cast a slur on the annual Festival Of Kerry – the self
same jamboree that each year selected one maiden as an
ideal of womanhood and honoured her as Rose Of
Tralee. The Dean knew that he would be accused of small
town small-mindedness, but what was wrong with that? He
pointed out that in the big smoke of Jerusalem they'd said
of Jesus: 'What do you expect from him? He comes from
Nazareth.' The Dean stressed that he was not an intellectual, but he knew that if his parishioners worshipped
Christ in the morning, they could not play with the Devil
in the evening.

That same afternoon the placebo Monroe met the press
at Dublin Airport while she awaited her transfer to
Shannon. Caressing the mandatory pet Chihuahuas with
rhinestoned fingers, the emerald-garbed star presented a
pair of impeccable credentials – she never missed Sunday

mass and she'd been Queen of the previous month's Saint Patrick's Day parade in Sacramento, California. 'I wore a green mini-skirt,' she smouldered.

Informed of the Bishop's ruling of that morning, Jayne declared herself 'quite surprised'. 'My show is not *risqué*,' she insisted. 'It's satirical. My clothes will be tight-fitting but high-necked, especially because it's Sunday. I think it's much more elegant, and sexier, to be fully clothed.' She outlined an alternative theory for the cleric's hostility. 'I did make a big mistake once,' she giggled, 'and maybe the Bishop remembers.' It transpired that on her first visit to Ireland, eight years previously, she'd remarked fawningly upon the beauty of her 'British' surroundings.

A huge crowd of well-wishers awaited Mansfield at Shannon. 'Isn't it wonderful,' she gushed, leaning against a counter to take in the scene. Within minutes of her chauffeured departure, an Aer Lingus clerk had erected a sign on the counter proclaiming 'JAYNE RESTED HERE'. When the star's vehicle caught a flat near the town of Castleisland, Jayne made straight for the only place open on a Sunday afternoon. In the parish church she lit a votive candle for her young son who'd recently been mauled in a lion-petting incident.

Arriving belatedly into Tralee, the actress learned that the venue's directors had just emerged from an emergency meeting. They'd issued a terse statement. It said: 'Owing to the controversy caused by the visit of Jayne Mansfield, the management of the Mount Brandon Hotel has decided to cancel her appearance.'

Mansfield responded with a statement of her own. She said: 'There seems to be a problem. Nobody cancelled my act tonight.' In her version of events: 'The musical arrangement for my act was sent on in advance so that an

Irish band could practise it. The band, I have been told, broke down somewhere and cannot be located.

The Brandon's dashing manager, Mr Patrick White, leapt to the rescue. *Of course* that's exactly what had happened. He'd appreciate it if everyone could just ignore the original statement which said the cancellation was due to 'controversy'. 'I had the statement done up and it slipped out by mistake,' he pleaded. The Dean of Kerry presumably didn't buy the missing musicians story. This was a victory for Christian decency and a personal triumph for himself and the Bishop. At high mass that evening the Dean expressed his gratitude to Mr John Byrne, the hotel's managing director, for 'cancelling this special entertainment'.

Jayne Mansfield jetted off for Paris the following day. She'd netted the hefty sum of £1,000 plus generous expenses for her flying visit. Even as the star hightailed it out of town, some Tralee folk were still spoiling for a scrap. The *Irish Press* reported that: 'Tralee residents were considering lodging a protest with RTÉ over Saturday night's sketch on *The Late Late Show* which depicted three people with placards in protest against Miss Mansfield's visit in the town. One local resident said: 'This type of thing is not funny. If RTÉ want to laugh at Miss Mansfield, alright, but they should leave the people of Tralee out of it.'

Rarely has The Point been missed with such aplomb.

A ROW IN THE HOUSE

Damian Corless Vs *Into The Heart*.

Who? Martin, Kathleen, Bono, Niall.
When? February, 1981.
What? A car hit a pole which hit Kathleen then Martin.
Where? Willow Park Road, Dublin.
Why? Some days are better than others.

It all began on a bleak morning in early 1981 when middle-aged Dublin couple Martin and Kathleen Corless pulled out of their driveway to go to work. After travelling a few yards, they joined a line of stalled cars. A bus had come to grief at the end of the icy road.

There were other routes off the estate. Martin flicked the indicator and began to turn the car around. A motorbike speeding down the wrong side of the street braked hard to avoid a collision. Martin rolled down the window to remonstrate with the reckless rider. The term 'road rage' was unknown at the time, but the semantics of the situation couldn't shield Martin from a barrage of hysterical punches.

By teatime Martin was sporting a horrific shiner and cursing the seatbelt that had rendered him a sitting target. The table was being cleared after the evening meal when an excited neighbour rang at the door. Come see! More motor mayhem! Just outside the front door, a car had swerved suddenly across the oncoming lane and ploughed into a telegraph pole.

Martin and Kathleen joined the knot of concerned neighbours at the scene. In the confusion, nobody paid much heed to the phone cables trailing from the felled mast. These cables, shrouded in dusk, now formed a tripwire across the road. The first passing car sprang the trap.

The car, when it came, snagged the fallen wires and lurched onward like a harpooned whale. High on a nearby gable the wire strained at its bracket. The bracket formed the third point of a triangle completed by the moving car and fallen pole (see p. 644, Fig.1a). As the cable jerked rigid, it shot the pole into the air. As the pole flew upwards, a steel foothold struck the back of Kathleen's head. The projectile reached its maximum altitude and the cable snapped. The mast fell to Earth, pinning Martin to the ground.

An ambulance whisked the injured couple away. The onlookers' attentions turned back to the driver who'd crashed in the first place. He'd emerged from the car crash unscathed. After dusting himself off, he'd dashed back home around the corner to phone the gardaí. The kids milling around identified him as Bono out of U2.

My parents survived to tell the tale. Naturally, over the years, I told it to anyone who'd listen. Hard as I looked, though, I could never find a good enough reason to put it in print. It was just a freak incident completely unrelated to U2's soaraway success story. Until the publication of Niall Stokes' 1996 U2 hagiography, *Into The Heart*.

In the book, Bono's friend and collaborator Gavin Friday discusses the U2 song *I Threw A Brick Through A Window*. As Gavin relates it: 'Bono was going to a party with Alison and he decided to splash out on a bottle of wine . . . There was this couple up the road called Mr & Mrs Curley, and Bono was driving this crock of a car – and whatever he did he crashed into Mr & Mr Curley's gate and the whole fucking post fell into the garden. The wine spilt all over the car and the gardaí thought he'd been drinking. And there were all these fucking neighbours, all these two-faced Catholics, standing in judgement. And it was, like, "I have to get out of this fucking kip". So there was this sort of brick through the window of that Gay Byrne world that was closing in on us all. And the feeling was: Sorry, Cedarwood has to go.'

This is surprising. At the time of the accident, sightings of U2 were very rare in the Dublin suburb of Cedarwood. A major British, European and US tour had kept them beyond the gaze of the local window-squinters for most of the previous six months. A long slog around Europe beckoned within days.

Back to the book. In the very next paragraph, Bono explains that the song in question was about 'a row in the house'. End of story. So Gavin's garbled outburst was just a gratuitous car-crash anecdote – like this one, but not as good – a jigsaw piece that didn't fit but was bunged into place anyway. And Niall Stokes let the name Curley pass when he knew full well it was Corless, having been at the receiving end of the anecdote many times.

Perhaps Niall would argue that these are trifling details, that an impressionistic mish-mash is even better than the real thing. To do so, however, he'd have to apply a different set of standards to those brought to bear by his own magazine on Eamon Dunphy's *Unforgettable Fire* biography.

'FOUL!' screamed the *Hot Press* headline. Dunphy's tome was gleefully savaged as an 'ill-researched' error-riddled 'travesty'. 'The pettiness of each of these errors does not mean they can be simply disregarded,' censured the mag. 'The truth is that they combine to distort the big picture.'

Dunphy's book got Niall's school wrong. This was seized upon by the writer of the critique, Neil McCormack, as evidence of a deeper failing. 'In getting his facts wrong,' he charged, 'Dunphy not only insults the people involved, he throws entirely false light on the picture with a simple fact that, if he was not entirely certain of it, he need never have included in the first place. It suggests a lack of knowledge, a lack of research – and ultimately a lack of care.'

Enough said. Oh, except that the prototype U2 first gigged in 1976, not 1974 as Niall's book states. And U2 have a song called *Some Days Are Better Than Others*. Towards the end of Stokes' exhaustive study – p.119, to be precise – that title is rendered as 'Some *Songs* Are Better Than Others'.

Doctor Freud was unavailable for comment.

HE BELIEVED HE WAS GOING TO BE THE NEXT JEFFREY ARCHER

The Exceedingly Strange Life And Times Of Michael Keating.

Who? An ex-Dublin Lord Mayor and PD Deputy Leader.
When? 1977–2002.
What? A novel, a baldness cure, a mystery diary, a tax bill.
Where? Fine Gael, the PDs, Fine Gael, movie sets etc.
Why? Movie director Neil Jordan detected a 'fanciful' streak.

In May 2002, following a five-year investigation into the laundering of drugs money, Michael Keating agreed to pay €250,000 to the Criminal Assets Bureau. In return, the CAB left Keating with enough cash from the enforced sale of his luxury home to purchase a more modest family dwelling. For the former Lord Mayor of Dublin and deputy leader of the Progressive Democrats a long, strange trip had come to a sorry pass.

Keating's predicament would have been beyond his wildest imaginings back in 1977 when the voters of Dublin's north inner city swept himself and arch-rival Bertie Ahern into the Dáil for the first time. Ahern had the momentum of a massive Fianna Fáil landslide behind him. Far more impressively, Keating delivered a new Fine Gael seat in the midst of a rout.

The rising twin-stars, both councillors, would compete to be the first to tell the local community association that its annual Corporation grant had been approved. The pair

would vie to propose the grant at the Corporation – in fact
it was a formality – and then they'd race to get off the first
mailshot claiming credit for the handout. Five years older
than Ahern, Keating already had one career behind him.
As a journalist he'd edited *Woman's Way* and several other
publications.

Keating's electoral heroics in 1977 didn't earn him a
seat on the front bench, but Garret Fitzgerald's 1979
reshuffle rectified that and he was made party spokesman
on human rights and law reform. He sparkled in the role,
dismaying Fine Gael's hang 'em, flog 'em rump with far
sighted proposals on prison reform, child protection, gay
rights and freedom-of-information.

When Fitzgerald's first coalition government came to
power in 1981, Michael Keating was made minister of
state at the Department of Education with responsibility
for youth and sport. A survey that same year named the
cherubic Dubliner as the third most photographed politician
in Ireland after the Taoiseach and Charles Haughey. But
while his career graph was shooting off the chart as far as the
public were concerned, behind the scenes Michael Keating
was in a hole and digging furiously.

Trouble first reared its head when Keating made a
unilateral decision that the State should purchase Adare
Manor in Limerick. His party leader Garret Fitzgerald
told him to forget it, and to cancel a planned trip to
address a meeting in Adare. Keating carried on regardless.
Furious, the Taoiseach dispatched a garda patrol car to
intercept his minister, unaware that Keating had pressed
an Air Corps helicopter into service. Despite everything
Fitzgerald had said, Keating assured his audience in Adare
of the government's 'genuine' interest in retaining the
house for the nation.

There were several other run-ins with the party hierarchy, but the final straw came with Keating's campaign for the first of 1982's two general elections. In the 1981 election Bertie Ahern had topped the poll, but Fine Gael's Alice Glenn had made it into the Dáil on Keating's coat-tails, just ahead of independent Tony Gregory.

Alice Glenn would later run the Irish chapter of the hard-right World Anti-Communist League. Keating had a personal distaste for the views of a woman who once boasted: 'The past two referenda showed we are not yet a modern sophisticated people – thank God for that.' Increasingly intolerant of Glenn, Keating ran a highly personalised campaign in February 1982 leaving his party colleague out on a limb. Tony Gregory took full advantage to oust Glenn. It was a crunch result in the Fitzgerald government's fall from power and the episode marked Keating as Fine Gael's dead man walking. When the coalition returned to office in the second general election of that year, he was left to stew on the backbenches.

Denied a place at the cabinet table, Keating had to pick at the leftovers and in 1983 he began a hectic year as Lord Mayor of Dublin. After leaving office he complained that his allowance had been 'woefully inadequate', cribbing that it wasn't proper for the Lady Mayoress to spend 'a full day slicing up almost sixty catering pans in the basement of the Mansion House to prepare sandwiches'.

Fitzgerald's cabinet reshuffle of February 1986 sealed Keating's internal exile. With nowhere to go in Fine Gael, Keating looked towards the upstart Progressive Democrats for rescue. Fine Gael's standard put-down of the PDs was to dismiss the year-old party as a Fianna Fáil dissident group. If Keating were to defect, it would not only reduce Fitzgerald's Dáil majority to a precarious margin of one, but it would give the lie to the 'dissident' claim. There was a price to be paid, however. Keating demanded, and got, the deputy leadership of the Progressive Democrats, leaving Mary Harney and Bobby Molloy to bite their lips for the greater good.

The Taoiseach received Keating's 'Dear John' letter only after the nation learned of his treachery on the main evening news. Fine Gael's press officer, Peter White, fumed that Keating had okayed a statement saying he was staying just hours earlier. In welcoming Keating on board, the PDs – the self-proclaimed party of standards and integrity – had to issue a denial that their new star signing had 'lied to the media about his intentions'.

Keating had barely arranged the pencils on his new PD desk when he set off on another damaging solo run. He announced that his new party backed proposals, by Liam Skelly of his old party, to spend £200 million on regenerating inner city Dublin. His new leader, Des O'Malley, was left to shoot down the plan amid much embarrassment.

In November 1986, with an election in the air, the *Sunday Press* ran a big splash breaking details of the mad dash to Adare Manor five years earlier. And there was more. According to the same *Sunday Press* report, Keating had improperly spent Department of Education money on personal election literature. Keating branded the story an 'exercise in political knee-capping' and said he'd be suing the newspaper for libel, but he never pursued the case.

Keating retained his Dáil seat in the 1987 general election, but by now he was regarded as damaged goods by both Fine Gael and the Progressive Democrats, and even as a possible impediment to any future coalition deal between the two.

As he became an increasingly isolated figure in the Dáil, Keating kept an interest in a publishing company, Timeplan. He was 'very hands on' according to one employee. But in a 1989 *Hot Press* interview, Keating insisted he had no involvement in publishing. It was pointed out to him that his wife's name was on the company stationary. He said a friend had put her name on the letterheading 'without my knowledge and without my agreement' as part of the friend's efforts to get Keating on board, 'but I said I'd no interest in that'.

It wouldn't be the last time that Michael Keating would be asked to explain incongruous documentation. Nor would it be the last time his choice of acquaintances would let him down. The friend who urged him to join Timeplan was Jim Booth, who was later Chairman of the Inner City Traders Association until his arrest on charges of handling stolen goods and possession of a firearm. In December 2000 Booth was convicted of possessing stolen mobile-phone accessories, a revolver and crossbow.

Keating's souring love affair with the PDs ended in tears (for them) when he jilted the party on the opening day of the 1989 general election campaign. 'He left us in an awful mess,' said one party activist, who added: 'We didn't feel we'd lost a great politician, just a candidate who happened to be deputy leader.'

After his sudden retirement from politics, Michael Keating quickly recast himself as a wannabe best-selling author. 'He really believed he was going to be the next Jeffrey Archer,' remarked one acquaintance. *Day Of Reckoning* was hyped as 'an international super-thriller' about a brave and cunning individual who takes the big institutions for a ride. It was launched by the Taoiseach of the day, Charles Haughey. The book fared no better than Keating's slightly earlier attempts – which included an appearance on *The Late Late Show* – to market a miracle cure for baldness.

In 1991 he retired from political retirement. Remarkably,
Fine Gael took him back. He was parachuted into Dublin
South West where fully three percent of the electorate
welcomed his return with their first preferences in 1992.
At the count in Tallaght, Keating said he was personally
disappointed but that he was in the constituency 'for the
long haul'. He returned to the council circuit.

That same year Keating formed Atlantis Business
Consultants with an old political adversary who'd once been
active in the Bertie Ahern camp. Atlantis was set up to
tender for FÁS training schemes. Keating's new partner was
surprised when an employee told him that Keating was using
Atlantis stationary for unrelated projects. Surprise turned to
shock when the partner learned that the Department of
Trade & Enterprise had received 'supportive documentation'
from Atlantis linked to an application for beef export
insurance. The partner asked Keating if it was true that he'd
been using Atlantis stationary to tender for non-FÁS
projects. He recorded Keating's nonchalant response as:
'Maybe I have.' The company was shut down.

Keating lowered his profile as the Nineties wore on.
However, on Good Friday 1995, he surfaced in the
proximity of movie director Neil Jordan who was making
the biopic *Michael Collins* at the time.

Jordan wrote in his diary that he met Keating who was
accompanied by a journalist. The entry read: 'They told
me that a friend of Mr Keating, a solicitor, is in possession
of Emmet Dalton's diary. (Dalton was an aide of Collins).
In the diary, the unnamable friend claims, there is an
admission that Dalton shot Collins at close range with a
Luger pistol.'

According to Jordan's diary, Keating told him that his
solicitor friend was dying with cancer and didn't know

what to do with the sensational document. Keating told him that the dying solicitor had sat on Dalton's diary because it revealed that Michael Collins was an enthusiastic homosexual and that Dalton's main job had been to pick up young privates for his commander.

At this point, Jordan asked the pair if they'd actually seen Dalton's diary. They told him no, but that they'd seen copies of some of the pages. Jordan felt that 'the whole scenario is far too fanciful' and he asked Keating and friend why they'd decided to share the secret with him. They answered that one, he said, with 'an indeterminate reply'. So Jordan told them that if the diary really existed they should publish it themselves. He then pressed them on why they hadn't insisted on seeing it with their own four eyes. At that point, he wrote: 'They tell me, solemnly, that the cancer was misdiagnosed and the solicitor was no longer in fear of death, so no longer felt the burden of revealing his terrible secret.'

Jordan closed his diary entry by saying that the pair then departed, leaving him to muse as to what a former Lord Mayor was doing 'peddling such extraordinary stories'.

In September 1997 Michael Keating was arrested by the Criminal Assets Bureau, along with his business partner, Peter Bolger, for their part in a money-laundering operation. When apprehended, Keating was holding £48,000 which had passed through Bolger's company, Louiseville, on behalf of the drugs-trafficker George Mitchell AKA 'The Penguin'. Louiseville traded as Eringold. Keating was a director of Eringold, although once again his name was curiously missing from the company records.

Keating had used his political connections to get a letter of recommendation for Bolger and Eringold from the Minister of Agriculture, Ivan Yates. What he hadn't told

Yates was that Bolger had fourteen convictions for theft, fraudulent trading and forgery. Bolger had been convicted in his absence by a British court, having fled Britain three days before his trial ended.

While Keating and Bolger were under investigation in Ireland by the CAB, it emerged that they had been involved in a £20 million VAT fraud in Britain during the early 1990s. The fraud, involving the claiming of VAT on imaginary exports of computer parts, led to the convictions of an Irish man and woman.

During his trial for the fraud, Limerickman Daniel O'Connell, told the jury that he'd tried to pull out of the racket, but that Keating had threatened to break his legs. According to O'Connell's evidence: 'Keating said, "If you don't get on with what I've told you to do, you will be in serious trouble." He told me I would be in a wheelchair. He said, "We know where you live. We know where your wife and children are", and "Your girlfriend will end up with a lot of stitches in her face".'

According to Peter Rook QC, prosecutor for HM Customs & Excise, Keating had been 'well involved' in the fraud. Rook identified Keating as a director of one of the firms which placed bogus orders for computer chips. The trial heard that millions of pounds were moved to offshore bank accounts in the Bahamas, Central America and Belize and that British police were extremely anxious to question Michael Keating as to the money's whereabouts.

Unfortunately for their investigation, the former deputy leader of the party of fiscal rectitude was staying put in Ireland.

THE SCREWS WERE ALL ASTOUNDED

Official Ireland Vs *The Helicopter Song*.

> Who: The Wolfe Tones entertainment group.
> When: Late 1973.
> What: The Tones' latest release was banned.
> Where: From the airwaves and newspapers.
> Why: For celebrating an IRA jailbreak.

The Austerity Christmas of 1973 put a full-stop on a decade of Irish economic boom. The first of the great oil crises was biting deep, and short measures were the order of the day. The three-day working week had arrived. People queued for rationed petrol. Late night TV was deemed an extravagance so RTÉ scrapped a lump of its Christmas schedule. School holidays were extended by a week to save the state fuel. At a time of enforced absences, Ireland's unique contribution to the global missing list was a huge hit.

Some background. Mountjoy Prison was in the news throughout 1973. In the spring, two prisoners escaped over an exercise yard wall. Then, in July, a routine garda patrol surprised a gang about to throw a rope ladder into the same yard. The men got away. A summer of riots and hunger strikes ensued, as prisoners agitated for political status. An uneasy peace was restored when the authorities allowed that the Republican prisoners would take care of their own wing of the prison.

It was the calm before the storm. In mid-October a man with an American accent phoned Irish Helicopters at Dublin Airport. Giving his name as Paul Leonard, the man – who claimed to be a movie producer – arranged

to take aerial photos of monuments in Co Laois, followed
by a sight-seeing jaunt over Co Wicklow. On Tuesday,
October 30th, Leonard – 'a prosperous looking man in his
mid-twenties' – called to Irish Helicopters and selected
their most manoeuvrable aircraft, the Alouette 2.

The exotic stranger returned the following day for his
£80-an-hour trip. As arranged, the helicopter flew to
Stradbally, Co Laois, where it landed in a field belonging
to Tommy Kelly, a bachelor farmer. Two men emerged
from nearby trees and notified the pilot of a change of
plan at gunpoint. 'Mr Leonard' departed with one of the
men, advising the pilot that if he knew what was good for
him he would do what he was told.

The helicopter's new passenger gave directions for
Mountjoy. It was still bright when the aircraft set down in
the exercise compound at 3.35pm, just as a group of
Republican inmates were stretching their legs. Seamus
Twomey, JB O'Hagan and Kevin Mallon hopped on
board while the other prisoners formed a protective
cordon around the helicopter.

The prison staff seemed mesmerised by the whirring
blades. 'Some of them shouted to the warders at the main
gate to lock it,' testified a man visiting at the time. He
witnessed 'a huge cheer from the prisoners' as the craft
took off. Within ten minutes the fugitives were hopping
into a stolen taxi at Baldoyle Racecourse.

Meanwhile, back at Mountjoy shellshocked warders
compared notes. It emerged that some guards assumed the
helicopter was an Army chopper come to pick up a sick
prisoner. At least one warder thought that the visitation
was the Minister For Defence making a surprise inspection.
As the apparition hovered the guard was heard to mutter:
'Nobody tells me anything around here.'

The country was convulsed, mostly with laughter. It would be months yet before the Dublin and Monaghan bombings brought the bloody reality of the Troubles down South. There was a broad consensus that Robin Hood had put one over on the nasty Sheriff. *The Irish Times* reported a scintillating new joke sweeping across party lines in Leinster House. Q: 'Tell me, d'ye think it would have happened if Fianna Fáil was in power?' A: 'Not bloody likely! Twomey and the boys wouldn't be in the Joy in the first place.' An emergency cabinet meeting appeared to conclude that the audacious breakout was just one of those things. 'They regard it as something unlikely to happen a second time,' surmised one reporter.

Checkpoints crisscrossed Dublin. Gardaí suspected that Twomey, the most wanted of the three, was holed up in the capital. He was a slippery customer. British soldiers had once raided a Belfast house looking for him. After a fruitless search they'd apologised to the villain in disguise for disturbing his peace.

Ten days after the escape, Mountjoy's remaining Republican prisoners were transported to the high-security jail in Portlaoise. For reasons best known to himself, Kevin Mallon trailed his former cellmates to the town. He was having a ball at the Hotel Montague's GAA dance when an observant off-duty garda reunited him with his comrades.

It's not known whether Mallon was at the dance long enough to join in the raucous chorus of the country's Number One hit. Performed by The Wolfe Tones it was called *Up And Away (The Helicopter Song)*. The record's execution had been as speedy and slick as the feat of criminal derring-do it celebrated. A mere twenty-two days after the great escape, *Up And Away* crashed into the Top

Ten. Its potent combination of topicality and cutting edge technology (a whirring-noise sound effect) quickly airlifted the song to the top of the charts.

The tune had all the subtlety of a swinging lump-hammer, but the lyrics compensated by fusing a good storyline with that rarest of qualities in Irish rebel songs – a happy ending. The result was a jarring mid-air collision between *Boolavogue* and *Chitty Chitty Bang Bang*.

The first couplet got the effort off to a flying start, rhyming 'the year of '73' with 'longing to be free'. As the narrative unfolded 'the screws were all astounded' and 'just stood there dumbfounded', while 'the traitors' in the Dáil 'were quite aghast' to see 'the Provies flying past'. Needless to say, 'cruel Britain' was 'furious' with the escape, adding to the goodwill 'everywhere in Ireland' going out to the 'gallant three' and their 'marvellous flying bird'.

The Mountjoy escape had been an acute embarrassment to the authorities. The Wolfe Tones' rousing anthem was insult heaped upon injury – the solemn offices of the state made an all-singin', all-dancin' laughing stock. Piqued, Official Ireland reacted the only way it knew how and banned the cursed thing. For weeks, Larry Gogan's Top 30 countdown climaxed prematurely with the Number 2 hit in the land. Newspapers were scrawny because newsprint was scarce due to the oil shortage, but lack of space wasn't why a most newsworthy phenomenon got zero coverage in the nationals.

Needless to say, the blanket ban merely increased the disc's outlaw cachet and sales soared accordingly. Soon, every ballad group in the land were featuring the toe-tappin', knee-cappin' *Up And Away* in their set. The song was recorded by several acts, eventually getting temporary release on an album entitled *The Lid Of Me Granny's Bin*. Future singles by The Wolfe Tones included a nifty ditty articulating Ireland's territorial claim to Rockall and a timely intervention into the Falklands' War on the side of Argentina.

A few years after defeat in the Falklands conflict the Wolfe Tones mounted a one-band cultural boycott on Radio 2 (now 2FM), refusing to supply the station with copies of their latest album, *Sing Out For Ireland*. They claimed that they and other domestic acts had been 'victimised' by the national broadcaster which was 'depriving young people of the right to hear Irish music'.

The Tones accused the station of poisoning young minds with foreign records that 'mainline in sex and drugs'. And if the young people *were* mad for the likes of the Beastie Boys and The Smiths, the Tones argued: 'It's only because the youth aren't getting the chance to hear any other sort. If we got equal billing on the national station with, say, Madonna, we'd be selling a lot more records and the money would be staying in the country.' Cruelly, the station continued to deprive the youth of their right to hear the Wolfe Tones on the playlist.

More than a decade after the runaway success of *Up And Away*, the Wolfe Tones' Derek Warfield glumly reflected: 'Our audience in the North now would be ninety-nine-percent Nationalist. It's totally gone that way now, which is a tragedy.'

Explanations on a postcard, please. Best entry wins a copy of the seminal Sixties Wolfe Tones' album *Rifles Of The IRA*.

IF MY WIFE ONLY HAD ONE OF YOURS I'D DIE HAPPY

The Daniel O'Donnell School Of Go-Go Dancing.

Who? Toni The Exotic Dancer.
When? The Toni phenomenon peaked in 1986–87.
What? Two breasts wobbling in a gauze vest. 1 feather boa.
Where? The Lower Deck, Dublin, and all over Ireland.
Why? 'They're there to be used. They're making me money.'

In the age of innocence that was the 1980s, a thirty-something housewife and mother billing herself as Toni The Exotic Dancer drew big crowds to the Lower Deck in Rathmines every Sunday lunchtime for a spectacle which essentially consisted of two pendulous breasts wobbling haphazardly in a gauze vest. Toni's dancing, which involved a feather boa and much writhing, was limited in style, but she didn't cover for this by doing anything as coarse as removing her clothes.

She explained: 'I do not take me clothes off because there's no reason to take them off. Between the boobs and the legs and everything, I show enough . . . I feel it would have nothing to do with my act to drop my top. It would just be a thing on the side. Anyway I need to keep them closer together or else they'd be bouncin' all over the place.'

Reports of Toni's 'outrageous' and 'raunchy' gyrations were carried by the *Sunday World* on an almost weekly basis, and thrill-starved males flocked to cast an eye over her credentials. One group made the long haul to Dublin from Carlow on the strength of some exposure in the *World*. Asked what they expected to see, an elderly day-tripper nursing his pint replied: 'She'd want to show something to cover the cost of the petrol at least.' A short time later, the show over, the senior citizen from Carlow was asked if he'd had his petrol money's worth. 'I'll never believe the fuckin' *Sunday World* again,' he growled.

Those who came to Toni's performances purely to letch were missing the point. Toni The Exotic Dancer was no purveyor of in-yer-face filth, but a graduate of the Daniel O'Donnell tea-and-biscuits charm school. 'I use no vulgarity,' she pointed out. 'I don't believe a woman should be vulgar. I'm still a lady and they know that. The fan letters I get, they say, "we know you're a lady and we know you're a mother and a damn good one as well".'

After each show Toni would quickly emerge fully-clothed from her dressing room to distribute signed photos of herself and have a cosy chat with her fans. Describing the men who came to see her as '*the crème-de-la-crème*' she explained: 'I get some great comments, like "If my wife only had one of yours I'd die happy". I gave a photograph to one guy and I signed it for him, and the guy just looked at it very, very dry and says, "It's hard to believe that you and the wife are the same sex".' Admirers showered Toni with flowers and wrote her poetry.

During her meet-the-audience sessions, Toni would engage in question-and-answer sessions with her admirers: 'Not personal questions about my body by any means, they ask questions about your life, and is your husband jealous, and they're honest too – they say if you were my wife I wouldn't allow you to do that.' The niceties out of the way, the fans would then frequently inquire whether a shag was out of the question. 'A lot of men ask you to go to bed,' she confessed. 'I say no thank you, and thank you for the compliment.'

Toni started in showbiz when, aged seventeen, she got work as a go-go dancer at Sunday morning stag shows in pubs around Dublin. She retired to become a housewife and raise children, but when she went looking for work after twelve years in the home she found that her options were limited. 'I went out to look for a job and it was a cleaning job and it wasn't good enough.' So she put an advert in the *Sunday World* and, with that organ taking an active interest in her unconventional line of work, the bookings started pouring in.

Husband Brian remained constantly on hand to keep a watchful eye on the show. 'I criticise her,' he revealed. 'If I feel she's not putting enough into her act I tell her, I lift her out of it. But if she's putting *too* much in, well, she knows were to draw the line – *we* know where to draw the line.' The lines were firmly drawn in their domestic arrangements too. Dismissing suggestions that Brian might get jealous, Toni observed: 'I live with this man, I wash for him, I cook for him, why the hell should he be jealous?'

Toni viewed her exotic dancing as a stepping stone to greater things. 'I want to have my own band,' she said. 'I want to start singing. I want to go into acting . . . I want to go into television and films . . . In the end I want to write a book.' She admitted: 'I can't do a Harold Robbins. It'll be an entertainment book about how it all started and how the men came to see me . . .'

WE'D NEVER HAVE GOTTEN TO THE BOTTOM OF IT

The unsolved mystery of the €70 million black hole.

Who? Six politicians, CIE's top brass, Denis O'Brien's Esat.
When? 2001.
What? A key inquiry is shunted aside.
Where? The main players were summonsed to Kildare Street.
Why? Something very disturbing had happened inside CIE.

In 1997, the state's public transport body, CIE, signed a deal with Denis O'Brien's Esat phone company which was to deliver a complete safety upgrade of Ireland's railways by the end of 1999.

Instead, it led to public inquiry which exposed scandalous cost over-runs, breached procedures, missing documents, allegations of intimidation and much, much more. The affair, almost certainly, drove one man to his death.

The deal in question allowed Esat to lay fibre-optic cable along the country's rail-lines, turning the national rail network into an electronic 'spine' for the company's budding mobile phone service. CIE's *quid pro quo*, it was reported at the time, would be to get a new Mini-CTC signalling system 'for virtually nothing'.

With the deal done, CIE could now hold up the contract as its riposte to a host of doomsayers. One scathing report that same year warned of a 'predictable' risk of fatalities within two years unless urgent repairs were made. The report found that some 'highly suspect' signal-box wiring at Heuston Station dated back to 1936.

But the dream date with Esat turned into a nightmare for CIE, and for the taxpayer. The initial projected signalling cost of €17.78m had surged to €70m and rising by the start of 2004. By that late stage the timetable was in tatters and the original 1999 completion date had been pushed back to 2005.

CIE and Esat unveiled their joint-venture in June 1997. Esat's cable-laying operation pressed full-steam ahead. Meanwhile, CIE's parallel project quickly ran off the rails, burning cash in shovel-loads. But it was late 1999 before news of the over-run leaked from the state-run company to taxpayers in the outside world.

Fine Gael's Jim Higgins got wind of a rail disaster in the making. He tabled a question in the Dáil. To his surprise, Mary O'Rourke, the Minister for Public Enterprise, said she was glad he'd raised the matter. In her two years in the post, O'Rourke's relations with some CIE executives had become openly fraught.

When the politicians began poking around, they discovered a Bermuda Triangle at the heart of CIE. Millions of taxpayers' money was going into the signalling upgrade. Very little progress, or information, was coming out. An Oireachtas Committee of Inquiry was established, chaired by former Justice Minister Sean Doherty.

The Department of Finance stepped in with an offer. It was prepared to cover the cost of legal representation for all parties. It was an offer the six Inquiry TDs were determined to refuse.

One explained: 'We wanted to run a quick, efficient investigation like the Public Accounts Committee did into the DIRT tax affair. The offer from Finance would have turned it into a fully-fledged tribunal, with lawyers taking over and raising objections at every turn. We'd never have gotten to the bottom of it.'

In the event, they never did get to the bottom of a mystery that might have bamboozled Sherlock Holmes. Holmes, famously, had to solve the case of the dog that didn't bark. The six TDs faced a similar task. Tried and trusted civil service early-warning systems had mysteriously gone on the blink.

The mystery was never solved because the Inquiry was shut-down in November 2001. An unrelated Oireachtas committee was investigating the role of gardaí in the shooting dead of Abbeylara man, John Carthy. The gardaí went to court with a claim that politicians sitting on Oireachtas committees have no right to pass potentially damaging judgements on members of the public. The court agreed.

The Rail Inquiry was stopped in its tracks.

Before it was derailed, the Committee met for 235 hours in private and public sessions, the latter televised daily by TG4. As it probed, the Inquiry shone a torch down some dim corridors of power. Caught in its beam, it glimpsed figures 'running for cover'.

That phrase was used by ex-CIE Chairman Brian Joyce, explaining how the company's chain of command failed to alert him to the mounting millions. 'There is usually a lot of running for cover,' he said, 'a lot of people anxious about their future, and you find it very hard to extract bad news as opposed to good news from them.'

Precisely how much effort CIE's top brass had put into extracting bad news became a key issue. Some witnesses conveyed the impression that CIE's management structure was a sort of commune where everyone, and no-one, was leader.

Areas of managerial responsibility appeared ill-defined and confusing to the curious TDs. CIE's chief financial officer, Jim Cullen, maintained that his job was to monitor expenditure, but not costs.

What did become abundantly clear was that standard semi-state fail-safe procedures were flouted, taking some senior personnel out of the loop. Worker-director Bill McCamley of the SIPTU union claimed that when 'vague rumours' of a signalling scandal reached him, he started asking awkward questions. This, he said, exposed him to 'psychological intimidation' by other board members.

McCamley claimed that CIE's then chief executive, Michael McDonnell, warned him to leave off being so nosy, telling him 'you are not doing CIE any good'. Another witness said that McDonnell had 'spiked' a report which might have jammed the breaks on the runaway costs.

As the head of CIE, Michael McDonnell was the top dog that failed to bark. McDonnell was appointed to the post in 1995 by the then minister, Michael Lowry. A career civil servant, McDonnell stepped across from Lowry's own department.

In December 2002, businessman Mark Fitzgerald (son of former Taoiseach Garret) told the Moriarty Tribunal that Michael Lowry attempted to interfere with a process, led by independent consultants, to fill the top CIE post. He said that Lowry, while minister, asked him to recommend McDonnell for the job.

Fitzgerald was criticised by some for the delay in going public with this claim. One ex-Inquiry member confirmed that if the committee had known about Fitzgerald's assertion even a year earlier: 'It would have been put to Lowry as a priority when he attended the Inquiry.'

Sparks flew when Denis O'Brien's turn came to face the investigators. The simmering hostility between O'Brien and the Chairman, Sean Doherty, erupted into white-hot volcanics. At one point, O'Brien told Doherty: 'You're not fit to be Chairman . . . All you're interested in is abusing people.'

After a short time-out, Doherty asked O'Brien if he wished to withdraw the remarks he'd made about the committee. No, said O'Brien, he hadn't criticised the committee, just its Chairman. O'Brien then questioned Doherty's fitness to sit in judgement over others 'given your past involvement with phone tapping and other matters'. As Minister for Justice in Charles Haughey's 1982 GUBU government, Doherty had authorised the illicit tapping of journalists' phones by gardaí in an effort to settle internal Fianna Fáil feuding by rooting out a mole.

Leaving the hearing, O'Brien was asked if his attack on Doherty's credibility had been calculated. No comment. However, those attacks were repeated in a press release which was issued within hours.

O'Brien and Doherty had clashed previously at the hearings. Doherty had asked O'Brien if he'd struck a 'sweetheart deal' with CIE in order to have his fibre-optic spine laid. It was 'absolutely disgraceful to even suggest it', replied O'Brien. 'If you wanted a headline, you've got it.'

For the Irish tax-payer, the deal soon turned sour. For reasons which will maybe always remain clouded, CIE prioritised Esat's cable-laying project over its own urgently-needed safety signalling upgrade. As a result, Esat's cable went into the ground quickly and efficiently by mechanical plough.

Now CIE was sunk. Once the Esat cable was laid, the same ground couldn't be ploughed again. This meant that long stretches of CIE's signalling cable would have to be laid by hand – a slow and far more costly process.

When Esat began laying its cable, the company was preparing for flotation on the US Nasdaq stock exchange. The flotation, in November 1997, was a success. O'Brien told the Inquiry that the cabling deal with CIE was not a crucial factor in the highly profitable outcome.

However, CIE's group solicitor pointed out that Esat's own published flotation prospectus, designed to attract investors, stressed the importance of the cabling deal. The prospectus said: 'Based on a signed letter of intent, the company expects to use CIE's rights of way to construct the network.'

Astonishingly, the CIE solicitor told the Inquiry that he'd neither seen nor heard of this 'signed letter of intent' between CIE and Esat. He'd scoured CIE's files but found no trace of any such letter. But the letter was referred to three times in the Esat flotation prospectus. 'I certainly want to get to the bottom of it,' he remarked.

There were other striking aspects to the affair, including a series of notable overlaps in personnel. CIE negotiated the deal with Esat while operating under a new procurement policy aimed at keeping close tabs on how the company was spending public money. That policy had been proposed in 1996 by a consultant hired by CIE, Leslie Buckley.

The following year, Buckley had moved over to Esat where he was Acting Chief Executive. He and Denis O'Brien negotiated the cabling deal with his former employer, CIE. The deal to which CIE agreed was in breach of the newly-adopted procurement procedure which had been designed by Buckley to cut costs.

Another key figure, Dr Ray Byrne, worked for both CIE and Esat for an overlapping period. The Inquiry heard that a series of scheduled CIE monthly meetings, which might have identified the huge over-run, were all cancelled. It heard that they were scratched because the man who would have chaired them, Dr Ray Byrne, was repeatedly unable to turn up. Dr Byrne said he doubted he was responsible for every cancellation.

In his opening statement, Chairman Sean Doherty said he would be trying to find out why four senior figures linked to the signalling project left CIE's rail division, Iarnród Éireann, to join the signal-laying contractor Modern Networks Ltd (MNL).

The Inquiry heard that Iarnród Éireann's contract with MNL had been 'impaired' by the dropping of a clause obliging MNL to notify it in advance of any 'unforeseen ground condition' which would require hand-laying. A performance bond was also waived by Iarnród Éireann, weakening the company's entitlements from the deal.

The Inquiry also heard that the MNL contract wasn't put to tender, when – by the book – three suitors should have been sought. It also heard that invoices from MNL didn't separate work done on Esat's giant phone aerial and on CIE's rail safety upgrade, blurring the true picture of CIE's costs.

The buck for CIE's disastrous signalling deal was passed horribly on to its Chief Executive, Michael McDonnell. As a public inquisition before the Inquiry loomed, McDonnell took his own life. He was found hanging in the locked garage of his Terenure home in April 2001. He was 58.

At the inquest, McDonnell's daughter Orla said that her father had never suffered from depression until two months before his death when he was 'forced to leave' his CIE post.

The Rail Inquiry had just one more day of public hearings to go when it was flagged to a crashing halt by the

ruling in the Abbeylara shooting case. The Committee's
unfinished report is a catalogue of mixed signals, cold
trails and dead-ends.

Reams of collected documentation which never
reached the public domain lie stored in a Leinster House
limbo. The general consensus around Kildare Street since
then has been that there's little political appetite for re-
opening this particular can of pickles.

MORAL DEPRAVITY, MY LORD

Holy Ireland Vs The Lesbian Nuns.

> Who? Lapsed Catholic sisters Nancy and Rosemary.
> When? September 1985.
> What? The pair received a hostile reception in Ireland.
> Where? In central Dublin and later outside RTÉ.
> Why? They were plugging a book on convent sexuality.

Friday the 13th of September 1985 was going to prove unlucky for one side in the keenly fought tug-of-war for Ireland's immortal soul. The lesbian nuns were coming. After days of breathless speculation, a Thursday morning radio interview confirmed that lapsed Catholic sisters Nancy Manahan and Rosemary Curb would arrive the following day to plug their US best seller, *Breaking Silence: Lesbian Nuns On Convent Sexuality*. An appearance on *The Late Late Show* was in prospect, although the programme had a policy of keeping its guest-list top secret until transmission time. Aghast protesters jammed the Montrose switch. Just in case.

What gave? The infamous Bishop And The Nightie scandal of two decades before had long since acquired comedy cult status. Gaybo himself had interviewed a lesbian on the show six years earlier, eliciting barely a whimper of 'Sodom and begorrah' from his public. But these were changed times. Here, at the mid-point of the Eighties, the rancour of the first abortion referendum still lingered, while the first divorce poll was bearing down hard. A state of most uncivil war obtained between

Irelands old and new. And besides, lesbians were one
thing, but lesbian nuns . . . Was nothing sacred?

On the Thursday morning of the radio interview,
Dublin customs seized 1,500 copies of the offending book,
seemingly unaware that 3,000 copies were already on full
frontal display in bookshops around the country. An
official announcement was hurried out on Thursday night.
Its tone was unmistakably one of 'oops, there's been a
ghastly mistake'. The seizure was pinned on a lone zealot.
No need to panic. The impounded tomes had now been
'cleared by reference to a higher authority'.

The book itself chronicled the experiences of 49 nuns
and former nuns across North America. Each had a
remarkably similar story to tell. Namely, that: 'Our
devotion to our girlfriends and the nuns, along with our
discomfort on dates with boys, was not, as we suspected at
the time, an unmistakable sign of religious vocation, but a
premonition of our late-blooming lesbianism.'

A press conference was arranged for three o'clock on
the Friday afternoon at a top Dublin hotel. However, upon
arrival there, the former sisters were flatly informed that
the room they'd booked was unavailable. The nuns, their
publishers, a coterie of journalists and half of Dublin's gay
community were summarily dispatched onto the street.
There they remained for some time, hanging around.
There was nowhere to go because the pubs were shut for
Holy Hour. A vengeful God couldn't have fashioned a
more poetic justice. The Pink Elephant bar eventually
provided a makeshift press HQ when the pubs reopened
at 3.30.

At this juncture the action shifted across town to the
High Court where Thomas O'Mahony, a solicitor and
director of the little-known Christian Community Centre,

was seeking an injunction to keep the ex-nuns off the airwaves. O'Mahony argued that if the *Late Late* appearance was allowed to go ahead, 'it would greatly undermine Christian moral values in Irish society'. In addition, he claimed: 'The respect of the general public for nuns would be greatly undermined.'

Justice Barr wasn't having any of it. He couldn't even ascertain for certain that RTÉ were going to interview the renegade sisters that night. In a nutshell, the judge decided that the arguments for the proposed ban amounted to too little too late. Justice Barr added: 'RTÉ have in the past interviewed leading homosexuals, giving them the opportunity to express their views and explain their . . .'

'Moral depravity, my lord,' pressed O'Mahony.

In the hours before the show, RTÉ's top brass convened and gave the nuns their blessing. In a terse statement they said they were 'satisfied that it will be presented in a responsible manner'. Thomas O'Mahony was far from satisfied. Hotfoot from his failed High Court challenge he arrived outside RTÉ. There, in the words of the *Irish Press*, he 'led the crowd outside the studio in reciting decades of the Rosary and in hymn singing'.

The pocket-sized multitude in question consisted of the singing solicitor, Fianna Fáil TD Michael Barrett, eighty civilians, several bull-horns and one portable Virgin Mary. Leaflets issued by Christian Community Action said the purpose of the high-decibel vigil was to persuade RTÉ 'to desist from offending the Christian moral values of the Irish people by glamorising the heinous sin of Sodom and Gomorra'. Mrs Elizabeth O'Hanlon, a 'concerned mother of three' was worried that the item might put young girls off vocations. A number of callers to the station expressed the view that if

Gay Byrne wanted to preside over this sort of heresy, he might consider a new career in the States.

The ex-nuns were visibly shaken by the hostility of the picket. In the face of adversity, Nancy Manahan gallantly turned the other cheek. She remarked: 'I admire them for coming out to stand up for what they believe in. They too are breaking silence.' Gaybo was more concerned with Christian activists breaking the law. Leaving the studio under Garda escort after the show he fulminated that: 'During the past week there have been several threats on my life, on my children, on my wife and on my home.'

The item itself was televised Purgatory, lacking any redeeming raciness. There were no lewd tales of cloistered capering, just a restrained five-way discussion radiating stifling sweetness and light. The phone calls to the station after the show were overwhelmingly sympathetic to the ex-nuns. Gaybo surmised that most viewers would have found the whole affair 'very boring'.

The day's escapades provided an excuse for a slew of 'GAY AND LESBIANS' headlines in that weekend's newspapers. By Monday, normal service had been resumed. 'NO MOVING STATUES, SAYS BISHOP' trumpeted the *Irish Press*. It was the start of another normal week in inter-referenda Ireland.

ONLY MESSING . . .

The Case Of The Drugged Ice Cream.

Who? Dubliner Tony Murphy. Ireland's Hare Krishnas.
When? September 1987.
What? An alleged kidnapping using doped dessert.
Where? From a Dublin restaurant to a Fermanagh island.
Why? The nation wanted to suspect the worst.

It was a three day wonder, but for that short duration 25-year-old Tony Murphy from Rathfarnham in Dublin was the most talked about man in Ireland. There was plenty to talk about, including abduction, captivity in a remote hideaway, indoctrination, and a daredevil escape. What really caught the public's imagination, though, was the drugged ice cream.

It was September 1987. Murphy, a former supermarket worker, had been on the Garda missing persons list for over a week when he reappeared with a sinister and shocking tale. His story began with a visit to the Hare Krishna restaurant on Crow Street in central Dublin. There, he'd hoped to alleviate a temporary cashflow problem by cadging a few bob. The kindly Hare Krishnas didn't give him money, but they treated him to some vegetarian soul-food and an ice cream dessert. Drugged ice cream, Tony later surmised. He blanked out.

His next memory was of being in a different room where he was offered more food. Perhaps surprisingly, in the light of how his last snack had disagreed with him, he ate it. Next thing he knew he was on an island, which he learned was Inisrath, on Upper Loch Erne in

Co Fermanagh. In all, he spent eleven days there. Tony repeatedly pleaded for his liberty, he said, but he was told that Krishna was anxious for him to stay. Apparently it was also the will of Krishna that he'd be given a few thumps and locked up.

During his time on the island, Tony received a neck injury which necessitated a visit to Enniskillen General Hospital. He blamed this injury on a pair of roughnecks who'd accosted him in a bid to shave his head against his will. Another version of events later emerged – that he'd been hurt during a bout of playful wrestling. No matter. At least the hospital visit would put an end to his ordeal, wouldn't it? Incredibly, no. He didn't breathe a word of his predicament to the doctors or nurses because he feared they were 'in cahoots' with the Hare Krishnas. So he meekly returned to his island captivity.

But Tony Murphy did escape, and in a style befitting James Bond. He climbed out of a window, shinned down a pillar, navigated a leaky boat, stole a car (which, as fate would have it, belonged to a Hare Krishna) and headed south for the border. Eventually he found refuge at a Monaghan Garda station. Reunited with his parents, he went to Rathfarnham Garda Station to declare that he was no longer a missing person. He told gardaí that he didn't want to press any charges, nor did he want his adventure publicised.

But Tony's parents weren't going to take their son's kidnapping lying down. They insisted he tell everything to his parish priest, Fr Paul Murphy. In turn, Fr Murphy arranged for Tony to be interviewed on RTÉ Radio 1's *Liveline* programme. Tony glued the ears of the nation. A Hare Krishna spokesman, Shaunaka Ram Das, denounced the whole tale as a pack of lies. He said that Murphy had come to the island voluntarily and had later concocted a Baron Munchausen-scale fantasy to mollify his concerned parents.

The saga would consume a second *Liveline* programme, and then a third. Tony's torrid tale came as no surprise to many callers, who had always suspected so much. The terms 'cult' and 'brainwashing' were much bandied about. Besides, any group who could do *that* to an innocent ice cream clearly possessed a limitless capacity for evil. On the second show Fr Murphy said he knew nothing about the ways of the Hare Krishnas but it seemed obvious that Tony Murphy was telling the truth.

What happened next recalled the famous Monty Python sketch where a man claiming to have written the works of Shakespeare is reminded that the works in question were composed 300 years before his birth. He concedes: '*That* is where my claim falls down. I was hoping you wouldn't make that point.'

Tony Murphy's whereabouts on the day he claimed he'd first gone 'missing' were no longer a mystery. He'd been on the telly. An RTÉ crew had filmed him demonstrating outside the Russian embassy in support of imprisoned Soviet Hare Krishnas. The *Irish Press* also had photos of him there. In fact, Murphy was holding aloft the main banner at the assembly. This revelation pushed the drugged ice cream scenario back to the top of the agenda for a third *Liveline* running. Rather than accept that Murphy had led everyone a merry dance, diehard callers argued that his amnesia actually *proved* he'd been acting under the influence. The harassed Hare Krishnas eventually got their wish and the gardaí launched an official investigation.

Tony Murphy's statement took three days to complete and ran to thirty-three pages. Investigations revealed that

Murphy had previously told friends he'd been involved in
the murder of a man in the Dublin mountains. A detective
questioned him about this. He said he was 'only messing'.
Officers told Murphy that if he brought the Krishnas to
court on kidnap charges, he would land himself in trouble.
He brought them anyway, telling the judge that for him to
recant now would be 'unfair' to other potential victims.

Judge Gerard Buchanan dismissed Murphy's allegations
as 'outrageous'. The smear of unsubstantiated coverage
the Hare Krishnas received was a regrettable case of 'trial
by media'. After the judge delivered his verdict, Hare
Krishna spokesman Shaunaka Ram Das gave his. He
stated grimly: 'The involvement of the Catholic clergy in
this case merits further investigation.'

The end of the line for Tony Murphy's bogus journey
was a three-year suspended sentence for wasting Garda
time.

I DON'T KNOW ANYTHING ABOUT THESE SINGING GROUPS

The Law Vs Adam Clayton.

Who? The bass-player with U2.
When? Twice. 1984 and 1989.
What? £225 increasing to £25,000.
Where? A car, another car, and two courtrooms.
Why? For setting a bad example for the young people.

Adam Clayton was ever the outlaw. Two secondary schools tired of his insolent tomfoolery and bade him a premature farewell. During U2's dogmatic Christian phase his imperviousness to the authority of scripture severely tested the unit's all-for-one, one-for-all ethos. He built a reputation for haircuts which defied convention, not to mention belief.

The law and Adam Clayton came eyeball to eyeball on March 2nd 1984. The bassist was driving to his Southside Dublin home from a wine reception when he happened upon a Garda checkpoint in Harold's Cross. Adam drove blithely on.

Garda Gerald Walsh straddled his motorbike and set off in hot pursuit. Clayton was pulled over. Garda Walsh asked why he hadn't stopped at the checkpoint. 'Clayton replied that he was a celebrity in this country and asked how was he to know if they were gardaí or not.'

It was a philosophical humdinger worthy of the influential Irish thinker Bishop George Berkeley himself.

Who can really, *really*, say if a cop is a cop in this illusory world? However, if the bassist had taken the time to verse himself in the Bishop's writings on Subjective Realism – 'To be is to be perceived.' – he would have deduced that in all likelihood the man in uniform *was* a real policeman. Worse, Garda Walsh was not in a philosophical frame of mind, especially after Adam told him to 'quit messing' and that 'he hadn't time to talk'. The hole was getting deeper but the star kept digging, insisting 'that Garda Walsh would do himself a lot of harm as he (Clayton) was well known high-up'.

Point made, Clayton switched on the ignition. The Garda asked him to turn it off. No go. Garda Walsh told the court that: 'When he leaned in the window to turn off the switch, the car drove off and he was dragged along the road for about forty-five feet.'

Dusting himself off, the Garda trailed the fugitive musician to his Brighton Square address. This determined sleuthing did not impress Clayton. 'You'll be sorry for this,' he told his captor, explaining that 'he was the bass player with U2 and he wanted to go home to go to bed'. He again asked the Garda to desist from his messing.

Reinforcements arrived to 'assist' the musician to Rathmines Garda Station. It was a contrite Clayton who pleaded guilty to dangerous driving and driving with excess alcohol. Indeed, so impressed was the District Justice with his contriteness that he reduced his driving ban from three years to two. The rising star left the court £225 poorer with the stern admonition that he 'should be setting an example for the youth of the country'.

Four-and-a-half years later Adam Clayton was a megastar. Perhaps his fabulous wealth and fame aroused a twinge of begrudgery in someone less well-endowed. In any case, 'a complaint' was made which led one Garda Moody to a black Aston Martin in the car park of the Blue Light pub in the Dublin Mountains.

A man was sitting in the open boot of the car, surrounded by others. Garda Moody announced that he was going to search the car for drugs. 'On hearing this, the man in the boot stood up and walked away.' Adam Clayton, for he was that man, should have remembered the lesson of the U2 song: '*If you walk away, walk away / I will follow.*' Adam walked into a buzzing courtroom on September 1st 1989 to face charges of possession and intent to supply. Nineteen grammes of cannabis resin was a weighty matter.

Justice Windle, presiding, inquired as to how many 'cigarettes' the haul amounted to. He was told 150. The judge remarked: 'Oh, people are allowed to bring 200 cigarettes through customs from Duty Free – but not cannabis.' In the public gallery U2's drummer Larry Mullen had to chuckle. Beside him U2's manager Paul McGuinness didn't. Beside him a little gouger in a Guns 'N' Roses jacket entertained the throng by mimicking the manager's crossed arms and grave expression.

Justice Windle continued to extemporise for no-one in particular. 'I don't know anything about these singing groups,' he stated in time-honoured judgely fashion, 'but I understand that they have some influence on children, youths and – how long do they listen to this stuff? – until they're about thirty I suppose.'

So Adam got another lecture about influencing young people. With the State withdrawing the trafficking charge, there remained the possession case. To the astonishment of many – doubtless including several people serving time for drugs' offences – Justice Windle announced that possessing nineteen grammes of cannabis resin was 'on a very low scale of importance'. Moreover, Adam had been given the drugs as a present, he was of good character, he 'bitterly regretted this incident' and he was now going to contribute £25,000 to the Women's Aid Refuge Centre.

Adam had found what he was looking for.

A waiting Mercedes whisked the bassist away to freedom. Ace reporter Liam Fay lingered on the courthouse steps with a senior citizen who'd earlier given Adam a congratulatory slap on the back. 'Ah, well, sure he's a great singer,' sighed the old man. 'A great singer.'

OBVIOUSLY THERE'S BEEN A LOT OF ATROCITIES OFF THE PITCH

The Irish Football Experience.

Who? The Irish FA, Belfast. The FA of Ireland, Dublin.
When? 1920–1993.
What? The repeated disfigurement of the Beautiful Game.
Where? On the pitch, off the pitch, on the streets.
Why? Sport and sectarianism make a volatile mix.

The Irish Football Association was born and reared in Belfast. Between 1880 and 1920, Dublin barely got a look-in when it came to staging international matches. The capital, being the capital, resented playing second city to Belfast. The 1920 Irish Cup semi-finals were the prologue to a bitter divorce.

That year Glentoran, with a support base in the staunchly loyalist Harland & Wolff shipyards, met nationalist Belfast Celtic. The match finished a draw. Twelve minutes from the end of the replay, Celtic's Gowdy was sent off. This sparked a pitch invasion by the team's strident Sinn Féin following. In the ensuing riot, several civilians and police were shot and many hundreds injured.

The second semi-final fared little better. It was between Glenavon and Shelbourne. Glenavon travelled south to Dublin for the tie. For ninety minutes the home support hurled dog's abuse and missiles. The Northerners scurried off the pitch a beaten team. With Belfast Celtic expelled from the competition for the treasonable behaviour of

their fans, Shelbourne lifted the Irish Cup for 1920
without the bother of having to turn-out in a Final.

The 1921 semi-finals once again brought Shelbourne
face to face with Glenavon, only this time the Northern team
had home advantage. The War of Independence was raging.
Mayhem reigned. Routine headlines of the day included
'EXECUTIONS IN CORK', 'CLERGYMAN'S HOUSE
BOMBED' and 'LIVELINESS IN DUNDALK'. The *Irish
Times* carried a regular Deaths Pending column entitled
'Courts-Martial Sentences'. Shelbourne emerged from a
fraught Belfast visit with a 0–0 result, sufficient to take
Glenavon back to Dublin. At this juncture, the Belfast-
based IFA put the boot in. Inexplicably, they ordered
Shelbourne to return North for the replay.

The Dublin clubs rallied around their top team. The
IFA decision was denounced as 'unjust'. The Dublin clubs
demanded that the IFA's clearly partisan Protests And
Appeals Committee be disbanded. The IFA's Chairman,
Mr Wilton, refused. At the same meeting, the Dublin
delegation sought clarification of a 'flag incident' at a
recent international in Paris. Chairman Wilton explained
that the dastardly French had made elaborate arrangements for the Irish players to parade onto the pitch behind
an Irish flag. Over his dead body, he'd told the Frenchies.
He was sure that the IFA's Dublin branch would
'deprecate' the introduction of politics into football.

That was the final straw. The divorce was finalised two
months later, in May of 1921. Complaining that they were
'smarting under an injustice', Shelbourne had already
withdrawn from the Irish Cup. Now, the south split from
the Irish League to form the 26-county Football
Association of Ireland. The partitioning of Irish football
virtually eliminated sectarian riots at club fixtures, with

one glaring exception. Violence and official censure
continued to dog Belfast Celtic, now virtually alone and
friendless in a hostile jurisdiction. The club was finally
hounded out of existence in 1950.

Three decades after the split, the IFA and FAI could still
dip into a common pool of players for international duty.
The Southern association discouraged its players from
turning out for the North, but internationals paid a
handsome match bonus. With the players manfully
resisting the FAI's appeals to boycott its Northern counterpart, a mysterious campaign of intimidation started up
towards the end of the Forties. Anonymous threats were
issued against the Republic's double jobbers. When the
players showed no sign of caving in, the scare tactics were
extended to their families and clubs.

The Southern players eventually caved in. In February
1950 Sean Fallon told the IFA to exclude him from the
North's game against England. Many years later he
admitted: 'The pressure put on my family was too much.'
At the time, though, Fallon's decision was held up as an
affirmation of faith and fatherland. One month later, Con
Martin chose St Patrick's Day to announce that he was
jilting the North. The FAI applauded his 'spirited action'.
Seventeen other players jumped on the bandwagon over
the following days. 'Many people consider this to be a very
patriotic gesture,' observed the *Irish Times*, 'as an international appearance means £20 to a selected player.'
However, the newspaper felt bound to point out that the
sacrifice being made by most of the seventeen was roughly
zilch, since the prospect of the North ever picking any of
them was 'rather slender'.

Several times from the Fifties to the Seventies, the FAI
and IFA trotted out various chat-up lines to each other. But

neither was really interested in a relationship. For one thing, a unified Association would mean half the number of prestige posts. And anyway, Northern Ireland did very nicely on its tod. The British Home International Championship each spring guaranteed glamour ties with England and Scotland, plus a run-out against Wales. Northern Ireland even mounted a respectable campaign in the 1958 World Cup Finals. Meanwhile, the Republic's famous capacity to laugh in the face of defeat made the team a great favourite across Europe. In 1973 an All-Ireland XI stretched world champions Brazil as a curtain raiser to new North/South negotiations. The reconciliation process didn't last much past the final whistle. It was formally abandoned in 1978, the year that the two Irelands met for the first time.

That year, the neighbours were drawn together in a qualifying round for the European Championships. The first meeting took place at Lansdowne Road late in 1978. Up to 10,000 Northern supporters alighted in the heart of Dublin. Gardaí mounted a huge security operation. No spectator would be left un-frisked. Both teams dutifully conspired to dampen any excitement, producing a drab 0-0 draw.

Bored into submission, both sets of fans traipsed out of the ground. Everything had gone perfectly to plan. Under heavy Garda escort, the northbound hordes made their way towards the train station. And then it all went horribly wrong. '*Ars-en-all, ars-en-all*' – there before their eyes was an arsenal! The gardaí had confiscated anything that could possibly harm a fly, from flagpoles to pencils to fly-swatters. But nobody had thought to clear away the mounds of fist-sized stones lying around Lansdowne Rugby Club's newly built clubhouse. The rioting raged for hours.

The return tie in Windsor Park was set for November 1979, but before that, in September, Belfast's Linfield FC were drawn to face Dundalk in the UEFA Cup. It was a match made in Hell. RTÉ's radio coverage of the first leg, played in Dundalk, was disrupted when broadcaster Philip Greene had to be rescued from his commentary box which was being dismantled by Linfield fans. The flow of play was disrupted by squads of riot police crossing the pitch. The last twenty minutes was played out before empty terraces vacated by fleeing Linfield supporters. As the Northern coaches left town, they shed a ballast of petrol bombs via the back windows. Their hosts reciprocated by lining the route out of town and hurling deadly missiles.

The result was a 1–1 draw and a fine of £870 on Dundalk 'for insufficient security service'. Europe's football authorities slapped a two match home ban on Linfield and ordered the club to pay for the damage to Dundalk's Oriel Park ground. Linfield's home leg against Dundalk would now take place in a continental country of Linfield's choosing. They picked Holland, spiritual homeland of all Orangemen. Dundalk FC released a statement insisting they were 'confident that the good relationship between Dundalk and Linfield would continue'. To quote the broadcaster Ronan Collins: 'As they say in football, it's a funny old world.'

The same class of 'good relationship' was on show weeks later when the Republic arrived in Belfast for their return tie with the North. Lord Mountbatten's murder just days before contributed to a poisonous atmosphere at Windsor Park. Tricolours were set ablaze on the terraces. The Republic midfielder Gerry Daly was carried off after a spectator attempted long distance brain surgery on him with an unsterilized projectile. The North won by the game's only goal. The final whistle heralded a five-year lull in cross-border football hostilities.

By 1984 the penny had finally dropped with the Irish authorities. Glasgow Rangers were coming to Dublin to face Bohemians at Dalymount Park in a UEFA Cup game. As sure as night followed day, Linfield fans would arrive in their thousands to pay homage to a club regarded as the Swiss Guard of Loyalism. The gardaí, club officials and British Embassy representatives drew up a set of precautionary measures to prevent violence, including extra fencing and segregated entrances.

The Bohemians fans had drawn up their own precautionary measures to ensure that the visitors had no monopoly on thuggism. The home support burned Union Jacks, chanted IRA slogans and joshed their counterparts that they'd be going home in a fucking ambulance. 'THE BATTLE OF DALYMOUNT', as the newspapers dubbed it, haemorrhaged onto the surrounding streets. Four out of every five Glasgow Rangers fans charged at the Bridewell Jail that night were from the North. A fleet of up to eighty Loyalist coaches ran a gauntlet through ambushes at Finglas, Ashbourne, Drogheda and elsewhere. For many, the drive North was most inconvenient, since they were Scots who'd landed in Dublin via Liverpool. They'd simply been herded onto the coaches by Gardaí. One officer grunted: 'They'll all go to the North whether they like it or not.'

Nine years later, in November 1993, Windsor Park was the venue for the last fixture of Northern Ireland's qualifying campaign for the 1994 World Cup Finals. The North had already missed the boat for the USA.

Their visitors from down the road could still qualify if they got a result in Belfast and Spain nobbled Denmark in Seville. The handful of incognito Republic supporters dotted about the terraces fooled no-one. The smell of fear gave them away. Before the game Alan McLoughlin, one of Jack's Anglos, gave a footballing perspective on the political situation. 'Obviously there's been a lot of atrocities off the pitch,' he observed.

Northern Ireland's Gerry Taggart would later offer his own unique take on the South's policy of recruiting British-born players, observing: 'In the Republic of Ireland a lot more people live outside it than in it, so they are more used to it. In the North there's not so much of that.'

It was like 'Twelfth Night' in the pocketsize stadium, which was a serried sea of orange flags, red hands and Union Jacks. *The Sash* segued into *God Save The Queen* which rose to a crescendo of *No Surrender* and then back into *The Sash*. Derailing the Republic's bandwagon would be fair return from the qualifying campaign. The home fans cheered the visitors with cries of 'Fenian scum', 'Hello England's rejects' and 'Bonner ye Taig bastard'. With the match three-quarters done, Jimmy Quinn rewarded the faithful with a fierce volley past the same Bonner. Windsor Park erupted with bellicose glee. As the roar subsided, a massed refrain welled up: '*Always look on the bright side of life . . .*'

The Republic's American Dream was minutes away from extinction when the lad McLoughlin made his second memorable contribution to a memorable day. His first goal for Ireland sucked the life out of Windsor Park. The deathly silence that fell on the ground was drowned out in the explosion of noise that filled thousands of homes and pubs south of the border. In a post-match interview, the delirious McLoughlin completed an immortal hat-trick. Pulsating with emotion in the heart of Belfast, he told reporters: 'I'm glad for the fans back in Ireland.'

In changed circumstances, the Windsor Park faithful would have applauded the sentiment.

SHRUBS WERE ALSO PULLED UP

Peter Robinson Vs Inadequate Border Security.

Who? DUP MP Peter Robinson.
When? 1986–1987.
What? He was arrested during a Loyalist border crossing.
Where? The County Monaghan village of Clontibret.
Why? He claimed the mob was providing a public service.

'ULSTER HAS AWAKENED' was the slogan of the hour. In reality, though, the North's belligerent tribalism was just doing a spot of sleepwalking south of the border.

It was August 1986, the height of the Loyalist marching season. The Democratic Unionist Party's Peter Robinson had recently issued a dire warning that 'the hour of politics is past' in the fight against the hated Anglo-Irish Agreement. The hour for bedtime was well past in the sleepy Monaghan village of Clontibret when a large invasion force struck. The intruders were kitted out with 'paramilitary-type jackets, masks and balaclavas and were carrying sticks and cudgels'.

The mob marched, military style, three times around the village, daubing graffito and making a general nuisance of themselves. They blocked the Dublin road. They tore the Garda insignia from the wall of the village station. 'Shrubs,' noted the *Irish Times*, 'were also pulled up.' Two-uniformed gardaí who attempted to intervene were set upon and beaten. Plain clothes reinforcements eventually sent the invaders scurrying back towards the border by firing pistols over their heads.

The normally dapper Peter Robinson was wearing a navy jacket with the hood pulled up when gardaí plucked him from the retreating ranks. Things weren't how they looked, explained the DUP MP. The civic minded object of the exercise was to expose inadequate border security. The mob which penetrated into Clontibret unchallenged had actually provided a valuable public service. As for Robinson himself, he insisted that he was only present in an observer capacity.

Overnighting at Monaghan Garda Station, the captive refused food and 'Barry's tea', a calculated snub to Irish Foreign Minister and tea tycoon Peter Barry. Robinson broke his fast the following afternoon when his wife, Iris, brought him 'good wholesome food from home'. The stroll into Clontibret had produced two notable cases of swollen feat. Gardaí and RUC numbered the marchers at a maximum of two hundred. Speaking from his cell, the MP reckoned there'd been five hundred. Meanwhile the DUP's Nigel Dodds triumphantly cited 'one thousand men'.

Robinson's incarceration threatened to prevent him from making a speech in the Northern village of Keady that evening. A planned Orange procession through Keady had been banned by the RUC. Orangemen were going to assemble in defiance of the ban. Robinson wanted to be there. Iris complained that her husband's release was being deliberately delayed. She objected that the banning of the march in the first place was an RUC 'surrender' to 'sectarian bigotry'.

Robinson was told to remove his 'ULSTER SAYS NO' lapel badge before entering Ballybay District Court that evening. Once inside the courtroom the badge reappeared. He pleaded not guilty on all charges. Bail was set at £10,000. Robinson's team had anticipated only half that amount. The judge allotted half-an-hour to raise the shortfall. With five minutes to spare, the DUP's Reverend William McCrea arrived clutching a bag containing sterling, punts and travellers' cheques. Liberated, Robinson hastened North to give his speech. His words failed to prevent a riot in Keady that night, as the gathered Loyalists left no stone unhurled.

Displaying instincts more suited to big fight promotion than the efficient dispensation of justice, the Republic's authorities chose Dundalk as the setting for Robinson's next court appearance. The defendant wondered aloud: 'Why it should be that my court case should be in a town that the world knows is an IRA dormitory town?' Close friends advised him to stay home on British territory on the date of his court appearance, but Deuteronomy and Genesis argued otherwise. Divine scripture told Peter Robinson 'that I should go to that other land'.

With his mind made up, associates urged him to at least wear a bullet-proof vest for the occasion. He preferred to place his trust in the Lord. 'The guidance was clear,' he later reflected, 'and it would have showed a lack of faith if I was going to wear it.' On the question of whether Jesus would have led marchers into Clontibret in the dead of night, he had no doubts. 'Jesus Christ disliked evil as much as the Protestant community dislike evil,' he stated. He didn't like the way that ecumenical churchmen 'would try to make Jesus Christ into some kind of namby-pamby'.

The DUP mobilised for a day-trip. Activist Jim Wells explained: 'We will be there to stand between a baying horde of Sinn Féin people and Mr Robinson . . . We will not be there to antagonise foreign subjects.' As they set out in bullish mood, Wells told his troops: 'If any foreign Paddies want to try to interfere with us we're ready for them.' A hundred yards into the Republic the Unionist convoy pulled over so that Jim Wells could address the Paddy press.

'What's the feeling . . .', a reporter began.

'Fenians, did you say something about Fenians?' snapped Wells.

Jim Wells' suspicions were well founded. According to several news reports, the crowd gathered in Dundalk was indeed of the baying variety. The most anticipated scrap since Ali Vs Foreman duly got underway. After several rounds of bloody street scuffles, the lobbing of a crate of Republican petrol bombs and scenes of wanton vandalism in a car-park, Robinson's Loyalist support group vamoosed without an intact no-claims bonus between them. And after all that, Robinson was simply remanded to Ballybay District Court for an October hearing.

Several adjournments later, the circus came to Dublin's Central Criminal Court in January, 1987. On day three of the trial, the MP changed his plea to guilty on the first charge of unlawful assembly. Ten other charges of assault and causing malicious damage were dropped.

After a night in jail awaiting sentence, Robinson stood in the Green Street dock where the brave but inept proto-Republican Robert Emmet had famously demanded that no man write his epitaph until the Union be sundered. Justice Robert Barr raised eyebrows by announcing that he felt the defendant was right. As in, Far Right. A 'senior extremist politician' to be precise. He promptly withdrew the 'extremist' bit after heated exchanges with Robinson's outraged counsel.

Justice Barr appeared to be enjoying the cut and thrust of the engagement. Robinson stated that he hadn't noticed anything odd about the Clontibret tour party – like the fact that they were wearing masks, for instance. The judge thought this strange, 'particularly and ironically in that he was there as an observer'. Robinson remained impassive throughout. Almost. According to one report: 'The composure cracked for just a few seconds and he appeared visibly shaken' when the judge said that his role in the invasion merited 'a substantial term of imprisonment'. Robinson was acutely aware that a sentence of more than one year (even if he didn't serve the year) would automatically disqualify him from his Westminster seat and bar him from standing in the next British election.

He needn't have worried. The judge fined him £15,000, plus £2,588 damages. He was bound over to the peace for ten years. The *Irish Independent* reported that a few loiterers jeered as he left Green Street court with his 'well-attired and striking' wife, 'Irish'. News of Robinson's punishment crossed the border. Word of his guilty plea apparently didn't. The Orange Order warned citizens of the Republic to stay out of the North following the 'savage' penalty imposed on 'a totally innocent man'.

And a man of conviction to boot, as decided by an Irish court.

BOOGIE MAMA BOOGIE, YOU WILD BITCH

Fermanagh's Finest On Their Mettle.

Who? Pat, Tommy and John McManus AKA Mama's Boys.
When? The early Eighties.
What? They were kingpins of the new wave of Green Metal.
Where? On stage, on record, in the *Sunday World*.
Why? No-nonsense titles, breasts, motorbikes galore.

After a brief flowering in the late Seventies, the Irish music scene hit a slump as the Eighties began. Thin Lizzy languished in dismal self-parody. The Boomtown Rats couldn't get arrested. Nobody was in the mood for dancing to the Nolan Sisters anymore. U2 had flown the coop to pay their dues trudging around America. The New Romantic bandwagon rolled up and down Dublin's narrow Grafton Street, but there was a broad consensus that for men to wear mascara was a fundamentally un-Irish activity.

Into this vacuum stormed a swarm of mean metal muthas who would never, ever wear make-up and who rejoiced in hard, non-girlie names like Winter's Reign, Trojan and Sweet Savage. The new breed proved just how hard they were by paying into each others' gigs and then not smiling or clapping. Mama's Boys operated several notches above all this parochial handbagging. Hailed as the kingpins of the so-called new wave of Green Metal, they were a power-trio of brothers who'd cut their teeth playing Irish traditional music.

Having cast off their báinín sweaters, Pat, Tommy and John McManus from Fermanagh took a belt and braces approach to their new career in heavy metal. Long before Spinal Tap thought of it, they had the biggest hair, the darkest shades, the driest ice, the Flying-V guitars and the foxiest chicks. Their general business philosophy could be summed up as 'motorbikes-with-everything'.

They locked horns with premier leaguers like Accept – 'They weren't very nice to us. We were blowing them off most nights.' and The Scorpions – 'There was competition but it was friendly.'. They chose no-nonsense song titles – 'Midnight Promises', 'Runaway Dreams', 'Boogie Mama Boogie, You Wild Bitch' – that guaranteed to do what they said on the tin.

There were times when their literal approach got the better of them. They called their first album 'Plug It In' and there was something inevitable about the sleeve illustration – a three-pin plug going into a socket. 'Plug It In' was followed by 'Turn It Up'. Then, just as a pattern seemed to be emerging, they called their third album 'Mama's Boys'. Even at their most unpredictable – and that was them at their most unpredictable – they took care not to confuse their audience.

It's fair to say that Mama's Boys weren't big with militant feminist types. Their first two albums were released on the Pussy label. Asked on British TV where they got the name Pussy, one of them piped up: 'Because the music's cat.' While this at least had a plausible ring to it, accusations of sexism continued to dog the band, especially after they featured a scantily-clad woman on the cover of their third album. The *Sunday World* ran several shock-horror reports of women flashing their breasts at the Boys' gigs, which didn't deter hordes of young males from paying in. Some cynics theorised that these topless women were all, in fact, one versatile model who happened to be dating a member of the Boys' circle.

When Mama's Boys scaled the dizzy heights of landing the *Sunday World*'s front page it was in dramatic but perplexing circumstances. Pat 'The Professor' McManus was minding his own business outside the McGonagles venue in Dublin before a gig when he was bundled into a van and kidnapped. Needless to say, the show had to be cancelled.

The IRA were big into this sort of fund-raising scheme at the time, but Pat's disappearance was different in that there was no ransom demand. Then, days later, he reappeared unharmed but unable to say for sure what had happened.

The band's jealous rivals were at it again, casting unfounded slurs that ticket sales for the cancelled show had been poor. Mama's Boys stood over the truth. Another band, the elegantly named Muff Divers, publicised a forthcoming gig by pledging to show up on the night whether they were kidnapped or not.

Mama's Boys landed the big deal they craved and prepared to conquer America. Leaving nothing to chance, they decided to add some extra features to their logo, incorporating some eyes, some hands, AC⚡DC lightning bolts, Saxon-type wings, their own moniker and several kitchen sinks. However, one reviewer thought the whole idea smacked of overkill. He wrote: 'How are you supposed to get all *that* on the back of your denim jacket?'

Pat braced himself for fame, reflecting: 'Personally I'd be very satisfied if the album sells two or three hundred thousand copies.' Asked if he was prepared to submit himself to wild sex and drugs parties around LA

swimming pools, the rocker from Fermanagh responded:
'Ah sure, don't we have a lake out the back at home.'

At Christmas 1985 the music press reported that the
Boys had split from their management. 'Since then they've
been keeping a low-profile,' said the story, 'but hopefully
the up-and-coming dates will provide a springboard for
world domination.'

By then, however, Spinal Tap had stolen their thunder.

THIS KIND OF NEAR THE BORDERLINE ACTIVITY WON'T DO

The Bishop And The Nightie.

Who? Mr & Mrs Fox of Dublin. Bishop Ryan of Clonfert.
When? February 1966.
What? The bishop found himself surprisingly isolated.
Where? On a remote outcrop of high moral ground.
Why? Because a gameshow question disgusted him.

When it first went on the air in the summer of 1962, the premise of the *The Late Late Show* was to draw the viewers in for a traditional fireside evening, with Gay Byrne glad-handing guests and passing around the sandwiches. Everything went pretty much swimmingly until the beginning of 1966, when sparks started flying from the fireplace. In January a potentially lethal belt of the crosier was dodged when the show hastily withdrew its invitation to Victor Lownes, a *Playboy* executive visiting Ireland. In the run-up to his scheduled appearance, Lownes had told the press he was on a recruiting drive to snare Irish bunnies for England's *Playboy* clubs. Not on the national broadcasting service, he wasn't.

The following month the *Late Late* aped British TV's 'Mr & Mrs' gameshow, the nudge-nudge wink-wink hit of the day. It was quickly apparent that the Foxes from Terenure in Dublin were no swingers. Asked to pick a dream date from A, B or C, Mrs Fox believed her hubby would most like to treat her to a night in the pub with the lads. Thoughtfully, he selected the romantic dinner for two. Mr Fox was asked whether his wife would prefer a holiday in Spain, a Shannon cruise or a fortnight in New York. He correctly guessed that she'd select the sights of Roosky and Banagher over those of Manhattan or Madrid. At this point, the prospects of the item igniting into the stuff of Irish folklore seemed remote.

The tremors began when Gaybo asked Mr Fox the colour of his wife's night-dress on their wedding night. 'Transparent,' he said, to a swell of tittering. Mrs Fox was ushered back in and asked the same question. 'And for heaven's sake,' clucked Gaybo, 'watch every word you say.'

'I didn't wear any,' confessed Mrs Fox.

When the shrieks of laughter subsided she changed her answer to 'white'. That night three people phoned Montrose to complain that the nightie material clashed with the nation's moral fabric. There was a single telegram. It read: 'Disgusted with disgraceful performance.' The sender was the Bishop of Clonfert, Thomas Ryan.

The next day Bishop Ryan let fly from his pulpit. The show had been 'objectionable', 'debasing' and 'disgraceful'. The bishop thundered: 'Surely, if we want to look at television, we are entitled to see a programme that is more in keeping with moral standards traditional in our Catholic country.' He called on all 'decent Irish Catholics' to protest. Mrs Fox declined to comment, except to say the fuss was 'too ridiculous for words'. Gaybo declared himself 'absolutely at a loss to know why there should be any objection by anyone'. The lead editorial in the *Irish Times* scolded that 'his Lordship is killing a fly with a sledgehammer'. The *Times* gave Gaybo its endorsement. The presenter was, it assured its readers: 'Irish, of the Irish, accomplished and bland.'

Having said initially that he couldn't see what the bishop's problem was, Gay was pushed into submitting a ritual apology by his station bosses. The item, he now accepted, 'was embarrassing to a section of viewers'. Bishop Ryan twisted the knife. He'd make no comment on Byrne's apology, but he would say that the Director General of Telefís Éireann, Kevin McCourt, had phoned him personally with an explanation he'd deemed satisfactory. A Montrose spokesman said the Authority had 'no knowledge' of any such communication.

The Bishop had made a wrong call. The general public was not outraged. In fact, the general public couldn't care less. On the day after Bishop Ryan's outburst Telefís Éireann received a modest sixty calls on the subject, and thirty-six of those were in support of the item. Letter writers to the press seemed bent on perpetrating lame puns about 'The Late Night Shift' and 'The Late Late Nightie Show'. Trinity students announced a march down O'Connell Street in protest against the Bishop's 'absurdity' and Gaybo's 'fawning apology'. The marchers would be dressed in white nighties. The modernising mohair men in government saw no percentage in getting involved and kept out of it.

As the *Irish Times* editorial had correctly surmised, the bishop had rashly left himself out on a limb. In the words of that organ: 'A lapse of taste has been treated as if it were an outrage to morals.' Delayed knee-jerk reaction fell to the middle ranks of Official Ireland who felt that, whatever the merits of Dr Ryan's stance, a bishop mustn't be left ignored and isolated.

Loughrea Town Commission came to the bishop's rescue with a motion that *The Late Late* was 'a dirty programme that should be abolished altogether'. Members of the Mayo GAA Board condemned it. Meath Vocational Education Committee passed a resolution deploring *The*

Late Late for its mediocrity, its low morals, and for its all-round 'anti-national' treachery. When Mr P Cahill of Waterford County Council proposed a motion congratulating Telefís Éireann for 'a good show', the Chairman stopped his mischief with the words: 'I don't think we should go that far.' The discussion was then declared closed.

Senator JB O'Quigley reminded the Seanad that the show's 'deplorable' fare was being funded by taxpayers' money. He insisted: 'This kind of near the borderline activity won't do.' Senator Sheehy Skeffington blamed the education system for failing the country. Because many citizens were 'an under-educated people' it came as no surprise that 'vulgarity' topped the viewing figures. Senator CB McDonald objected that far too often the show's guests and panellists seemed primed with 'one too many over the mark'. The only TD to speak out, Stephen Barrett, hoped that: 'with the passage of time Mr Gay Byrne's mind will become more enlightened'.

The deputy was to be severely disappointed. Within a few weeks, a *Late Late* panellist would call the Bishop of Galway 'a moron'. The Swinging Sixties had arrived, Irish style.

THEY'LL GO WILD FOR THIS IN AMERICA

The fall and fall of Lord Nelson.

Who? Self-appointed super-patriots. The Irish Army.
When? March 1966.
What? Nelson's Pillar AKA The City Sofa.
Where? O'Connell Street, Dublin.
Why? Because it was oppressing Ireland.

Dubliners had long been embroiled in a love-hate relationship with Nelson's Pillar. The monument had dominated the capital's main artery since 1809. It was known as the 'city sofa' because idle citizens would lounge on its steps watching the world go by. The viewing deck at the summit afforded unparalleled vistas of the capital for just 6d. It was a popular point of departure for Dubliners bading goodbye cruel world.

The Pillar was the enemy within. Yeats condemned it as 'a monstrosity'. Every few years its demolition was debated at official level. In 1891, Dublin's Lord Mayor introduced a removal bill in the Westminster parliament. Dublin Corporation opposed the motion on the grounds of cost. When they discovered that the pillar's trustees would have to foot the bill they did an abrupt U-turn. When the demolition was put to a vote, however, Lord Nelson was granted another stay of execution.

The Pillar saw out the Easter Rising, the War of Independence and the Civil War with barely a scratch. It survived periodic bouts of enthusiasm amongst Dublin

Corporation officials for blowing up imperial monuments. In 1929, for instance, King William was blasted from his plinth on College Green. In 1936, the city fathers marked the coronation of George VI by dynamiting his ancestor, George II, on Stephen's Green.

At 1.30 a.m. on March 8, 1966 Nelson crashed to earth with a bang. Suspicion fell on the recently dormant IRA. The usual suspects were rounded up and taken to the Bridewell. They were quickly released without charge. The Irish Republican Publicity Bureau issued an immediate denial of any IRA involvement. News of Nelson's downfall elicited an ambivalent mix of amusement, celebration and half-hearted condemnation. *The Irish Times* spoke to an architect surveying the debris. 'JA Culliton thought it tragic,' said the report. 'He seemed to be the only one who did.'

A Garda spokesman approvingly described the demolition as 'a thorough job'. The gardaí speculated that the bomb may have detonated prematurely. Anxious to give the bombers the benefit of the doubt, a Garda spokesman expressed the view that it had probably been timed to go off 'two or three hours later when there would be less danger of anyone being injured'.

The device exploded upwards and outwards causing minimal collateral damage. One Garda on the scene grinned broadly as he described it as: 'An absolutely perfect job. Not a window broken in the Post Office. Perfect.' Another Garda reflected gleefully: 'They will go wild about this in America!'

The country was abuzz with preparations for the Golden Jubilee of the Easter Rising. Nobody could be seen to mourn the passing of the Imperialist Sea Lord. Dublin's Lord Mayor, Alderman Eugene Timmons, focused his condemnation on the unofficial nature of the demolition, saying: 'No small group had the right to assume a responsibility which should have been the decision of the local community.' An ancestor of the fallen hero took the news graciously. The Honourable George Nelson said: 'I am sure there was nothing personal in it.'

A street carnival broke out around the scene of the explosion. A huge crowd of sightseers gathered for a gawk, their numbers swelled by an influx of country folk freed to travel because it was early closing day in rural Ireland. Foolhardy revellers played a game of dare, jinking through the police cordon to pose under the most unstable part of the stump. One report noted: 'The young gardaí were harassed and maddened by grown men who found the barrier as great a challenge as the children, and there were some fine displays of running and tackling which brought rousing cheers and jeers from the assembled thousands.'

An unidentified man wrapped Nelson's sword in his overcoat and drove off with it. According to one report: 'There were happy, smiling faces everywhere and witticisms like "poor old Nelson" were greeted with roars of laughter.' The bombing caught the imagination of the whole country. Within hours of the explosion punters were flocking into a Ballina pub – 160 miles away – to see a display of Nelson debris put on exhibition by scavenging lorry drivers.

The only moaners were the staff of a store in O'Connell Street which was behind the Garda cordon and therefore devoid of custom. The mendacious manager refused to shut up shop and give them the day off. Also hit were O'Connell Street's Nile-siders, the group of families who had for generations jealously guarded the 'privilege' of selling fruit and flowers under the shadow of the pillar. The late statue had commemorated Nelson's victory at the Nile.

When the dust settled, the Lemass government was caught in an embarrassing half-Nelson. Justice Minister Brian Lenihan's description of the event as 'reckless' and 'an outrage' was dismissed as 'tepid' in an *Irish Times* editorial. The newspaper summed up the administration's Catch 22 situation, explaining: 'The Government is in a sad case. What sort of celebration will it be if they catch the dynamiters and clap them in prison?'

There was no getting away from the Easter Rising and the tide of nationalist triumphalism sweeping the land. Telefís Éireann's new prestige documentary series was devoted to recalling the great battles against the English. The country's best selling records included a collection of rebel songs by Arthur Murphy and a compilation entitled 'From 1916: The Best Of Ireland's Music' featuring such splendours as 'Wrap The Green Flag Around Me Boys', 'Amhrán Na bFiann' and Pearse's touching poem, 'The Mother'.

But 1916 fever wasn't all beer and bunting. For the majority in the North the celebrations commemorated an act of treachery. 1916-mania in the South inevitably portrayed the Six Counties as a spot of unfinished business rather than a legitimate political entity. The Pillar bomb turned up the heat in Northern Ireland. Ian Paisley had already been sowing fears that the Taoiseach's recent ice-breaking welcome to Belfast signalled a Stormont sell-out. A few days before the Nelson explosion, the British Military Attaché's home in Dublin had been petrol-bombed. When the Admiral was tumbled from his perch, RUC stations across the North were sandbagged in readiness for an unknown onslaught. Austin Currie, the nationalist MP for East Tyrone, received a threatening letter. It informed him he'd be shot if there were any 'rebel celebrations of the murders of 1916' in the county.

The cabinet was in a pickle. The St Patrick's Day parade was one week away. It would be followed shortly by a huge march down O'Connell Street on Easter Sunday which would form the centrepiece of the 1916 commemorations. Members of the Old IRA were to provide the Guard Of Honour. It now seemed likely that they'd be filing past a pile of rubble – an awkward reminder that the aspirations of 1916 remained unfulfilled. Something would have to be done.

At a cabinet meeting within hours of the explosion the Taoiseach, Seán Lemass, pressed for the removal of the stump of the pillar 'as expeditiously as possible'. The following day he was told that the pillar was private property owned by trustees. On the same day the Army's director of engineering, Colonel RG Mew, sent the Department of the Taoiseach a detailed memo on how to blow up the stump.

Before that could be done, however, the government would have to strike a deal with the pillar's trustees, although some advisors to the Taoiseach raised the possibility that the trustees didn't actually possess any documentary proof that they owned the thing. Another possibility was that the trustees – if they were told the rest of the pillar was to be blown up – might look for an injunction to prevent the inevitable.

To move things on, it was decided that the state would indemnify the trustees of the pillar. Three days after the bombing, the Government Information Bureau announced that the remainder of the monument would be demolished.

Six days after the first explosion, the Army Bomb Squad completed the job begun by enemies of the state. In a flurry of last minute activity, members of The Royal Institute Of Architects had been denied a High Court injunction against the demolition. The unique Regency lettering at the base of the pillar was sacrificed to political expediency. As *Build* magazine saw it: 'The savages have triumphed . . . the deliberate act of destruction of Thomas Johnston's doric column has been encompassed by unknown elements and the government.' The army destroyed the stump in a controlled midnight explosion. Huge crowds gathered to watch and cheer. Radio Éireann captured the whoops and applause so the whole country could share in the fun the next morning.

Unfortunately the controlled explosion didn't live up to its name and, unlike the seditionaries, the army succeeded in wreaking wholesale damage to surrounding buildings, including the General Post Office. As the crowds surged forward for souvenirs, gardaí were deployed to prevent mass pillaging from shattered shopfronts. When St. Patrick's Day arrived, Official Ireland closed ranks on the touchy subject of the Pillar. Television and newspaper pictures of the Dublin parade were angled to omit the tarpaulined scar at the heart of the country's main street.

Over the following weeks, visitors flocked into Ireland to bask in the carnival spirit. Greasy tills rang ceaselessly as the 1916 industry slipped into top gear. Books about the Rising rolled off the presses. Nearly a million commemorative ten shilling coins bearing Pearse's profile entered circulation – via the Royal Mint in London. Eager philatelists flooded the GPO to buy up special edition stamps. CIE's fleet of tardy double-deckers displayed the Sword Of Light, the official 1916 symbol.

Newspapers strained to outdo each other in the scale and lavishness of their 1916 pull-out supplements. The fervour even spread to perfidious Albion where *The Telegraph* serialised the Rising exploits of de Valera and *The*

People cashed in with a pictorial tribute entitled 'SIX DAYS TO DEATH'. Sticklers for detail complained that the British troops featured in the *People's* 1916 souvenir publication were actually Irish Free State soldiers fighting in the Civil War of 1921–22. And that the photo of the Four Courts was actually of the Custom House. And that one shot – captioned 'A rebel leader brandishes a revolver as he cries "To your positions!"' – was actually from a Michael Collins election rally of 1922.

As Easter Week approached, Kilkee Town Commission patriotically passed a proposal to enact all its business in Irish. One member stormed out, protesting 'I don't know a damn thing you are talking about'. He wasn't the only one. The inaugural meeting *as gaeilge* lasted precisely twenty-one minutes instead of the usual two hours.

Croke Park was the venue for a major Easter Week entertainment extravaganza to commemorate The Rising. Seating was available for 18,000 people nightly. The spectacular pageant, entitled 'Aiseiri', was a joint production by the Army and the FCA. One first-night notice conveyed the tone of the event, citing, 'the torches, the rockets, the canons spitting fire, the Redcoats biting the dust on all sides'.

The infectious mood of good-natured Brit-bashing inspired many celebrations of an impromptu nature. Nelson's Archway in Skibbereen was blown up in the dead of night. 'UP THE REBELS' was daubed large on Cavan's Protestant Hall. In Dun Laoghaire, well-wishers painted the town green. Amongst an assortment of Republican slogans was the scrawl 'HITLER WAS A GOOD FELLOW'.

By the time the Easter holiday weekend arrived, the Stormont parliament had rushed through several new laws. The North's Home Affairs Minister was empowered to

translate the prevailing bunker mentality into physical fact.
The Stormont administration effectively closed the border
from the Saturday morning to Sunday night by cancelling
the North/South train service and manning all cross-
ings. Meanwhile in Dublin, a fair job had been made of
expunging Nelson's remains from the scene of the crime.
There were other embarrassments, however. The Protestant
Archbishop of Dublin, Dr Simms, found himself locked out
of the formal opening of the Garden of Remembrance. His
Grace stood outside for most of the ceremony while red-
faced officials searched for a key to admit him.

There was worse. The focal point of the Easter Sunday
commemorations was the Presidential viewing stand at
the General Post Office. When President de Valera took
his place to oversee the Easter Parade, wide open spaces
were clearly visible in the VIP seating around him.
Comical scenes ensued, as prominent guests were shooed
in from the margins to flesh out the President's television
backdrop.

And so the most lavish expression of national pride in
the history of the young state degenerated into a petty
political squabble over invitations. Fine Gael and Labour
expressed their disappointment that the Fianna Fáil
administration had been so small-minded as to snub
them. The relevant government department, Defence,
issued an apology saying it 'sincerely regrets this error'.
The ruling Fianna Fáil party pointed out that some of its
own ministers hadn't been invited, evidence of a genuine
mistake. They suspected that the Fine Gael and Labour
leaders had deliberately stayed away to generate a row.

In the weeks and months that followed, a stream of
missives arrived from home and abroad proposing what
should replace Nelson's Pillar. These included statues of

Michael Collins, Saint Patrick, Patrick Pearse, a winged figure, an eternal flame 'to commemorate all who died for Ireland', and an underground chapel dedicated to the blood sacrifice of Easter 1916. All were quietly filed away.

Lord Nelson's assailants saved the government further blushes by evading capture – at least until one of them decided to claim his footnote in history.

In September 2000, 67-year-old Liam Sutcliffe went on national radio to shop himself as one of the 1966 bombers. In the wake of the broadcast, Sutcliffe was arrested for questioning. He was later released without charge.

In January 2003, when the final section of Lord Nelson's replacement Spire was put in place, Sutcliffe was amongst the crowd of Dubliners gathered to witness the event. He described the new monument as 'magnificent' and 'a much better thing to have on the main street than an old foreign admiral with a broken arm and a missing leg'.

He said that the plot to blow up Nelson was hatched over a drink in the Cosy Bar on the Crumlin Road in Belfast. The drinkers were in agreement that the 1916 commemorations to date had lacked spark: 'And my friend's sister-in-law said it was shocking to see a British admiral in O'Connell Street. So I said we should remove it.'

He put the idea to a senior Republican who initially thought it would be too dangerous, but then saw the merits of the plan. Sutcliffe claimed: 'The first attempt was on the last day of February but the bomb didn't go off. So I had to go up on March 1st and remove it. I went into Clery's, bought a nail clippers and stripped it. I had a week then to drop it back. I went back on March 7th, had electrics in a briefcase. I connected everything up and placed it in an aperture – one of the widows at the top – that looked up Henry Street.

'I shook the hand of the man up guarding the platform and said "Cheerio". He went off after his shift that night and the bomb went off at 1.32 in the morning. I had it timed for 2 a.m. but I had it on fast and it gained 28 minutes.'

Asked whether he saw the bomb go off, he said: 'I did not. I was at home tucked up in bed. I didn't know it had gone off at all until I saw it on the front page of the paper that morning.'

His own personal preference to replace the monument he'd destroyed had been a statue of the seven signatories of the Easter Proclamation. After 34 years, however, he felt the Spire would do admirably, and it appeared to be 'explosion-proof' to boot.

PEOPLE WILL GET DRUNK...

A Pocket Of Turbulence Over The Atlantic.

Who? 18 Irish tourists Vs The US Olympic wrestling team.
When? Christmas 1995.
What? The wrestlers took on several of the tourists.
Where? 30,000 feet above the Atlantic.
Why? An in-flight food fight was a big downer.

'Travel,' wrote Mark Twain, 'is fatal to prejudice, bigotry and narrow-mindedness.' At Christmas 1995, an expedition from the travelling community went to extraordinary lengths to prove the great man wrong. Eighteen members of the Connors, Cash and Purcell families were embarking on the winter break of a lifetime, a trip to Disneyland in sunny California. Travelling on Irish and British passports, the tourists set off from London's Gatwick Airport in high spirits.

Shortly after the Northwest Airlines flight passed its point of no return, so did the behaviour of its Disney-bound party pack. Thirty thousand feet above the choppy Atlantic, members of the traveller families developed a drink problem. The problem was that the flight attendants had called closing time. The Connors, Cashs and Purcells were politely told that they'd had enough. Some of the group begged to differ. When this brought no joy, some felt they had no option but to borrow or steal. Young children were dispatched down the aisle – 'Fagan-style' said the press – on an undercover mission to liberate shorts from the service trolleys. The vigilant flight attendants repulsed

their advances. The plane people of Ireland stood up for
their rights. The captain was summonsed from his cockpit
to tell them to sit down again. He beat a hasty retreat
when the pocket of on-board turbulence turned out to be
unexpectedly severe.

As the shouting and swearing escalated, some of the
travellers discovered a practical use for aeroplane food. A
portion of potato, for instance, could be easily converted
into a crude but effective spud missile. Some of the
travellers implemented a boycott of the toilet facilities,
leading to eye-witness reports that brought vividly to mind
the words 'slash' and 'seats' in a novel setting. 'The seating
area was soiled,' said a shocked airline official, Doug
Killian, 'people were urinating by their seats.' A teenage
boy had to intercede on his mother's side when a bout of
fisticuffs broke out between his parents. The final,
unforgivable, affront to the American Way was perpe-
trated by a number of miscreants who lit up cigarettes on
the non-smoking flight.

A male flight attendant decided to fight fire with fire.
The holiday makers soon had him rolling in the aisle. As
chance would have it, several members of the United
States Olympic Wrestling team were on the flight. The
wrestlers moved in and subdued the troublemakers. The
worst offenders arrived in the States handcuffed to their
seats. The eighteen travellers never got within a thousand
miles of the theme park of their dreams. They were hauled
off the aeroplane in Minneapolis. One of the party, Michael
Purcell, was carted away by the FBI. The others were held
pending deportation on the next available departure for
London. In-flight drinks would not be served.

The deportees were furious. They felt that the airline
was clearly culpable of igniting the mayhem. Eileen Cash,

one of the group's elders, had no doubt where the blame lay: 'Northwest Airlines gave us drink on the plane, they shouldn't have. We were going on holiday and something happened on the plane. We feel ashamed and embarrassed over it, but we never did anything.' Her daughter, Eileen Connors, added: 'We are embarrassed by what happened. The man arrested was nothing to do with us. We were all separate. We were just a bit noisy. We never did anything.' The man arrested for assault and intimidation, Michael Purcell, didn't exactly have 'nothing to do' with Eileen Connors, as she claimed. He was Eileen Cash's son-in-law while she was Eileen Cash's daughter. What Eileen Connors meant to say, perhaps, was that she was not her brother-in-law-in-custody's keeper.

Anyway, Eileen Connors wanted the blame redirected at the real villains of the piece, Northwest Airlines. 'My little girl, Eileen, who is three,' said Eileen, 'was punched on the back by an air hostess. The children were very disappointed, it was a Christmas holiday. They gave us a lot of drink. Why were they giving out drink? People will get drunk, people are not used to drinking shorts.'

Meanwhile, the deportees turned their thoughts to Michael Purcell, still pondering the error of his ways in a Minneapolis clink. When Michael got home he would face a stern reminder that violence is never the answer. 'All the family are going to kick up over this,' said the man's irate mother-in-law. 'He'll get some hiding.'

RADIO DOWNTOWN FUCKING BURBANK

2FM Survives A Sickly Infancy And A Near-Death Experience.

Who? Larry Gogan. Gerry Ryan. Dave Fanning. Ray Burke.
When? 1979–2004.
What? The station saw off several threats to its existence.
Where? From pirates, super-pirates, and a bent Minister.
Why? The pirates were more fun, the Minister on the take.

'I wonder if the housewife has the time for discussions. What is often called wallpaper radio, with time signals, may be a good answer to her problem.' The speaker was Donncha Ó Dulaing, head of RTÉ's radio features in 1970.

The housewives of Ireland never did get their own wallpaper service to solve that particular woman's 'problem'. When a less demanding alternative to Radio Éireann did come on air nine years later, it was dedicated to the youth of both sexes. 2FM passed its quarter-century in May 2004, having survived a sickly infancy, several personality crises and one near-death experience.

From birth, the second national station was widely regarded by grown-ups as the idiot bastard offspring of legitimate wireless. One commentator reassured the public: 'As many proponents of liberal birth control say, the fact that it's there doesn't mean you have to use it.' Others welcomed it as a septic tank to drain off Radio

Eireann's creeping pop content, thereby helping to restore the cultural purity of the flagship service.

The new station was flung together in the spring of 1979 with what Gerry Ryan later recalled as 'very, very indecent haste'. Sensing the winds of change, RTÉ executives had actually proposed a music station as early as 1977. The Minister for Posts & Telegraphs, Padraig Faulkner, dismissed that plan out of hand. Two years later, with pirate stations popping up all over the place and stealing listeners and advertising revenue from the state broadcaster, the same Minister Faulkner ordered RTÉ to get a music service on the air, and pronto!

Almost 600 hopefuls – almost all of them from the pirates – applied for sixty new jobs. The selection process wasn't an exact science. Ex-insurance man Marty Whelan sent in seventeen demo tapes before he got the call. Gerry Ryan, in marked contrast, turned up for a job interview on a tip-off from a friend who'd told him the standard was such that a basic grasp of English should see him through. 'I didn't have a script,' he later recalled. 'I read the sleeve notes on the back of a Glen Campbell album.'

The remit of Radio A Dha, as the putative station was tentatively titled, was to blast the buoyant pirates off the airwaves. The government coveted the mavericks' advertising revenue but was equally concerned to eliminate unregulated sources of news. The new station was supposed to win over the country's under-25s, but its earliest schedules proved comically unsuited to the task. The programming suggested that Radio 2's target audience was a bilingual student priest with 'The Boomtown Rats', 'David Soul' and 'The Gallowglass Ceili Band' inscribed on his satchel.

While the pirates were cominatcha with a frothy diet of Rod Stewart, The Police and Gary Numan, the new station sought to seduce the Young People of Ireland with a music policy resembling a twenty-car-pile-up. 'Toss The Feathers', 'Anonn Is Anoll', 'The Heather Breeze', 'On The Boards', Larry Cunningham, Diana Ross and The Jam were all grist to the mill. Sunday mornings were set aside for 'Sounds Religious', a 'meditative' oasis of edification which aimed to woo the youth with 'the sound of Sunday in words and song'.

RÉ2, as it was now briefly dubbed, did occasionally trespass into territory broadly recognisable to real young people. Jimmy Greeley and Marty Whelan brought a veneer of exotic mid-Atlantic slickness to their shows. Gerry Ryan was permitted to hone his frippery undisturbed in a weekend graveyard slot. The biggest cult to emerge from the Dublin pirate scene, Dave Fanning, went on air at midnight in the time-honoured tradition of his pirate escapades. Trouble was, 'The Rock Show' on Radio 2 was only transmitted on VHF, so his legions of fans relying on the MW 'trannies' of the day were left to whistle.

The celebrations to mark Radio 2's first birthday in 1980 were muted. The schedules were a mess, the ratings dismal, the mood mutinous. In Madigan's pub of Donnybrook, two bickering factions muttered darkly about each other's cluelessness. The old Radio Éireann hands and the ex-pirate crew had split over musical differences. The old guard wanted to scrap the patchwork of specialist programmes and fight the pirates on their own terms with wallpaper pop.

The ex-pirates, in contrast, mostly felt that this was an lazy cop-out and that the resources of the state broad-caster ought to be put to more imaginative uses. Unhappily for them, they were on short-term contracts while the former Radio Éireann stalwarts were permanent civil servants. There was only going to be one winner. The most outspoken dissenter, DJ Declan Meehan, was let go when his contract wasn't renewed. Dave Fanning's airtime was curtailed. Gerry Ryan's recently introduced 'Rock-steady' was scrapped. Radio 2 switched to a diet of popcorn for breakfast, dinner and tea.

And still the pirates grew and prospered, particularly in the advertising-rich 'Bay Area' of Dublin. The pirates' very illegality gave them several advantages. For a start, it gave them a rebel cachet. The Radio 2 presenters, under their new dispensation, were afraid to say 'boo!' on air. It was James Dean against Ken Barlow. Additionally, the pirates were free to broadcast at one million on the Richter Scale, and they egged-on each other to see who could make the loudest racket. Frustratingly, Radio 2 had more poke under the bonnet than any of the outlaws but was forbidden by statute from using it.

As the Eighties progressed, the super-pirates emerged, gorging themselves on the rich pickings of clutter-free radio and great cash giveaways. Disillusionment in Radio 2 was rife. Marty Whelan later explained: 'The DJ was the one who went around the country meeting listeners face to face. You got the feedback on the spot.' DJs and producers would lobby for change, but to no avail. In the bureau-cratic graveyard of Montrose, he complained: 'A lot of ideas got buried.'

The cabaret fraternity were deeply disenchanted with the station's mainly British and American bill of chart fare. Protests were mounted outside RTÉ by people who didn't see why Radio 2 should play Queen's *Radio Ga-Ga* when an act like The Memories might have an equally good Irish version on release. Jim Hand, a well-known owner and trainer of showbands, summed up the prevailing mood in his sector when he dismissed the station as 'Radio Downtown Fucking Burbank'.

Across rural Ireland, in the absence of a strong pirate presence, Radio 2 fared much better, but the morale of the crew remained becalmed in the doldrums. Whole years passed by uneventfully during Radio 2's whatever-you-say, say-nothing phase. On-air spontaneity was frowned upon, innovation was stifled. When Mark Cagney let slip a 'fuck it' on his show in 1985 it was Radio 2's JFK Dallas moment – everyone remembered where they were when they heard it. Things were that dull. It was left to Joe Public to puncture the relentless timidity of it all, most often from the end of a phone-line.

Ian Dempsey solicited listeners' suggestions as to the ideal royal wedding present for Britain's Andrew and Sarah. 'I'd like to give Fergie AIDS and put a bomb up Andy's hole,' enthused one caller on air.

For consistent hilarity, however, Larry Gogan's *Just A Minute Quiz* became the jewel in the crown. For instance . . .

Larry: With what town in Britain is Shakespeare associated?

Contestant: Hamlet.

Larry: What was Jeeves' occupation?

Contestant: He was a carpenter.

Larry: What is the international distress signal?

Contestant: Help!

Larry: Name the BBC's Grand Prix commentator . . . I'll give you a clue, it's something you suck.

Contestant: *Ooh*, Dickie Davis!

Larry: What 'S' is a native of Liverpool?

Contestant: Scumbag!

Larry: What fairytale character said, 'All the better to see you with my dear'?

Contestant: Was it Bruce Forsythe?

Somewhere, the penny dropped that the listeners themselves might be the untapped resource that could rescue
the station. If years of wallpaper pop hadn't worked, it might
be time to try discussion radio, whatever the risk to the
mental balance of the nation's housewives. The break-
through came in 1988 when Gerry Ryan was transplanted to
a morning slot with the simple brief to listen to the listeners.

Radio 2 had begun to stir from its torpor the previous
year. In the summer of 1987 the station began broadcasting around the clock and dropped the chart-driven
format which had served it so poorly since the acrimonious
in-house split of 1980. In a bid to reposition Radio 2
closer to the wallets of the affluent 25–40 market segment,
more airtime was allocated to classic hits. DJs were even
granted permission to play three records of their own
choosing per two-hour slot.

But it was Ryan's knockabout morning show that
worked the miracle. Within a matter of months his Dublin
audience had soared by 50%. One jock displaced in the
reshuffle and dismayed by the rush of new blood,
objected: 'The lunatics have taken over the asylum.'

Radio 2's belated entrenchment in the Dublin area
came in the nick of time. The independent local radio
stations were on their way. In 1989 Radio 2 streamlined its
moniker to 2FM and mounted assorted revelries to
celebrate its tenth birthday. It finally had something to
celebrate – it could now claim to be a truly national
station. The quartermasters of the new independents
waved chequebooks frenetically but there was no major
exodus of 2FM talent. Marty Whelan broke ranks to join
Century and was summarily ostracised for his treachery.
He was 'surprised and disappointed' not to receive an
invite for the 2FM tenth birthday party.

Justice Minister Ray Burke was now about to do his damnedest to ensure that 2FM snatched defeat from the jaws of victory. It was 1990. After less than a year on the air, Century, the first independent national station, was in dire straits. The political and financial machinations of the Burke/Century/2FM love-hate triangle are tortuous, but again Dublin was the key. Century had less than 10% of the 15-34 Dublin audience which was crucial to solvency. Century's staff were already referring to their workstation as 'Cemetery Radio'.

The capital's two new local independent stations, 98FM and Capital, had legally enforceable contracts with the state. 2FM only had the protection of public opinion. Minister Burke effectively tried to kill off 2FM to save Century. In 2002, the interim report of the Flood Tribunal found that Burke had received large 'corrupt' payments from two of Century's directors, Oliver Barry and James Stafford.

This finding shed new light on an incident during the launch of the state's first licensed independent station, Capital – later rebranded as FM104 – in July 1989. The station went on air at 8 a.m. At 8.40 a.m. Capital broadcast its first news bulletin, leading with a political bribes scandal story. Minutes later, the man known as Rambo breezed into the studio and complained to the producer: 'The first morning, the first news bulletin and what do we get? A quote from the Workers' Party!'

On the eve of 2FM's eleventh birthday, Ray Burke unveiled bizarre plans to transform the station into an 'education and public information' service. His vision for 2FM included providing instruction in 'continental languages, the Irish language, the rural and farming sectors, business and trade union affairs, social welfare and social affairs'.

2FM boss Cathal McCabe cheered up his shell-shocked troops with an internal circular requiring DJs to translate a passage of Hungarian, draft a request for headage payments, and pencil-in three suggested halting sites on a map of Dalkey. Fine Gael's Jim Mitchell charged that Minister Burke was 'screwing' 2FM by trying to turn it into 'a drudge station'. The stars of RTÉ descended on Leinster House to register their outrage. Gay Byrne and Gerry Ryan's shows were flooded with calls of support for 2FM just as it was.

As the debate raged, Ray Burke shot himself in the foot. He turned up at Century to host his own show, a xerox of 'Desert Island Discs'. As Burke was going on air, Gerry Ryan was on 2FM inciting the listeners to 'give it to him between the eyes'. Burke's pompous Century broadcast only served to harden public opinion against him. One radio critic wrote that the Minister was: 'trying to give the impression that he was somehow a great rock'n'roller and ex-hippy . . . The show came across as arrogant and enormously patronising.'

The public outcry saved 2FM. For all his efforts, Ray Burke was unable to stop Century from failing, together with his own memory. In 1997, Burke was sure that the 'largest contribution' he'd ever received was £30,000. In 2001 he remembered that the biggest figure was actually £35,000 from Century's Oliver Barry.

A few months later he was reminded that in 1984 he'd opened a Jersey company, Caviar, to receive a lump sum of £60,000 from the builders Brennan & McGowan. When it turned out Tom Brennan and Joe McGowan had had faulty recollections of where all that lolly had come from, Ray Burke had to rack his brain once again.

He did his best, and managed to remember an alternative source for the money, but by now a tribunal

lawyer felt obliged to point out: 'Mr Burke, it is one thing
not to remember something. But I suggest to you that to
remember things which *didn't actually occur at all* is a very
odd kind of failure of recollection.'

I WILL HAVE YOU SHOT

Alex Higgins Vs Dennis Taylor.

Who? Two former snooker world champions.
When? 1990.
What? Higgins launched a furious tirade against Taylor.
Where? At the close of snooker's World Cup Final.
Why? It was partly to do with a non-existent £6,000.

It was billed as the OK Corral of the green baize. The fixture itself was of modest import, a quarter-final tie in the 1990 Irish Masters at Goffs. But this time Alex Higgins had really, *seriously*, gone beyond the beyond. Mild-mannered fellow northerner Dennis Taylor was gunning for him.

Only six days earlier the two former World Champions had been team-mates in the Northern Ireland side which had contested the final of snooker's World Cup. Higgins, Taylor and third man Tony Murphy presented a picture of beaming harmony during their run of victories in the competition. Then, within minutes of their defeat by Canada in the decider, the chummy facade disintegrated in a sudden eruption of searing bile.

The tremors had begun the previous evening. Having just won their semi-final, the Northern Ireland trio posed for photographs. Higgins picked that moment to tell Murphy: 'You played like a shit.' Team spirit wasn't improved the following afternoon when, during the first session of the final match, Higgins hijacked two frames allotted to Taylor. Taylor and Murphy bit their tongues and twiddled their thumbs 'just to keep peace and quiet'.

That fragile peace and quiet was in smithereens mere
moments after Canada's victory. Higgins tore into Taylor
with a torrent of verbal abuse. Taylor then understandably
declined to share a press conference platform with
Higgins. An emotional Higgins went on a solo run before
the media scrum, accusing Taylor of wanton greed. Taylor
had stood to collect a £6,000 bonus for the highest break
of the tournament. That prize had been snatched away in
the very last frame of the night when one of the Canadians
bettered Taylor's modest 71 with an unbroken 124.

Higgins' beef was that Taylor had intended keeping the
hypothetical bonus prize. 'I've known this guy for twenty-
four years,' he groused. 'I didn't know anybody could be
that greedy. He has put money before everything, he has
put money before his country. In my estimation, Taylor is
not a snooker player, because the more money he gets the
more he wants.'

The Hurricane raged hard. 'I'm absolutely disgusted
with him,' stormed Higgins, 'and he doesn't deserve to
wear the badge which shows the Red Hand of Ulster. If
he ever speaks to me again I will pretend to be deaf and
dumb. I gave him my room number at the hotel if he
wanted to get into fisticuffs. We've had a fabulous week in
Bournemouth, but there has just been one fly in the
ointment and he comes from the pits of Coalisland.'
With that, Higgins announced that he was off to a
nightclub.

Taylor then had his say. He told astounded journalists
that Higgins had threatened him. He quoted Higgins as
saying: 'I come from Shankhill, you come from Coalisland
and the next time you are in Northern Ireland I will have
you shot.' Taylor was horrified, less by the shadow of the
gunman than by Higgins playing the sectarian card.

Scrupulously apolitical, Taylor prided himself on his hard-won cross-community esteem.

Taylor revealed that: 'During the first session interval of the final, Alex even dragged Tony and myself into the Ladies' toilet for a team talk. A lady came in and Alex told her to go to the gents. Alex called me a thirteen-and-a-half stone bag of shit and said that he wanted me back in his hotel room to sort out the problems.' Crude remarks about Taylor's late mother had really twisted the knife.

And as for the £6,000 that never was. Taylor said that the Northern Ireland team had a long-standing agreement that where bonuses were won, the winner takes all. 'It was Alex's idea in the first place,' he explained, adding, 'I'm supposed to be the captain of the team, but we have always gone along with Alex rather than cause the team to be in disarray.'

Taylor was at a complete loss. He'd helped out Higgins in the past. He'd tried to see the best in his capricious team-mate. 'You grin and bear it for all those years,' he sighed, 'then you get this thrown at you.' Throwing was by now second nature to Higgins. A year previously, police had been called to the star's Manchester flat complex during a protracted bout of furniture flinging in a blazing row with his girlfriend. The police were questioning neighbours on the ground floor when they saw Higgins plummeting past their window. Incredibly, he survived the fall from his second-floor window with negligible injuries. 'He was paralytic,' observed a neighbour. Days before his World Cup outburst he'd been fined £50 for hurling a skateboard through an ex-wife's window when she refused to let him deliver presents to his kids.

'I'll never speak to him again,' insisted Taylor, irritated that 'The majority of people side with him because they don't know what sort of person he is. If they did, he wouldn't get the support he does.' Higgins' support was indeed phenomenal. His speed, skill and audacity had once moved the game to a new dimension. Twice a world champion, he was snooker's first and greatest people's hero. Insiders knew otherwise. In the words of Stephen Hendry's manager, Ian Doyle: 'With Higgins around the tension quadruples. He poisons the atmosphere.'

Now, even the public could see it. When the pair locked horns at Goffs, the home crowd froze him out for the first time ever. The eagerly anticipated showdown was a damp squib. Taylor studiously ignored his opponent throughout a dull contest. As if sensing he was on a hiding to nothing, Higgins meekly capitulated.

The Higgins-Taylor bust-up was another painful round in the sorry saga of Higgins Vs Higgins. In 1972 The Hurricane captured the World Championship with a verve never witnessed before or since. A decade later, in 1982, he again lifted the crown in dashing style. Fifteen years on, he sank seven pints and little else while crashing out of a qualifying match five games removed from a first round appearance in the 1997 competition.

A long time on the ropes, The Hurricane was sliding groggily towards the canvas. He'd been rooming in a cheap hotel, his rent paid from a benevolent fund set up to aid players who'd fallen upon 'genuine hardship'. On the eve of his latest humiliation he'd been turfed out of his lodgings for disruptive behaviour. Somewhere, somehow, he'd squandered some two million pounds along the way.

While he searched for a new digs, the BBC began filming a new series entitled 'Senior Pot Black', showcasing a dozen of snooker's first television stars. Alex Higgins had been the brightest of them all. For him, the call never came.

A FAIRLY AVERAGE REPUTATION FOR RELIGIOUS TOLERANCE

Ireland Inc Vs The Jehovah's Witnesses.

Who? Two Jehovah's Witnesses. One Catholic mob.
When? May 1956.
What? A Sunday afternoon book-burning.
Where? The townland of Clonlara, Co Clare.
Why? The men were guilty of worshipping false gods.

Stephen Miller and Henry Bond were just going about their daily business as Jehovah's Witnesses, knocking on doors and asking if people had heard about the One True God. Unfortunately for Miller and Bond, they were in the wrong place at the wrong time to be trying on that sort of thing.

The Witnesses were at the point of knocking off God's work on Sunday, May 13, 1956. They'd spent a passable afternoon doorstepping the householders of Clonlara, a small townland in County Clare. They'd been well received. Quite a number of people had heard them out. Nobody had slammed the door or fetched out the pitchfork.

The pair clambered astride Miller's motorcycle and set off for home, but as they hit the road a car suddenly pulled up in front of them, blocking the way. A group of men began closing in on the motorcycle evangelists. Sensing trouble, Miller scrambled the motorbike over a grass margin in a bid to escape. One of the encroaching men grabbed at Bond's arm, nearly yanking him to the ground.

The Witnesses drove the short distance to an establishment called The Angler's Rest. They needed to use the phone. They were told there was none. Caught in a dead end, there was nothing for it but to face the approaching mob. At the head of the gang was Father Patrick Ryan, the parish priest. 'Are you the men going around distributing and selling heretic books and articles?' he asked, not particularly looking for an answer. The Witnesses were relieved of their bags and briefcases. Miller demanded that the guards be called. The priest replied that no guards were needed to deal with Miller.

One of the parishioners brandished Miller's vacuum flask and asked the priest if he should break it. He was told not to. Another man thought it would be appropriate to punch Miller on the chin. This was the signal for the mob to give the strangers a good roughing up. The visitors' books and pamphlets were ceremonially burned in the street and the pair were sent packing with a stern warning never to set foot in Clonlara again.

Miller and Bond weren't found wanting for the courage of their convictions. Two months after the Clonlara showdown, Limerick District Court was packed to the rafters for the rematch. Fr Ryan and ten accomplices were charged with assault and malicious damage. The Bishop of Killaloe, Dr Rogers, arrived to lend his support from the public gallery. It was reported that: 'The crowded courtroom rose to their feet as His Lordship entered.' The Bishop had made a submission letting the judge know that he stood foursquare behind his curate. Counsel for the defence began by producing a Jehovah's Witness text entitled 'Let God Be True'. A passage from the book was read out. It stated that the doctrine of the Blessed Trinity was of pagan origin and that Satan was its author. Miller told the court that this was so.

It was pointed out to Miller that he was seeking legal redress under the Constitution of the Republic of Ireland. Did he realise that the self same Constitution commenced with the words, 'In the Name of the Most Holy Trinity, from Whom is all Authority'? He replied that he did. The defence put it to Miller that he was of the view that 'the laws of the land and the Constitution of this country are under the authority and authorship of Satan, the Devil himself'. Miller replied: 'It is not surprising when you see the conduct of its ministers of religion.' He was in a hole and taking digs.

The defence turned to the conduct of Pastor Charles T Russell, a founding father of the Jehovah's Witness movement. Was it not true that Russell's wife had accused him of infidelity? Miller replied that he didn't see what this had to do with a mob beating him up at Clonlara.

Henry Bond then told the court that the pair had spent a few hours in Clonlara, giving away books to people who either wouldn't or couldn't pay for them. He told how, at the Angler's Rest, a group of men had seized their bags and burned them. He agreed that the men might have taken exception to a remark of Miller's to the priest. Miller had said: 'Look here chappie.' This form of address clearly didn't extend due respect to a parish priest at the head of a belligerent mob.

Henry Bond told the court that he had been raised a Catholic but had been a Jehovah's Witness for the past three years. Hearing this, counsel for the defence told him: 'I cannot but feel sorry for you, and I will not cross-examine you.' Bond replied that he was 'honoured' to have become a Witness and reminded the court that the issue at hand was an 'unwarranted' attack on himself and Miller. Margaret O'Donoghue of The Angler's Rest testified to seeing a barracking mob surround the two men. She'd heard one man give the warning: 'Do not say "my dear fellow" to the priest. Address him in the proper manner.'

A garda sergeant said that he'd called to Fr Ryan's house shortly after the incident. The priest had bluntly informed him that the Jehovah's Witnesses would not be allowed to distribute their literature. Their kind had been expelled from the parish the previous year and he had instructed his parishioners that if any returned he was to be told straight away.

Counsel for the mob rested his defence on the incontrovertible fact that blasphemy was a crime punishable by statute under the Irish Constitution. He branded Miller: '. . . an unusual and an unholy and an unprecedented witness in the witness box, who sees nothing wrong and does not feel in error in telling your worship that Satan himself discovered the doctrine of the Blessed Trinity and therefore commits blasphemy against God and His Blessed Mother'.

The defence cited a directive in the Constitution ordaining that public homage was due to Almighty God. Furthermore, the defence argued: 'This witness is prepared to dishonour the Christian religion, making no distinction between Catholics and non-Catholics.' This was a black mark in a country where Catholics and non-Catholics had fought relentlessly for the exclusive franchise on honouring the Christian religion.

Before delivering his verdict, Justice Hurley stressed that the courts were obliged to be non-sectarian . . . BUT . . . 'We have,' he contended, 'a fairly average reputation for religious tolerance in this country, but is religious tolerance to be extended to accept the gospel which Mr Miller and his companions were disseminating? . . . The Irish faith is something that has been tempered by the fires of history. It is a tradition, a legend, a way of life. It has its roots in lovely villages and mountains, in prison cells and on the scaffold, and in sorrowful mothers' hearts.'

Miller and his fellow-travellers sought to destroy that picturebox religion, said the judge. They were guilty of blasphemy in the Catholic understanding of the word. In this light, even though the charge of assault was proven, he would dismiss it under the Probation of Offenders Act. As for the other charges against the mob, he'd dismiss them too.

The judge didn't want any repetition of this case. As a preventative measure he bound both Miller and Bond over to the peace on sureties of £200 each, a massive sum in 1956. He warned that if they were involved in any more incidents they'd go to prison for three months. The Witnesses' solicitor asked the judge to fix recognizances in case of an appeal. The judge rebuked him: 'Sit down, you have no standing in this court.' The solicitor countered: 'Your worship's decision is unprecedented and contrary to the law of the country. I say that without fear of contradiction.' He was wasting his breath.

There was no public outcry over this glaring piece of rough justice. Only the *Irish Times* raised the civil libertarian angle, and that paper's leader writer was careful to express an appropriate level of disdain for the ill-done-by religious weirdoes. The paper's editorial noted: 'The consequence seems to be that people going peacefully about their work not merely can have their property seized and destroyed, but need not consider themselves entitled to the protection of the law.'

It stressed: 'We know little about the particular tenets of the Jehovah's Witness, and that little we dislike.

Nevertheless, these men have the same right as any other religious sect, whether Christian, Jewish, Mahommedan, Taoist or Hindu, to propagate their faith by peaceful means. Any denial of that right is a reflection of the state of freedom in this country. Most Irishmen feel a sense of outrage when a Christian priest is prohibited from pursuing his sacred mission in communist countries; yet what so often and so deplorably happens there has been re-enacted in County Clare and endorsed in Limerick.'

But if the *Irish Times* was the conscience of trendy liberalism in Ireland, its time had yet to come. A simple truth prevailed – God was a Catholic. And so long as that remained the case Jehovah's Witnesses and their ilk would be unwelcome interlopers, at large in the State with no invisible means of support.

THEY SAID IT COULDN'T BE DONE

The Pint That Was Light Years Ahead Of Its Time.

Who? The Guinness Group.
When? 1979–1981.
What? Guinness Light.
Where? Astronauts in space loved it. Pintsmen on Earth didn't.
Why? It had an insurmountable image problem.

The Guinness Group end-of-year report for 1978 made grim reading. In Britain, sales of the famous stout had nose-dived for the third year running. True, the company had been expanding into Nigeria, Malaysia, Cameroon, Ghana and Jamaica, but the governments of those countries were tugging at the company's purse-strings, demanding a bigger state cut of the brewing plants and the profits.

But the brainboxes at Guinness had a cunning plan. In the summer of 1979 Guinness Light was launched with such hullabaloo as hadn't been seen since the unsinkable Titanic squealed down a Belfast slipway in 1912. The space-age adverts featured an astronaut boldly going where no man had gone before, and the fate-tempting slogan: 'They Said It Couldn't Be Done . . .'. They, whoever they were, would turn out to be dead right.

There was little, if anything, intrinsically wrong with Guinness Light. As the name suggested it was a less-creamy, more gravity-defying version of Uncle Arthur's dense black brew – Guinness for a hot summer's day if you like. But nobody liked.

Guinness Light's real failing was that it was an idea whose time had not yet come. Fifteen or twenty years later, it would have found a ready niche amid the bamboozling profusion of Lite American-style beers and day-glo kiddies' concoctions, but Guinness Light was born into a pub culture – in Ireland and in Britain – that was stubbornly set in its ways. Drinking was a manly pursuit, typically carried out in dank, grubby surroundings smelling of stale booze, mildew and smoke, and where the sandwiches came with a side-serving of dead bluebottles. 'Men Only' signs were still a common sight on the doors leading into bars. Ladies were tolerated in the lounge.

Choosing a drink was easy. There was one tap for stout, one for ale and one for Harp. Lager was generally only considered suitable for puny L-plate drinkers and women – it was house policy in some pubs to refuse pint glasses to the fair sex for fear their unladylike appearance would lower the tone of the place. Into this world of time-honoured ritual came Guinness Light with its astronomical launch budget, its astronautical imagery and its cryptic message: 'What one small step did for mankind, we've done for beer.' (Actually, it wasn't so much cryptic as plain daft.)

Even the very name Guinness Light was just asking for trouble. For the average stout-slurper of the day, the term 'light' just meant 'weak'. To even suggest that he'd consider drinking a watered-down brew was tantamount to calling him a sissy. But Guinness had spent a fortune developing and marketing the accursed stuff, so the company wasn't going to give up without a fight.

The *Sunday World*'s Pub Spy was dispatched to get an early reaction to the new arrival. Before he set out, Pub Spy was reminded that the launch of the new product was of huge importance to Guinness and that if he was able to report a positive reaction that would be great. Pub Spy came back and tendered a report that was candidly critical rather than glowing. The review ran, warts and all. So, by way of editorial balance, the newspaper commissioned another hack to do a vox pop on the streets of Dublin. The journalist returned with slim pickings. He'd only managed to find two people who weren't hostile to Guinness Light, and even they were faint in their praise. So another journalist was sent out in the hope that his mission might prove a case of third time lucky.

Happily, the third hack came back with the goods, but the National Union of Journalists chapel at the *Sunday World* was concerned that the methods used had not been entirely scientific. The NUJ insisted that the positive piece on Guinness Light must not be published. The editor pleaded with the union not to be so bolshy. The NUJ said that unscientific reporting had no place in the *Sunday World*. At this point senior management intervened, opening up the appalling vista that Guinness might withdraw its advertising from the newspaper. The NUJ remained steadfast – the unscientific story must not run.

When the next edition of the *Sunday World* appeared, there was a glamorous dollybird draped seductively across the front cover. Nothing unusual there. Except that foxy chicklet Mia Murphy was clad in a figure-hugging tee-shirt bearing the legend 'Guinness Light: Light Years Ahead'. Crisis averted – at least for the newspaper's management. But, ultimately, there was to be no solution to Guinness Light's image problem. In 1981, fed up with flushing good money after bad, Guinness pulled the plug on the drink that the public just wouldn't swallow.

Ireland had seen failed launches before, but no previous miscalculation had been as monumental. At the more modest end of the scale was the short-lived 'Korona Programme' which Radio Éireann began broadcasting in the autumn of 1959. 'The Korona Programme' was a live show sponsored by Korona watches. The format of the programme called for the presenter to give the listeners regular time-checks – demonstrating the accuracy of Korona's timepieces. Unfortunately, reading the time accurately wasn't one of the presenter's strongpoints. After six episodes of unplanned comedy the programme was scrapped well short of its projected thirteen instalments.

Twenty years after Guinness Light, the company launched a Guinness white developed at St James' Gate in Dublin. The pale Breo beer – 'breo' is the old Irish word for 'glow' – which cost £5 million to develop, was withdrawn in 2000 after just a year on the market.

IT IS AN UNPLEASANT DUTY TO CRITICISE FOUL PLAY

The GAA Vs The Dublin Media.

Who? The Tipperary GAA County Board.
When? 1968.
What? The board slapped a blanket ban on six journalists.
Where? From all Gaelic games activity throughout the county.
Why? For reporting facts instead of accentuating the positive.

The earliest known hurling contest took place in 1272 BC. The match report appeared, two millennia later, in the Mediaeval 'Book Of Leinster'. It makes rousing reading. While the native Fir Bolg and the invading Tuatha De Danann were killing time before the Battle Of Moytura, it was decided to have a 27-a-side limber-up. There was no time limit. Both sides simply hacked at each other 'until their bones were broken and bruised and they fell out-stretched on the turf and the match ended'. In place of the modern lap of honour, the victorious Fir Bolg hurlers fell upon their crippled opponents and slew them.

While the primal bloodlust at the core of most sports has become stylised and diluted out of all recognition, hurling has retained much of its untamed purity. But in this cosseted age of dental floss, men's deodorants and brain-scan machines, hurling's deep entanglement with violence has increasingly become the love that dare not speak its name. There was a time, not so long ago, when it was all very different. In 1965, for instance, Mr M Costigan didn't feel in the least bit ridiculous telling the Laois GAA County Board: 'The (foreign games) Ban should be retained. Men like Davis, Pearse and Wolfe Tone died for its retention.' It wasn't strictly, or even remotely true, but everyone knew what he meant.

Some years later an internal GAA document echoed the language of the gun when it said: 'We would like to emphasise that the spirit as well as the letter of our amateur status rules and regulations should be appreciated and honoured by all our units.'

The GAA first started getting sensitive about its violent reputation at the peak of the Sixties' peace'n'love fad. LSD provided the Association with a powerful motivation. They saw they could make serious pounds, shillings and pence by pushing their wares in the schoolyards. A new Hurling Revival Plan was launched with spectacular success. Orders for juvenile hurleys from January to July 1968 were up ten thousand on the same period in 1967. But there was still resistance to the ancient game from modern parents who wanted their little Sean Óg to go out into the world with a full set of teeth, ten working fingers and an outward-facing nose.

Parents with reservations would not have been won over by the 1968 National League Hurling Final, a game worthy of that first legendary clash between the Fir Bolg and Tuatha De Danann. The combatants were Tipperary and Kilkenny. Recent meetings between the sides had produced several hospitalisations and a catalogue of standing vendettas. Before the Final was very old, the thin line between healthy competition and faction fighting had evaporated in a red mist. 'TIPPERARY VICTORS IN GAME OF UGLY INCIDENTS' was the *Irish Times'* verdict. According to that paper: 'The needle which has marred a number of recent matches between these counties again thrust up its ugly and malicious spike.'

The first outbreak of extra-curricular violence came when Tipperary's Len Gaynor was felled by a blow on the head. 'A short fracas ensued.' Moments later, the hapless Gaynor was whacked by a spectator as he shimmied down the touchline. Shortly afterwards there was an off-the-ball incident in the Kilkenny goalmouth. Kilkenny goalkeeper Ollie Walsh 'was laid prostrate by a blow from behind'. The match official had no sympathy for the poleaxed goalie. 'As Walsh lay on the ground the referee ordered Jimmy Doyle of Tipperary to proceed to play the ball.' This, felt the reporter, was 'the limit of absurdity'. As a sporting gesture to the horizontal goalkeeper, Doyle put his shot over the bar for a point rather than going for goal. 'Had he scored a goal, a riot could have developed.'

The following week, the GAA's Central Council convened at their Croke Park HQ to review the carnage. The Association's President, Mr F Muldoon, took pains to point out that – leaving aside the assault, fracas, spectator ambush, attack and counter-attack – the game was *mostly* played in the right spirit. Michael Maher of the Tipperary County Board rounded on the press. By drawing attention to the violence, the newspapers had passed up a golden opportunity to showcase the sportsmanship on view. The Kilkenny Board Chairman, Nicky Purcell, didn't see what all the fuss was about. 'These things will happen,' he said.

Six weeks later, the GAA's Central Council announced its verdict. Tipperary's John Flanagan and Kilkenny's Ollie Walsh were meted out six-month suspensions. The Tipperary County Board fingered the blame for the suspensions firmly on the press. The newspapers had 'created a climate of public opinion' which had forced the Central Council down this appalling vista.

'JUST WHO DID THE PRESS STRIKE?' countered the *Irish Independent*, accusing the GAA officials of 'an astonishing lack of knowledge of, or disregard for, the rules of hurling'. The *Independent* threw the rulebook at Tipperary. Rule 96 clearly stated that: 'A player deliberately striking an opponent or deliberately kicking him shall incur suspension for not less than six months.' So there.

Ollie Walsh appealed against the severity of the ban. His county Chairman, Nicky Purcell, came to his defence. A main plank of Purcell's argument was that the people of Kilkenny were against the six month suspension. He got no joy. Nicky Purcell was furious. He demanded to know: 'Why was not last year's All-Ireland Hurling Final between the two teams investigated? During it, one Kilkenny player lost an eye, another received multiple fractures to his wrist, another finished the game with concussion and a fourth had an index finger broken.' And now, suddenly, hurlers were to be bound by namby-pamby rules! Three thousand years of tradition was being turned on its head.

Purcell's lines of reasoning didn't sway the GAA's Central Council. Both suspensions stood. Tipperary's only sensible option now was to knuckle down and concentrate on the impending All-Ireland Championship. Instead, the county slapped a ban on six Dublin-based journalists who'd penned blow-by-blow accounts of the rumble with Kilkenny.

Weeks passed. The Dublin chapel of the National Union of Journalists finally retaliated on August 25, 1968, instructing its members not to handle any Tipperary GAA news. The Tipperary board picked that same day to announce the lifting of its ban on the six. The county said it would reinstate normal relations with the NUJ from the following Wednesday, four days before Tipperary were to meet Wexford in the 1968 All-Ireland Hurling Final.

If only it were that simple. The national press was out to teach Tipperary a lesson. In the run-up to the All-Ireland Final, the Wexford team's build-up was given blanket coverage, with daily reports and individual player profiles. Tipperary were mentioned strictly in passing. The big game produced a shock. There was more than a hint of glee in headlines like 'WEXFORD TORPEDO TIPPERARY' which greeted the underdogs' triumph.

It was the end of the Championship line for Tipperary, but not for the anti-Dublin resentment they'd stirred-up. In a wildcat strike, Derry's GAA Board notified the NUJ that the county would be imposing a news ban on the Republic's national newspapers. Cork were next to air festering grievances. Three days after losing the 1968 Minor Hurling Final to Wexford, the Cork Board attacked the Dublin newspapers for pinning nasty 'incidents' on their minors. Cork selector Frank Murphy complained: 'The reports are typical of those of the past four All-Ireland Finals, when lavish praise was given to Wexford and little to Cork.'

Cork's criticism stung the *Independent*'s Mitchel Cogley into a bizarre rebuff. He wrote: 'Where minors are concerned, it is an unpleasant duty – but a duty, nevertheless – to have to criticise foul play.' Press relations with Tipperary reached a new low when the Dublin branch of the NUJ extended its own boycott to include any written or photographic evidence of GAA activity in the county, from Senior matches to pub raffles.

Wexford were next to take a swing at the press. Apparently, the routine mayhem of a hurling final in

Enniscorthy had been blown out of all proportion by
reporters who seemed to have an unhealthy fascination
with gore. One member of the County Board objected
that: 'A lot of commendable things happen in County
Wexford that do not get half enough publicity. It is not
good enough.' Mr P Codd complained: 'It was stated that
one man was kicked in the face on the ground, and
everyone here knows that is not true.' Inconveniently, the
Board's Chairman, Sean Browne, felt honour-bound to
point out that it *was* actually true. The referee had noted
the assault in his match report. Still, the weight of opinion
on the Wexford Board was that the press had let the sport
down yet again.

   In Christmas week 1968 the NUJ lifted its embargo on
Tipperary as a gesture of goodwill and reconciliation. The
bloodshed continues.

THERE ARE CERTAIN THINGS IN LIFE THAT CERTAIN OTHER THINGS JUST DON'T APPLY TO

Ken McCue Hands In His Notice.

> Who? Layman Ken McCue. Dublin's Catholic Chancellor.
> When? 1992–93.
> What? A confirmed atheist and top cleric held a summit.
> Where? The Catholic Archbishop's Palace, Dublin.
> Why? McCue wanted to resign from the Catholic Church.

Dubliner Ken McCue started his secondary education left-handed and finished it ambidextrous. Far from being grateful to the Christian Brothers for putting him right, McCue took away a lifetime resentment of their school-of-hard-knocks regime.

By the time he'd reached his mid-thirties, Ken McCue had been a devout atheist for more years than he cared to remember. In the late Eighties, he wrote to the Archbishop of Dublin seeking to cancel his membership of the Catholic Church. He waited for a reply. And waited. And waited. McCue let the matter slide until a brief encounter with the health system pushed it back onto the agenda. Someone, he discovered, had taken the liberty of listing his religion as 'RC' (Roman Catholic) on his hospital admission card. He asked for the entry to be erased.

Two weeks later, Ken was back at the hospital for tests. He noticed that he was still listed on the computer register

as Roman Catholic. He asked the registrar to change the
entry to 'atheist'. The nearest category to 'atheist' on the
hospital system was 'agnostic', charitably suggesting a
category of people who are confused rather than damned.

Stung into action by his hospital experience, McCue
again attempted to formalise his defection from the church
which had claimed him as an infant. It was late 1992. He
tendered a letter of resignation to the offices of the
Catholic Archbishop of Dublin. The Archbishop's newly
installed Chancellor sent a prompt acknowledgement,
enclosing a 22-page internal discussion paper to illuminate
McCue's position.

From the document, McCue discovered that the Church
of Rome, in common with another celebrated Italian
brotherhood, doesn't let its initiates walk away lightly. The
paper was firm on this point: 'Loss of faith, for example, does
not result in a loss of membership. The Catholic Church still
claims jurisdiction over all those baptised in the Catholic
Church or received into it (Canon II) . . . It by no means
follows that because the subject is instrumental in forging
membership that he also has the capacity to dissolve it.'
Ken McCue believed his membership had indeed been
forged, while he was an innocent bystander at the
baptismal font. He eventually found a get-out clause.

Ken learned that he could make a 'formal act of
defection' by uttering heretical pronouncements or by
'notorious rejection'. The latter option entails making a
public and hostile repudiation of Catholicism. But even at
this break-point in the relationship, the Church reserves
the right to refuse a divorce. In the jargon of the
document: 'Church involvement and analysis of the act
must inevitably become part of the process . . . The will of
the agent alone effects nothing at the visible juridical level.'

Ultimately, the paper suggested that the best way to get out of being a Catholic was to tender 'an application informing or requesting church authorities of departure'. The Church could then launch 'an investigation to determine what weight should be given to the application'. This investigation 'would normally involve requesting an interview with the applicant . . . in the course of which one could discover whether or not the request is genuine, or that of a disturbed or perhaps annoyed person'. This implicit admission that the Church cherished 'disturbed' members over ones who fully knew their own minds confirmed McCue's decision to quit.

An interview was duly arranged for the beginning of 1993. The Chancellor of the House of the Archbishop of Dublin welcomed Ken into the Archbishop's Palace. The Chancellor outlined four possible exit routes. Ken McCue could embrace a different religion. He could voluntarily sign a renunciation of the Catholic faith. He could post a formal affidavit of defection. Or he could make a solemn profession of atheism before witnesses.

McCue told the Chancellor that he very much liked the sound of the solemn profession before witnesses. By its very nature, atheism lacked the social get-togethers that the members of organised religions took for granted. Ken told the Chancellor he wanted to go public. The Archbishop's man expressed stern disapproval. No-one in Ireland had ever done such a thing.

The Chancellor wanted to know why his visitor was so anxious to quit the Church. McCue replied that there were various articles of faith he just couldn't accept, like the existence of angels, the infallibility of the Pope and the sacrament of transubstantiation where bread and wine become the body and blood of Christ. The Chancellor

granted that there would be scientific problems with the
latter but that 'there are certain things in life that certain
other things just don't apply to'. So there.

Shot down on that one, McCue bounced back with a
demarcation line. Why, he asked, does the Lord's Prayer
involve the faithful asking God to 'lead us not into
temptation'? Surely, said Ken, it was a given that leading
us into temptation was strictly the Devil's work? The
Chancellor replied that Jesus told us to pray in that
manner, matter closed.

The Chancellor drew the discussion to a finish by
urging Ken to 'think it over' for a while before doing
anything drastic. McCue had covertly recorded the
conversation. He gave the tape to a journalist who wrote
up the story. Meanwhile, he sent a letter to the Chancellor
seeking to set a date for his formal profession of atheism
before witnesses. He got no reply. McCue phoned the
Chancellor, who was mightily miffed at the publication of
the article. He was not willing to discuss setting a date.

In the years that followed, McCue sent intermittent
letters to the Archbishop's Palace without reply. His
detention in the Lord's mansion of many rooms put him
in mind of two hotels. One was Fawlty Towers. The other
was The Eagles' *Hotel California*, a place where – as the
song famously put it – you can check out any time you like,
but you can never leave.

COUP D'ÉTAT OF THE YAHOOS

The Minister Of Defence Vs The President.

Who? Paddy Donegan TD. President Cearbhall Ó Dálaigh.
When? 1976.
What? The President of Ireland made a shock resignation.
Where? Appropriately, it began at the opening of a mess.
Why? Donegan called the President 'a thundering bollocks'.

If they only knew it, a lot of people had good reason to curse the name Cearbhall Ó Dálaigh. As Chairman of the Commission on Income Taxation, he was chief architect of the penal and discriminatory PAYE tax system. However, by late 1976, after almost two years as President of Ireland, it was generally agreed that Ó Dálaigh was doing a fine job. A font of culture and erudition, the President had been putting his multi-lingual skills to good use on a series of high-visibility friendship visits to Ireland's new EEC partners.

But admiration for the cosmopolitan head of state wasn't universal. Ó Dálaigh had become President without an election in 1974. Fianna Fail had proposed him. Fine Gael Taoiseach Liam Cosgrave had accepted the nomination reluctantly. Cosgrave's party were in government with Labour. It was an uneasy right-left balancing act. If Fine Gael had contested the Presidency, Labour would have been obliged to follow suit. The government was susceptible to a stress fracture. Ó Dálaigh got the nod as a non-party candidate, but for some Fine Gaelers with long memories the new President came with a flawed pedigree. Back in the Forties he'd stood for election to the Dáil as a Fianna Fáiler.

A former Chief Justice and twice Attorney General, President Ó Dálaigh knew a thing or two about the law. He was particularly keen on human rights and civil liberties. Back in 1971 he'd made a daring suggestion that Ireland could benefit from incorporating various progressive European and UN conventions into the law of the land. Ó Dálaigh became President at a time when the Cosgrave government was drafting reams of legislation clamping down on personal liberties under a 'Law & Order' slogan.

In March of 1976 the President referred the government's Criminal Law (Jurisdiction) Act to the Supreme Court to test its constitutionality. It passed the test and he promptly signed it into law. Whatever his personal feelings, Justice Minister Paddy Cooney put a brave face on the intervention. Better to have the Act tried out by the President, he said, than by someone with a serious charge hanging over their head.

Then, in September 1976, Ó Dálaigh did it again. This time he had reservations about the government's Emergency Powers Bill which allowed a person to be detained for up to seven days without being told why. Again, the bill was found to be constitutional and the President signed it into law at midnight on Saturday, 16th October 1976. His reservations about the legislation had delayed its passage by perhaps a month. He'd only been doing his job. For some members of the government, however, he was becoming a major pain in the Aras.

Precisely 36 hours after the bill was signed, the Minister for Defence, Paddy Donegan, arrived at Columb Army Barracks in Mullingar. The Minister was there to open a new cookhouse and mess hall. Nobody in his audience could have been prepared for what happened next.

'It was amazing when the President sent the Emergency Powers Bill to the Supreme Court,' blasted the Minister, launching into a short sharp rant. He concluded by declaring: 'In my opinion he is a thundering disgrace.' At least, that's how the newspapers delicately reported the phrase. Later that year Ó Dálaigh would tell a dinner party that the exact words used were 'a thundering bollocks', although he wasn't actually on hand to hear what was said. Minister Donegan was addressing an Army assembly. The President, under the Constitution, was the same Army's Commander-In-Chief. Paddy Donegan had dipped an elbow in hot water before, but this was a breath-taking triple-somersault from the high-board.

A year after the event, Donegan told a reporter that he'd been badly jarred in a severe car accident the night before his outburst. 'I was concussed and did not know it,' he said. 'I was like a zombie walking around.' He said he'd had two whiskeys at a reception before the official dinner, but he insisted there was no question that the drink had been talking. His track record supported this assertion.

The Oireachtas in 1976 was still a safe haven for a whole menagerie of 'colourful' deputies, but some of Donegan's utterances had an eerie glow-in-the-dark quality that was all their own. He was fond of telling people that the Irish Navy was several hands short of a full deck, and, indeed, several decks short of a proper fleet. While this was undoubtedly true, it was thought unseemly for a Defence Minister to belittle his own forces. When the gun-running ship, Claudia, was intercepted smuggling arms into Ireland in 1973, many felt the Minister's response failed to reflect the gravity of the situation. At a press conference he stated that no action would be taken against the Claudia or its crew. Outlining what he deemed a suitable punishment, he said: 'She'll get a boot up the transom and be told to get out of our waters fast.'

Four years earlier, Donegan had picked up a more severe penalty for his own breach of Ireland's gun laws. In 1969, when he was Fine Gael's spokesman on industry and commerce, he was fined £20 at Drogheda District Court after he admitted trying to run some traveller families out of Monasterboice by firing his shotgun outside their caravans. His cure for unemployment had a similar directness about it – put the jobless in the Army.

After his attack on the President, the Fianna Fáil opposition wanted Donegan's head on a spike. Instead, they got an apology-cum-excuse from the Government Information Service on the Minister's behalf. It merely said: 'I regret the remarks which arose out of my deep feelings for the security of our citizens. I intend to offer my apologies to the President as soon as possible.'

The President, though, wouldn't play ball. He cold shouldered Donegan's attempts to make contact. While President Ó Dálaigh played hard to get, Fianna Fáil tabled a Dáil motion calling on the Taoiseach to seek Donegan's resignation. Fianna Fáil leader Jack Lynch added that he did so with much regret, and not to score political points. Taoiseach Cosgrave replied that he was happy with Donegan's written apology to the President.

Fine Gael's John Kelly mounted an imaginative defence of Donegan. Kelly argued that the President's high profile meant he couldn't escape being a target for criticism. Mathematical probability dictated that some of that criticism was *bound* to be utter dog rot. The Minister's remarks were the result of strong, although completely wrong, feelings. The outburst was simply evidence of his 'passionate commitment' to his job and should be forgiven as 'the product of a hot and generous temperament'.

A vote was taken. The Dáil motion for Donegan's resignation was defeated by a margin of five. The government had stood by their man. The next day, President Ó Dálaigh resigned. The Cabinet was given a bare ten minutes notice before he went public with his decision. A civilian once more, Ó Dálaigh could now embarrass Donegan by releasing the texts of the Minister's apology, together with the dismissive snub it earned. 'Have you *any* conception,' he'd chided, 'of your responsibilities?' The government responded to the shock resignation by deeply regretting the President's decision and thanking him for doing a great job.

On December 3, 1976, Fianna Fáil's Patrick Hillary succeeded Cearbhall Ó Dálaigh as Head Of State. As was usual, the electorate had no say in the matter. The day before the new President took office, Liam Cosgrave shuffled his cabinet. Paddy Donegan was relieved of his Defence duties and packed off to the more tranquil pastures of the Lands Department. The so-called '*coup d'état* of the Yahoos' had claimed its second victim.

THE THIRD MOST FAMOUS WOMAN IN BRITAIN

Cold Feet Trip Up Mandy Smith.

> Who? The schoolgirl bedded by a rock'n'roll granddad.
> When? Late 1986.
> What? Mandy Smith's world TV debut was nixed.
> Where? She was axed from RTÉ's *Saturday Live*.
> Why? For fear she'd be 'a bad example to teenage girls'.

Mandy Smith banned by RTÉ. Ireland a laughing stock, again. It was pitiably absurd and demeaning, particularly by the marginally raised expectations of the day. It had been a year since the Lesbian Nuns affair. On that momentously silly occasion, the national broadcasting service had exhibited commendable maturity in the face of histrionic opposition. If that was one step forward, this was two steps back and a cream pie in the mush.

It was late 1986. Mandy Smith was big news. The stunning sixteen-year-old had turned down the Beeb's top-rated 'Wogan' show and flown instead to Dublin to make her first ever TV appearance. Her screen debut was to take place on 'Saturday Live', hosted by businesswoman Noelle Campbell-Sharp. In the event, Mandy ended up watching the show cooped-up in her Gresham Hotel suite surrounded by her hopping-mad entourage. She hadn't come to Ireland to undermine the state or promote cannibalism. The cute party piece she'd prepared for the show was to count to ten in the first national language – Aon, dó, trí – just like her Irish granny had taught her.

Mandy Smith's life had exploded across the front pages three months earlier with the revelation that she had been seduced by parchment-faced Bill Wyman of the Rolling Stones. At the time the furtive love affair began, she was a mature thirteen, he was a tearaway 47-year-old grandfather. Some men move their mistress into a nice apartment, Wyman installed Mandy in a swisher class of school. When the news broke, Wyman scarpered for France while Britain's Serious Crime Squad questioned Mandy and her Cabra-born mother Pat. No charges could be pressed against the wrinkly Lothario unless a complaint was filed. Three months on, none had been.

Noelle Campbell-Sharp had gone to a lot of trouble and personal expense to secure the most sought-after chat show guest in the Western Hemisphere. Mandy and a travelling party had been jetted in, limoed about and feted at the Gresham Hotel. Everything was fine and dandy until a phone call came from RTÉ saying could Mandy be in her seat by nine o'clock. Mandy's Dublin-born manager, Maurice Boland, wanted to know why they wanted her in place thirty minutes before the show went on air? The voice explained that Mandy was being downgraded to a seat in the studio audience.

Boland explained down the phone just who Mandy Smith was. 'She's the third most famous woman in Britain,' he pointed out, pausing to let this ace make its impact. Something came back from the other end. Maurice, teeth clenched, replied: 'The Queen and Princess Diana.'

Boland then rang the *Saturday Live* producer, who told him bluntly that he could withdraw Mandy if he didn't like the new arrangement. Shortly afterwards the producer would release an official press statement saying that Mandy Smith was 'not important enough' to be on the show.

Seething, indignant and bent on getting even, Boland took his troupe off to the Suesey Street niteclub on Leeson Street. They found the place strangely empty. Forewarned of Mandy's arrival, the bouncers had been overly rigorous in their application of the door policy. One person who was expressly to be allowed past the cordon was Ireland's premier Fleet Street stringer, Tom McPhail.

By Monday morning the British newspapers were having a hearty laugh at prudish Ireland's expense. Campbell-Sharp was quoted as admitting that: 'RTÉ got cold feet at the last minute. The production team had decided against her. They felt she should not give a bad example to young teenage girls. And I had to agree that by having her on the panel we would perhaps be giving her some kind of support.' RTÉ's Controller of Television, Joe Mulholland, cited a 'certain nervousness' about Mandy's scarlet past. 'We did not want to go into detail,' he stated, insisting that the post-watershed programme 'is supposed to be a family show'.

The *Saturday Live* Lolita-gagging botch-job petered out in an unseemly spillage of sour recriminations and disputed expense tabs, but it wasn't the last the world would hear of Mandy Smith. Within the space of a few more years she had launched a modelling career, become a pop singer, developed anorexia, become a recluse, made-up with Bill Wyman, married Bill Wyman, divorced Bill Wyman, written a book about herself and Bill Wyman, married footballer Pat Van Den Hauwe of Spurs, divorced footballer (to be continued) . . .

And RTÉ? Well, RTÉ gave the world *The Lyrics Board*.

ARMCHAIR LIBERALS WHO SIT AT HOME CONDEMNING APARTHEID

Hostile Trendies Vs Foster & Allen.

Who? Mick Foster. Tony Allen. The Dubliners. Paul Brady. U2.
When? The summer of 1985.
What? Demands were made that F&A never go back.
Where? To South Africa, from where they'd just returned.
Why? To rid the world of evil (and it was payback time).

Poor old Foster & Allen. There they were, polishing the gold discs and minding their own business. Then *whack!* They never saw it coming. The trendies of Ireland had been sniping at the popular Co Westmeath duo for years but this was different, concerted, an all-out assault.

It was the autumn of 1985. Life was good for Mick Foster (Favourite Film: The *Carry On* series) and Tony Allen (Unfulfilled Ambition: None). Conventional wisdom has it that a gentleman is someone who can play the accordion but doesn't. But Foster & Allen had never been cowed by convention, and their rewards were there for all to see. The pair had no fewer than three albums sitting pretty in the UK charts. They were gearing up for yet another sellout Irish tour. The world was their pearly oyster.

The spark that detonated the powder keg that shattered this state of bliss was a simple letter. The Irish Anti-Apartheid Movement (IAAM) wrote to the undynamic duo pointing out that their visits to South Africa 'provided great assistance' to that country's white supremacist junta. The IAAM cited The Chieftains, The Dubliners, Niall Tobin and other performers who had turned down lucrative offers to play Sun City.

There was nothing new in this. The IAAM had written to Foster & Allen before. The organisation's Chairman, Dr Kader Asmal, told the press that two previous appeals to the duo had yielded no response. This was hardly surprising. Foster & Allen were of the old school of Irish entertainers who respected the fact that deals and ideals are like men and women – one isn't necessarily better than the other, they're just different.

Contacted at a Tralee hotel, a bemused Tony Allen pointed out that Foster & Allen had, in fact, no plans for going to South Africa. This was true. The previous week they had announced details of their forthcoming world tour and the Dark Continent didn't figure. In fact, they'd only just returned from Sun City a few months previously, and nobody had raised so much as an eyebrow.

But something had happened in those middling months of 1985. Something big. Pop music had found its Manifest Destiny at Live Aid. Righting a wrong was now more intrinsic to rock'n'roll than writing a song. In precisely the same period, South Africa was coming to the boil as an issue in Ireland thanks largely to a spirited group of Dunnes Stores workers whose dogged efforts to keep South African fruit off the shelves gave the Anti-Apartheid cause ultra-high visibility.

As calls mounted for his resignation from the Seanad, Senator Donie Cassidy took the opportunity to point out that – contrary to a widely held belief – he was not the pair's manager. Meanwhile, Tony Allen spelled it out again for those who seemed determined not to hear – they had no plans to tour South Africa. Allen added that he 'did not see any examples of Apartheid on previous visits to the country'. That casual utterance set the musical trendies alight with moral indignation.

Whatever the state of Tony Allen's eyesight, the fact remained that Foster & Allen had no plans to return to South Africa. But that wasn't good enough for the trendies who demanded that the pair must swear an oath never to go back. Written in blood would be nice.

This was payback time for the men waggishly dubbed Voerster & Outspan by the rock critic George Byrne. Their flouting of the cultural boycott was bad enough, but there was a lot more on the charge-sheet. For years they'd converted maudlin tripe into multi-platinum success while musicians who were clearly their moral and artistic superiors struggled to command the attention of three drunks, a barman and a girlfriend who was getting far too chatty with the guy on the sound-desk. Most of all though, it was time to settle the score for *that* infamous *Top Of The Pops* appearance when the duo had dishonoured their caste and their nation by pretending to be leprechauns.

'It's a disgrace,' said Donal Lunny. 'They're sacrificing their morals,' reflected Those Nervous Animals. U2's Adam Clayton thought it was 'absolutely clear why they shouldn't go'. Dave Fanning employed the words 'ignorant', 'stupid' and 'disgusting'. Paul Brady – without providing any detail as to why   found it 'very hard to believe that a senator in Ireland could be entirely stupid'.

Chris De Burgh refused to issue a blanket condemnation. Having played South Africa himself, he knew 'more about the situation than ninety-nine percent of the Armchair Liberals who sit at home condemning

Apartheid'. As Chris figured it: 'Foster & Allen will be playing to multi-racial audiences, and even if that means only two percent blacks, it still proves that blacks are allowed in.' Meanwhile, Gavin Friday devastated South Africa's Electro-Da-Da fan-base when he confirmed: 'I wouldn't even allow a record of mine to be released there.'

Predictably, Foster & Allen's show at Dublin's Stadium was targeted by protesters. The audience cheered as the disruptive do-gooders were ejected. More accurately, it's probable that eighty-five percent of the audience cheered while the remainder didn't even hear the protest chants. A journalist once pointed out to Donie Cassidy that, in concert, the duo's vocals were far too loud in the mix. 'That's deliberate policy,' responded Donie. 'We did a survey and found that fifteen percent of Foster & Allen's audiences are deaf.'

After the token rumble at the Stadium, the row fizzled out. In the end, Foster & Allen's remarkable staying power saw them outlast many of the hostile trendies who'd taken them to task, along with the Apartheid regime itself. They're now free to play Sun City as often as they like, although nobody these days lashes out the rands quite like the old order did. Meanwhile Mick and Tony are probably still wondering what all the fuss was about.

A MIDNIGHT SWOOP ON A CONGESTED AREA

The Legion of Mary Vs Monto.

Who? Frank Duff, a civil servant on a mission from God.
When? 1922–25.
What? To shut down the largest red light district in Europe.
Where? In the heart of Dublin, just off O'Connell Street.
Why? With church & state in denial, Duff had to go solo.

It was quite by chance that Frank Duff got into the business of resurrecting fallen women. The thirty-something civil servant founded the Legion of Mary in 1921 to make the world a better place. At first, the organisation mainly ministered to the needs of the elderly patients of James's Street Hospital in Dublin's Liberties. One day in 1922 Duff set out to visit an invalid at No 24 Chancery Lane. By mistake he called on No 25. There, he encountered his first streetwalkers. And a sad, scrawny lot they were too. Duff saw a gap for a new saving scheme.

Frank Duff dispatched a brace of his priestly lieutenants around to No 25. The clerics asked the prostitutes lodging there to mend their ways. The young girls said they'd like nothing better, but how would they put food on the table? Do the done thing, said the priests, and enter one of the Magdalen Asylums. These nun-run sweatshops dotted around the country provided penal servitude for women afflicted with social leprosy. No thanks, said the girls.

They'd rather take their chances on the street. As a last
resort, the Legionnaires offered to cover the prostitutes'
weekly rent bill, a hefty £28, if they'd promise to mend
their wicked ways.

Duff convened a meeting to discuss the plight of the
girls at No 25. It was decided that the first step on the road
to redemption should be an intensive bombardment of
prayer. All that was now needed was somewhere to hold
the retreat. The capital's prim religious institutions didn't
want to know. Struck by this deficit of Christian spirit, the
Sisters Of Charity in Baldoyle pitched in with the offer of
a vacant classroom. One of the few girls who opted out
of the retreat went by the name of Honor Bright. She
stayed on the game and met a grisly end in the Dublin
mountains three years later. There was sufficient evidence
to bring a Garda Superintendent and a doctor to trial for
the murder. They got off.

Frank Duff made his case to William T Cosgrave, the
head of the new Free State government. Impressed,
Cosgrave gave the Legion a big house on Harcourt Street,
rent-free. The reformed prostitutes moved into the
building, now christened the Sancta Maria Hostel. Duff
extended his clean-up operation across Dublin's Southside,
but his sights were really set on the Northside's notorious
red light district, Monto.

Monto was part of the scenery, albeit a part that was
most clearly seen with the perspective of distance. Only
eleven years earlier, the 1911 *Encyclopaedia Britannica* had
marvelled at how Dublin's roaring skin-trade was 'carried
on more publicly than even in the south of Europe or
Algeria'. That writer lacked the practised blind eye of the
city's denizens. A new police chief had implemented a
zero tolerance policy some years before. His strategy of

surprise raids and constant harassment fell victim to its own success. Some brothels shut down, but the bulk of the displaced streetwalkers promptly moved their operations to the front of the General Post Office. Upstanding citizens were scandalised by the flagrancy, not to mention the pungent fragrance, of this display. Zero tolerance was quietly shelved and Monto got back to business as usual.

At its peak Monto covered a quarter square mile of buildings adjacent to the capital's main thoroughfare, Sackville Street. At the start of the Nineteenth Century thousands of British troops were billeted there in readiness for a Napoleonic invasion that never came. They, in turn, were sought out by young women who specialised in treating old war wounds and sports injuries. Eventually an elaborate three-tier system prevailed, with different classes of brothel servicing the needs of blue-ribband, white collar and no collar clients. Men of good reputation – including the future King Edward VII – entered the pricy Flash Houses through secret underground tunnels. Religious pictures decked the walls of the more shanty establishments.

Monto mushroomed into a carnal Klondike by the whiffy Liffey. Business especially boomed around the Dublin Horse Show, major Gaelic games finals and big race meetings. Alcohol sales generated more income than prostitution, a reasonable statistic when some establishments charged up to twenty times normal bar prices. Many premises operated a student discount scheme in the hopes of inculcating the bad habits of a lifetime.

The big losers in the system were the prostitutes. They handed over two-thirds of their earnings to their Madams. They were frequently in hock to moneylenders for the clothes on their backs. Disease was an occupational hazard. The bouncers attached to each brothel weren't just for unruly clients. They administered whatever beatings were deemed prudent to keep the girls in line.

The Legion held tactical talks for tackling Monto. There was no shortage of discouraging advice. Duff was told that his street missionaries would be risking life and limb. He was warned he could be set-up by prostitutes and blackmailed. The truth was, respectable Dublin had little enthusiasm for Duff's proposed do-gooding. Monto existed in a separate, parallel universe. Its presence wasn't regarded as a fit subject to be addressed from any pulpit. The civic authorities connived in this grand delusion. This policy of don't-mention-the-war benefited those members of Dublin Corporation who, as landlords, were collecting very lucrative rents from the brothels.

Duff pressed on regardless. In March 1923 he led a band of associates into the heart of Monto in search of a sick girl they'd been told about. The girl was removed to hospital where she eventually died of advanced venereal disease. The ease of the rescue encouraged the Legionaries to go straight back for more. On that first day alone, they signed up forty girls for a retreat at the Sancta Maria Hostel. The Legion Of Mary visited Monto twice a week after that. Less than two years later, Duff was able to claim that there were only forty practising prostitutes left in the area. He'd even initiated a resettlement scheme, planting ordinary decent folk in the vacated brothels.

The Jesuits finally weighed in behind the Legion in the spring of 1925, breaking the Church's vow of silence on the subject of Monto. The order was holding its Lenten mission in the Pro-Cathedral, on the boundary of the whore zone. On a February Sunday, the red light district was denounced from the Pro-Cathedral pulpit for the first time in living memory. Duff prepared for the main offensive. The next day, he led a big march into Monto, extracting promises from the remaining Madams that they'd quit the area. The marchers swept all before them except for two dug-in proprietors. At first, the pair said they'd go if the Legion paid off assorted debts of £75. Then they changed their minds and demanded £1,500 to get out. It was a move they would soon regret.

Duff went straight to Dublin Castle and enlisted the Chief Commissioner of Police. Thirty hours later, on the night of March 12, 1925, a large task-force swept into the area. The cacophony of gunfire, screaming and street scuffles roused sleepers for miles, and when the racket finally subsided 120 fresh arrests were squashed into the city's police cells. The rumour-mill went into overdrive. Everybody who was anybody was reputed to be snared. In the event, an unnamed Donegal TD turned out to be the only notary caught in the web. Like just about everyone else arrested, he claimed that his sole purpose in Monto had been an after-hours tipple.

From the remove of Cork, the *Cork Examiner* said: 'No citizen of Dublin will need to be told why a wholesale police raid was carried out.' And no citizen was told why the raid took place in that paper's report. The *Irish Independent's* coded story told of 'a midnight swoop on a congested district in the northern area'. The *Irish Times* simply ignored the biggest civil disturbance of the year, devoting its lead story instead to the number of spoilt votes in the recent by-elections. Ditto the *Evening Herald*, which instead devoted much of its front page to a report headlined 'CLOCKS AND COWS'. A pressing debate was underway in the British House of Commons as to whether the introduction of Summer Time would confuse the nation's cattle.

The only people charged in the wake of the raid were the two Madams. One was sentenced to three months' imprisonment, the other got off on a technicality. The victory was consolidated with a large procession through Monto. Each abandoned brothel was individually blessed and a holy picture nailed to the door. In the space of three years, Frank Duff had achieved a stunning victory over squalor, sin and official sloth. He'd shamed church and state into confronting the demons on their doorstep.

Ireland's homestyle prohibition era had begun. Within a few more years the Free State had clamped down on liquor sales and banned contraceptives, better known in official cant as 'instruments of race suicide'. By 1929 a catch-all Censorship of Publications Act was in place, and by the following year every last nude had been stripped from Dublin's Municipal Gallery.

Decades later, the English poet Donald Davie paid testament to the work begun by Duff and taken up with gusto by the new State. 'What I have always liked about the Irish Republic,' reflected the bard, 'is that it is, of all the societies that I know, the least "sexy".'

WHEN IRISH TEETH ARE SMILING

Bernie Murphy Vs *The Sunday Press*.

> Who? A Sandwich-board man turned councillor.
> When? 1985–1989.
> What? The illiterate Murphy went on the trip of a lifetime.
> Where? To join San Francisco's St Patrick's Day festivities.
> Why? 'They gave me teeth . . . a doctorate degree.'

Life had dealt Corkman Bernie Murphy a series of hard knocks. In his mid-teens his immediate family 'scattered', leaving him alone in the world. Unable to read, write or properly tell the time, his career options were limited. For years he lived hard and slept rough. Mostly, Bernie eked out a meagre living as a sandwich-board man on the streets of Cork.

Bernie Murphy's fortunes took a remarkable upturn in 1985 when he was elected to Cork County Council by an emphatic popular vote. His campaign had been orchestrated and largely funded by a disillusioned former Labour Party activist, John Lennon. Murphy's successful election manifesto had included the provision of a cable car for Patrick's Hill. It would go both 'up *and* down, as a tourist thing'.

1986 was to be Bernic Murphy's *annus mirabilis*. He found his long-vanished mother, he said, 'because I became a councillor'. A brother and sisters also materialised. His social diary bulged. Turning out for the Council in a charity football match – 'Cork's Maradona' was emblazoned on

his playing strip – he was sent off for abusive and
ungentlemanly language. Heading for an early bath, he
told his fellow players: 'Ye'll be laughing on the other side
of yer faces when I get elected to the Dáil.'

In truth, the upturn in Bernie Murphy's fortunes was
not welcomed by all his new colleagues in the chamber.
'The politicians were jealous,' he later claimed. So it came
as little surprise when Cork Corporation denied Murphy
permission to attend the San Francisco Saint Patrick's Day
celebrations as an official representative of the city. But
there was nothing they could do to prevent him travelling
in a private capacity. Bernie headed west on the trip of a
lifetime.

The councillor's American odyssey wound up in the
Dublin High Court in 1989. He was seeking damages
from the *Sunday Press* arising from a story headlined: 'SAN
FRANCISCO MAYOR ANGRY AT ALDERMAN'S
VISIT'. A number of leading lights in San Francisco's
Irish community had been quoted, none of them express-
ing unalloyed delight at Bernie's presence in their midst.
Murphy was unhappy with the report. He claimed that it
linked him with IRA fund-raising efforts, that it suggested
he'd only gone to America to get false teeth, and that it
inferred that he'd been conferred with an honorary
doctorate from a non-existent college. The newspaper
denied his interpretation.

The prosecution called John Lennon as its first witness.
Counsel for the *Sunday Press* noted that it is usual to call the
plaintiff – in this case Murphy – as first witness. Counsel
for the prosecution said he wouldn't call Bernie because he
was illiterate. Justice MacKenzie said he was sure the jury
would be disappointed as it would be difficult to assess
Bernie's hurt feelings at second-hand.

Lennon said there wasn't the remotest association between Bernie Murphy and the IRA. He said that Murphy had gone to a clinic shortly before his departure for the States and had all his teeth extracted. Under cross-examination, Lennon said that in the Seventies Bernie Murphy had been irresponsible. Back then, he had no self respect and didn't care how he dressed or what he said. By the early Eighties he began to calm down.

Asked about Murphy not giving evidence, Lennon said that his friend suffered 'an inability in the instant' to articulate his thoughts. In certain circumstances Bernie became frustrated and emotional. He wouldn't be able to tell the jury what he did and where he went in San Francisco in any chronological order. Lennon thought Bernie would contradict himself. That wasn't to say he'd tell lies, but he wasn't a competent witness.

At one point, the defence produced a photo from March '86 which featured Bernie in a nightclub. Lennon commented that it showed the alderman having a great time. This drew the enigmatic remark from the judge that: 'At least he has his trousers on.'

Bernie and several others had travelled to San Francisco at the invitation of Warren Hinckle, an American journalist. Lennon had no idea that Hinckle had written pro-IRA articles. Bernie had told Lennon that he'd enjoyed himself in the city's Dover Club. Lennon hadn't known that the club's exterior was festooned with IRA slogans. Lennon denied portraying his friend as a simpleton. He stressed that Bernie Murphy was 'ignorant but not stupid'.

Taking the stand, photographer Billy MacGill refuted the suggestion that Bernie had been 'shunned' as he marched past the San Francisco Patrick's Day parade viewing stand. On the contrary, he told the court: 'They cheered and clapped him. Mr Murphy broke into a little dance routine and waved the American flag.'

Bernie had been invited to City Hall. Journalist Hinckle told him it might be timely to remind the Mayor, Diane Feinstein, that on a previous visit to Cork she'd offered to help raise a million dollars for Leeside. So Bernie arrived at the Mayor's offices with a suitcase. The Mayor was nowhere to be seen, so Hinckle led the visitors to the Deputy Mayor's office. The Mayor wasn't there either. On the way out, empty handed, they met an NBC crew covering a different event. Hinckle drummed up an interview. The former sandwich-board man was broadcast coast-to-coast across the United States.

Photographer MacGill was asked wasn't it true 'that the unfortunate Bernie Murphy was brought to San Francisco to make a fool of himself for the private purposes of Warren Hinckle?' MacGill disagreed. He'd been unaware that Hinckle had been taking regular potshots at the Mayor in his newspaper column. He didn't agree that Bernie had been set up with the suitcase to embarrass the Mayor.

Counsel for the *Sunday Press* read from Hinckle's ongoing reports of Bernie's visit. One headline had proclaimed: 'WHEN IRISH TEETH ARE SMILING IT'S A GREAT DAY FOR A MURPHY.' Hinckle had elsewhere quoted Bernie as greeting one individual with the line: 'You're late, ye son of a whore!' The San Francisco *Examiner* had also reported that: 'The city councilman from Cork City, Ireland, cannot read or write and gets most of his information about America from violence-prone television shows. He expressed fears that he might be assassinated as he rode in the parade. He figured that if the crazy Americans did it to a Kennedy they might do it to a Murphy.'

The article continued: 'While Murphy was waiting for his bodyguard, Dr Charlie Tobin, the West Portal dentist, came to the bar to adjust the councilman's new teeth . . . "You're looking good Bernie" he said, after checking Murphy's new molars in a corner of the bar where they had set up a makeshift dentist's chair made of beer cartons.'

Billy MacGill disagreed that this type of publicity amounted to 'an unfortunate picture'. The *Sunday Press* side produced a photograph taken by MacGill featuring the Alderman in a clinch with two skimpily attired young women. The defence wondered what the people of Cork might think of Councillor Doctor Bernard Murphy appearing in that pose? 'That he was having a good time,' replied MacGill.

After four days in court Bernie Murphy settled his libel action against the *Sunday Press*, accepting £2,000 plus a contribution of £4,000 towards his costs. The judge deemed that Murphy and his friends had indeed been exploited by journalist Hinckle.

The wisdom of keeping Bernie Murphy off the witness stand can perhaps be gauged by some comments he made shortly after his return from San Francisco. Producing a photograph of a weightlifter named Nancy, the councillor sought the approval of one interviewer for his American sweetheart. 'What about getting up that one?' he enthused. 'I didn't get any jiggy-jig,' he added, putting the blame for that on Nancy's vigilant boyfriend. On another occasion he confessed his disappointment at 'not scoring' on the night of his election.

Bernie had had a ball on his American odyssey. He rounded on his fellow councillors who'd 'thought the Yanks were making a fool of me, but they weren't. They gave me teeth. They gave me a doctorate degree.' He had done his bit to maintain high standards in politics. He explained, with evident pride: 'I met a lot of punk rockers in America. They wanted me to go up and stay with them, but I'd say I'd end up smoking grass and all if I did.'

AN INCITEMENT TO CRIME

I've Just Become A Celebrity, Get Me Out Of Here!

Who? Gerry Ryan. A Cute Little Lamb.
When? The summer of 1987.
What? The details of a killing caused a wave of revulsion.
Where? The Inagh Valley, Connemara.
Why? The victim was cuddly, the tale was gruesome.

'If there's any blood coming out of that lamb I'd advise you to drink it.' The speaker was one Gerry Ryan, a Radio 2 nightshift deejay. Ryan's ability to spin a yarn had landed him the lead role in an early reality-radio soap. He was a natural. So darn good, in fact, that pretty soon the yarn was spinning a twister-like swathe through the affairs of the nation.

It was the early summer of 1987. The producer of Radio 1's flagship programme, *The Gay Byrne Show*, thought it would be a novel idea to abandon a bunch of city-slickers in a remote Connemara valley with just an SAS survival manual for guidance. The nation listened in rapt attention as a sorry tale of deprivation, disappointment and disunity unravelled in daily dollops.

The SAS booklet had primed the sextet with great expectations as they entered the Inagh Valley. Trout from the surrounding streams and freshly snared rabbit would crackle over blazing fires. Alas, it turned out to be an artist's impression. The rabbits were infuriatingly stand-offish. The fishing tackle snagged terminally on day one. The only things biting were dense clouds of tormenting midges. Gerry and his cousin Ciaran, a pianist, went hunting with rudimentary spears. They eventually settled for fern soup. 'It tasted like waxy paper boiled,' grimaced Ryan. The brackish broth was augmented with tiny minnows gulped down alive. On Monday evening Phyllis and Jean granted themselves a temporary derogation from the rules. The derring duo broke into a henhouse and poached themselves a square meal.

The six had opted to forage in pairs. So Gerry and Ciaran were unaware that Phylis and Jean had saved some leftovers. Had they known, they might have passed up Tuesday morning's breakfast of black slugs. From now on, they all agreed, teamwork would be their watchword. In Wednesday's dispatch to Gaybo, Gerry came good with a stirring tale of common purpose. The group had fanned out through the gorse, eventually separating a lamb from its mother. Ciaran had coshed the wee thing into oblivion by swinging a rock in a sock. Cathleen had slit its throat with a sheath knife. Man United 1: Untamed Wilderness 0.

Back at Montrose the phones started hopping. People were outraged by Ryan's account of the killing. Producer Philip Kamph assured listeners that the lamb's owner had been adequately recompensed, but for some reason this didn't calm the listening public.

Meanwhile, the survivalists carried on regardless. 'The group's falling apart,' muttered Gerry on Thursday morning. By the time the ordeal ended on Friday, the unhappy campers were at each other's throats. And it didn't end there either, as the one decent meal enjoyed by the famished crew began to repeat on them.

Disturbed by the lamb that got the chop, Dublin TD Tony Gregory tabled a Dáil question to the Minister for Justice. The Minister made inquiries. He was happy to inform the House that the circumstances of the lamb's death had been greatly exaggerated by Gerry Ryan. In fact, the ravenous hunters had met a woman named Ann Meis while traipsing across her land. Pick a lamb, she'd charitably told them, any lamb. Ann's husband then shot the popular choice, and she butchered it ready for cooking.

The Minister's revelation caused consternation in RTÉ. The station issued a statement regretting both the 'confusion' and the fact that it was not 'in a position to comment further'. RTÉ's news department sought to nail their radio colleagues without fear or favour. They interviewed the executioner, Hans Werner Meis, who confirmed the Minister's version of events. The newsroom contacted three unnamed survivalists. Two said they'd seen nothing. The third, intriguingly, argued that the farmer's account was true, but that the story told on the radio wasn't untrue. 'It was six of one and half-a-dozen of the other,' she said.

Unlike the unfortunate lamb, the 'Lambo' crisis now had a life of its own. It escalated further when footage of Ryan being cornered by an RTÉ camera-crew was axed from the *Newsnight* TV show without explanation. The next day it emerged that the Director General himself had ordered the cutlet to impose a cease-fire on his feuding minions.

The 'Lambo' affair moved to the letters pages of the national press where it quickly became all things to all men. For some, the episode was proof positive that Tony Gregory was just a malcontent, 'wasting Dáil time and the time of the gardaí'. For others it underlined the need for the Department of Health 'to publicise the proven fact that meat eaters are likely to spend longer terms in hospital and to die at a younger age than their vegetarian counterparts'. Meanwhile, the Kilkenny branch of the Irish Council Against Blood Sports warned the RTÉ Authority that the account of the killing could warrant prosecution as an incitement to crime.

In the heel of the non-existent hunt, the sacrificial lamb died for a greater good. Gerry Ryan's performance in pulling the wool over a nation's ears was the making of him. It's said that not long after, when he had his own personal stationary designed, it featured the image of a certain four-legged friend.

THIS IS NATIONAL MOOD DAY

In Dublin Vs Self Aid.

Who? U2. Van Morrison. Rory Gallagher. Elvis Costello.
When? May, 1986.
What? A galaxy of Irish musical talent.
Where? The RDS, Dublin. Television Centre, Montrose.
Why? Someone had to tackle Ireland's unemployment crisis.

It was the height of the mid-Eighties Aids epidemic. First Band Aid, then Live Aid, then Sports Aid, then Hear'n'Aid (spandex and big hair against want). Self Aid was a disaster just waiting to happen. *In Dublin* magazine was having none of it.

There are generally two reasons for doing anything – a very good reason and the real reason. 'The concert came first,' observed old-school leftie Eamonn McCann. 'The cause was attached later.' The idea of an Irish Live Aid had been floating around Montrose since Bob Geldof's global megabash the previous summer. All the vital elements were in place. In 1986 a dizzying proportion of young Irish people – 'our greatest national asset' – were signed to major British record labels. The rest could make up the audience. Best of all, the rotating Live Aid stage was available.

Nobody doubted the organisers' good intentions. It was just that their plan seemed largely based on the fable of the Pied Piper. McCann spelled out the obvious – this scatty attempt to attract 'pledges' of jobs and investment capital was doomed.

The jobs simply weren't there, he observed, and no amount of well-meaning diminished chords from Freddie White would subvert the basic rules of capitalism. State agencies were spending £450m each year trying, and failing, to create jobs. At tops, Self Aid would generate an extra £7m. It just didn't add up.

Worse, charged McCann, many of the companies involved in Self Aid were actively engaged in swelling the dole queues. RTÉ itself, the hub of all the hubba-bubba, was targeting 320 redundancies. The causes of unemployment needed to be clearly identified. At best Self Aid was a smokescreen, at worst an instrument for diverting blame away from the bodies responsible and onto the jobless themselves for being jobless. 'Major rock stars have become as lightning conductors,' he noted, 'attracting the energy of the urban young and running it safely to Earth.' They flattered themselves that they were part of the solution, when in fact they were part of the problem.

It was in this context that *In Dublin* editor John Waters launched a swinging attack on bill-toppers U2. The magazine's cover headline laid out the charge: 'THE GREAT SELF-AID FARCE, ROCK AGAINST THE PEOPLE'. Self Aid was a nonsense, Waters argued, and U2 should have known better than to lend it credibility through their endorsement. The newspapers reported that several companies had held back job announcements in order to garner free publicity on Self Aid day. The objectors were drowned out in the carnival spirit that prevailed as May 17th approached. Paul Cleary and his Partisans headlined an anti-Self Aid gig in Dublin's Underground venue, but they were no more than errant schoolboys larking around with pea-shooters while all eyes were on the big guns strutting at the RDS and television centre.

The big day came. A chill wind blew. The heavens opened. Ireland's massed troubadours played their hearts out, unaware that their monster meeting had caused metal muthas Dio to cancel two gigs across town, with a consequent dip in employment at the SFX Centre. Those Nervous Animals chugged through *The Business Enterprise (My Friend John)*. Leslie Dowdall modelled tight pants. Paul Brady played a set as dour and interminable as the nation's dole queues. Van was just Van. He growled into his microphone, alluding to a previous act: 'If Van Morrison was a gunslinger he'd shoot copycats.' No-one doubted he meant it.

U2 were angry. About the curse of unemployment and about *In Dublin*. Bono brandished a copy of the offending organ and the crowd booed on cue. 'He appeared hurt and stung by the gratuitous and ill-founded accusations that his band were partaking in "rock against the people",' scolded *Hot Press*, who produced the attractive Official Souvenir Programme of the event.

The grand finale was an ensemble rendition of *Make It Work*, the Self Aid theme song. It was awesome, but not in a good way. Feedback squalled. The singing was wildly out of tune. The seasoned performers melted into the background while lesser luminaries Deric Herbert and Philip King vied for a dubious posterity out front. Those tuned into RTÉ's fourteen hours of coverage at least had the ultimate sanction of the 'off' switch.

The Montrose studios resembled an open-plan hair salon, only with lots more telephones. A glamorous army of workers awaited the expected deluge of inspired job creation ideas and pledges. One switchboard operator confided to the *Irish Independent* that a large part of her day was spent fending off cranks, simpletons and callers with a conscription fixation. Short films highlighted worthy projects around the country. Gaybo auctioned his shoes for £300 but drew the line at kissing Mike Murphy for £50. Panel discussions on the topics of long-term unemployment, enterprise and venture capital set new records for brevity and tokenism.

The highpoint of the entire farrago was provided by a schoolboy from the Navan Road. He'd produced his own comic. A man with a mike asked where he'd gotten the idea. 'From me head,' came the withering reply. Music aside, the event hit rock bottom when one 'Ronald McDonald' strode purposefully into the studio and pledged 25 jobs in a fast food chain where, even in those dark times, 'Staff Wanted' signs were a regular part of the furniture.

At the end of the day the Self Aid totaliser had limped up to £500,000 in cash donations, a small fraction of Ireland's contribution to Live Aid for Ethiopia. The register of new jobs read 1,332, but this figure didn't bear close scrutiny. One hundred McDonalds jobs, 150 at Irish Life and twenty in the ESB had to be nixed because they would have existed irrespective of Self Aid. One caller from Harold's Cross had phoned in with an idea for creating one hundred jobs. These were mistakenly added to the total pledged.

'The figures are not a measure of success,' stated organiser Niall Mathews. Uncowed, U2 manager Paul McGuinness agreed. 'Fuck it,' he said. 'If Eamonn McCann thinks he was the first one to spot that this was unscientific, he's wrong . . . This is National Mood Day as far as I'm concerned.'

So that was that. McCann and Waters had been queering the wrong pitch. The original goalposts had long

since been uprooted and moved to the soon-to-close
Clondalkin Paper Mills, where they were pulped for paper
plates and party hats. Self Aid's tenth anniversary
occurred in 1996. It was an ideal opportunity to reassess
the event's impact, maybe visit some of the businesses
which owed their existence to that memorable day.

Nobody seemed to be in the mood.

THEY'RE A PACK OF FOREIGNERS

The Rise And Fall Of Catholic Marxism.

Who? The Catholic Marxists. God-fearing Dubliners.
When? The summer of 1968.
What? Ireland's first Pray-In turned ugly.
Where? In and around St Andrews Church, Westland Row.
Why? To put manners on 'snooty blow-ins'.

It was 1968. The forces of change, icebound throughout the de Valera decades, were beginning to thaw. But the warming winds weren't from hippy-dippy San Francisco or pagan Swinging London. Ireland's stiff collars were being tickled by a balmy Mediterranean breeze.

Since 1962 the Second Vatican Council had been doing for the Catholic Church what The Beatles were doing for youth culture. A Church defined along hard lines from time immemorial suddenly began to mellow out. Previously forbidden books flooded the seminaries. Fresh ideas began to circulate. Young priests began to experiment with mind-expanding notions.

The faithful weren't long in noticing the sea change. For generations, the function of the parish priest had been to play caretaker to the existing social order and obsess about sex. It was no accident that working-class priests and nuns tended to get shunted abroad to the missions while their middle-class brethren were slotted into the domestic scheme of things. But now, strange new concerns wafted down from the pulpits, about class and poverty and social opportunity on our own doorsteps. Even ecumenism, up to then tantamount to heavy petting with the Devil, was given a tentative embrace.

Then, in July 1968, Pope Paul VI threw a wobbler and slammed on the brakes. *Humanae Vitae* stopped the modernisers in their tracks. Artificial contraception, it stated, was a ticket to Hell. This didn't go down so well with those Catholics already using artificial birth control in the belief that it was cool with the new laid-back Church. Traditionalists rejoiced – the tinkering trendies in Rome had been mucking with their minds for far too long. But the genie was already out of the bottle. Liberation theology had established a toehold in Ireland. The Pray-In was born.

The Pray-In was the brainchild of a band of ecumenicists who were quickly tagged Catholic Marxists. The antics they provoked didn't recall Karl so much as Groucho, Harpo and Chico. In July 1968 the group produced a magazine, *Grille*, to fan the open dialogue that the Pope was now trying to suffocate. The first Pray-In was scheduled for an August Sunday afternoon in St Andrews Church, Westland Row, Dublin. A sizeable press corps turned up expecting a holy show. They weren't disappointed.

A group of perhaps fifty worshipers from the *Grille* camp entered the church and assembled in a small alcove. The Blessed Sacrament had been removed by Church authorities after the final mass of that morning, in anticipation of 'disrespectful' scenes. As the *Grille* contingent prepared to pray, a hostile crowd of parishioners assembled around them. After a few opening prayers, *Grille*'s John Feeney rose and spoke some words of welcome. He then started reading from the Bible.

This incensed the gathered locals who knew that good Catholics did not read the Bible – that was the clergy's job.

A middle-aged man sprang from the mob of parishioners and launched himself at Feeney, knocking his Good Book to the ground. Another *Grille* disciple, John Byrne, immediately took up the reading. At this point a woman collared the attacker and dragged him off his victim. It was the man's wife. 'You're making a show of yourself,' she chided. 'Let them go on with it. It'll all fizzle out.'

It didn't fizzle out just yet. No sooner was the first assailant led away than a force of parish vigilantes waded into the ranks of the prayer-group 'pushing them about, throwing punches and pulling women's headscarves off'. John Byrne's response was to strike up a hymn. If he hoped music would rustle-up the food of love, he quickly found out that the locals were fasting. Byrne was silenced with a fist in the teeth.

The parishioners hurled rhetorical questions at the invading peaceniks. 'Are you a Catholic?' they called. 'Are you Irish? Are you from this parish? Are you a Communist? Why don't you go and pray in your own church?' In fact, the Christian Marxists *had* asked for permission to hold their Love-In in a number of churches, with no success. Amid taunts of 'sacrilege!' John Feeney signalled the retreat. He told his battered crew that they would complete their Pray-In at the University Church on Stephen's Green a short distance away.

As they left the church, the pioneers of Catholic Marxism were jeered and heckled. One man, raised on the Latin liturgy, wanted to know: 'If you're Catholics why were you reading in English?' Another defender of the faith from Ringsend insisted: 'If this happened in our parish, we'd get them by the scruff of the neck and throw them out. Look at their faces, they're not Irishmen at all. They're a pack of foreigners.' A squad of gardaí had been assigned to shadow the Pray-In. They loitered with no intent of intervening.

A former Trappist monk and schoolteacher by the name of Louis Mulderry told reporters that the eviction was one-up for the common man. He said: 'The men who acted against these people look on them as a lot of snooty would-be intellectuals trying to take over their parish.' Shortly afterwards, over at University Church, John Feeney stood beneath the pulpit and began to read from the Bible. A man approached him. It was the former monk again, anxious to save another parish from snooty would-be intellectualism. He handed Feeney a note. Feeney read it aloud. It said: 'This church has been booked for a private christening. Can't you show some respect for the church, and the sacraments?'

In deference, the *Grille* refugees switched to silent prayer. The tranquillity of the scene was disturbed only by the incessant wailing of a waterlogged infant at the other end of the church. John Feeney then concluded the Pray-In by registering the group's annoyance with the Pope's birth control encyclical, the Soviet tanks bullying Prague, and the religious folk who'd beaten them up an hour earlier.

As the Catholic Marxists spilled out onto the street they were confronted by more opponents. Amused gardaí stood by as the two wings of mainstream piety jostled each other for over an hour. The gardaí had less cause to be smug shortly afterwards when the *Grille* group mounted a rather vague protest outside the Garda Club against the visit of some Chicago police to Dublin. The picket was 'in penance for the activities of Irish Americans generally'. *Grille* explained: 'These people are not noted for any great concern on Christian issues in the USA, such as Vietnam and race relations.'

It was a bad call. The protest's profound lack of impact simply demonstrated that nobody really gave a toss about the Catholic Marxists one way or the other, just so long as they kept out of other people's churches. Dublin's Archbishop McQuaid signed off the brief summer of Catholic Marxism by restating the church's free-market position on social issues. 'No measures of social security,' he proclaimed, 'can eliminate human poverty.' Advocates of an Irish welfare state could go back to Russia.

THE MURDERERS OF THE CHILDREN OF DUBLIN

Richie Ryan TD Vs Fluoridation.

Who? Future Finance Minister Richie Ryan.
When? 1962.
What? He battled to stop the fluoridation of water.
Where? In the county of Dublin.
Why? To prevent 'increases in the incidences of mongolism'.

At the dawn of the Sixties the nation's teeth were in a shocking state of disrepair. Health Minister Sean MacEntee envisaged one sweeping fix-it measure: fluoridating the water supply. But MacEntee faced a vocal and focused body of opposition. To buttress his case, the Minister needed figures to prove that a crisis existed. He ordered the Medical Research Council to assess the dental infirmities of 27,000 children in the cities of Dublin, Cork, Limerick, Waterford and the counties of Kildare and Wicklow.

The survey established that the Irish Tooth Fairy had a punishing work schedule. In Dublin and Cork the average ten-year-old had six teeth missing, decayed or filled. Worse, Irish teenagers had to negotiate their crucial snogging years with one third of their teeth blighted or gone. In October of 1962, Minister MacEntee unleashed these damning findings in a twelve page government information pamphlet. However, the publication singled out one fragrant exception, one glistening oasis of fresh breath confidence.

The nation must look to the village of Patrickswell in Co Limerick, said the booklet. There: 'Fluorine is naturally present in the public water supply. In this village the children's teeth were markedly healthier than elsewhere. It is clearly necessary to make a determined effort to curb this serious and widespread disease, one which may have far-reaching effects on general health, and which imposes an economic drain on both health services and individuals.'

The Minister's bulletin was a pre-emptive strike aimed at Dublin Corporation. The capital's local authority was about to debate the fluoridation issue at a special meeting. Legislation approving the fluoridation of water supplies had been passed in 1961 but a body calling itself the Pure Water Association had stirred up an effective poisoned-well scare. The Pure Water lobby charged that fluoridation amounted to an unwarranted 'mass medication' capable of producing untold horrors. The Minister harboured genuine fears that Dublin Corporation would throw out his measure.

In the run-up to the vital meeting, MacEntee put the Corporation members in their place. He warned that 'a partisan majority in a subordinate authority cannot be allowed to flout the law and defy the Oireachtas'. He demanded that Dublin Corporation find £11,000 to fluoridate Dublin's water supply for the first year, and around £4,000 annually after that.

The Minister contended that there were only two possible alternatives to his scheme, and that both were clearly impossible. One would be to treble the number of dentists in the state to 1,800 at an annual cost of £2,000,000. Apart from the expense, it would take years to train 1,200 extra dentists. Especially with the country's

600 existing practitioners fighting tooth-and-drill to preserve their closed shop.

The other alternative to fluoridation would be to improve people's eating habits and dental hygiene. Mountainous dollops of refined sugar were a staple of the Irish diet, in tea, porridge, cakes, pies, sandwiches and anything else that would bear sweetening. Toothbrush sales were dismal. The Minister ruled out getting people to take better care of their teeth. In his view, the Irish poor mouth was an inevitable by-product of progress. As the pamphlet explained: 'The fundamental cause of bad teeth is the modern diet – and this is something that cannot be changed substantially. Ireland is no exception here: all advanced countries must pay the penalties of the modern dietry and none has found a way of changing either the diet or the habits of eating, least of all among the children.' The pamphlet rubbished allegations that fluoridated water was the Devil's own brew.

Richie Ryan TD was an impassioned champion of Pure Water. The Minister's report, charged Ryan, was an unscrupulous effort 'to push fluoridated water down the throats of an unsuspecting public'. Ryan believed that imbibing fluoride was a matter for the individual conscience. He argued (deep breath): 'The addition of a chemical to piped water for the one and only purpose of ensuring that that chemical gets into the human body to be consumed by young, old, ill and healthy alike without regard for the specific doses suitable to each individual for the alleged purpose of reducing tooth decay in children only is indefensible.'

Ryan suspected that fluoride might merely delay the onset of rotten teeth. More fiendishly still, it might actually accelerate tooth decay in adults. The Minister had his statistics, but Ryan had his convictions. He insisted:

'Experience has demonstrated that . . . adults in a fluoridated area have many more decayed, missing or filled teeth than their counterparts in a non-fluoridated area.'

The night of the vital meeting arrived. Minister MacEntee had upped the stakes by threatening to abolish Dublin Corporation if it didn't do the needful. The three hour debate was stormy. Councillor Denis Larkin derided the Minister's booklet as: ' . . . the poorest attempt at documentation that he had ever seen.' He went on to say that 'something that was good for the teeth for a certain period might not be good later on'. Richie Ryan produced what he hoped might be a clincher, claiming to know of 'increases in the incidence of mongolism in areas where fluoridation had been introduced'.

A vote was called. Defiant to the last, Richie Ryan taunted his opponents on the Corporation with the cry: 'Let them stand up and be counted with the murderers of the children of Dublin.'

His impassioned cry was to no avail. The fluoridation measure was passed by a margin of 25 votes to fifteen. Dubliners' teeth began to improve dramatically, while water-related deaths remained largely confined to drownings. Richie Ryan overcame his problem with drink, in so far as any ill effects he suffered from fluoride didn't stop him from landing the Finance brief in the mid-Seventies austerity government led by 'The Minister For Hardship' Liam Cosgrave. Installed as the country's chief money-man, Ryan was fond of telling the plain people of Ireland to pull on the hairshirt, take their medicine and stop moaning. He knew what was best.

The electorate responded by burying the administration under the biggest landslide in the history of the state.

A LOT BETTER THAN SHOVELLING GRAVEL FOR A LIVING

The Rise And Fall Of The Showbands.

> Who? Donie Cassidy. Paddy Cole. Twink. Albert Reynolds.
> When? 1950s–1970s, with a break for Lent.
> What? Rock'n'roll found a uniquely Irish expression.
> Where? Parish halls to ballrooms to rubber chicken coops.
> Why? The music came to Ireland but its stars mostly didn't.

From the vantage point of the 21st Century, old photos of showbands with their cheesy grins, crooked teeth and gorse-bush hair can resemble gargoyle identity parades, but to Sixties Ireland these men were sex on legs. The showbands gave rock'n'roll a uniquely Irish expression and the draughty, hangar-size ballrooms which shot up in the Sixties represented fabulous pleasure palaces. This was largely because they were a vast improvement on the parish halls they'd replaced. A widespread practice was to douse the wooden floors of these halls with paraffin before a dance to keep the dust down. The atmosphere at a Saturday night shindig would consist in part of a nauseating petroleum haze.

They may not have all been 'lookers', but the top showband names were rolling in dough. It wasn't unknown for the biggest stars to spend a fortune flying to London just to take in a movie – grown-up films tended to be banned in Ireland. Indeed, the *Irish Times* film critic, Ken Grey, complained in 1970: 'How much longer can the censor protect film-goers from the facts of life with his scissors? How long before the BBC and ITV are showing uncut versions of *The Graduate*?'

In the early Sixties the best of homegrown talent would show off their customised Volkswagen Beetles outside Molly's of Portobello in Dublin. At dawn, the flashiest cars in the country would line up on the starting grid at Rathmines Bridge for a spot of drag racing before the guards got out of bed. By the end of the decade the Beetles had been traded-up for Mercs and Jags.

The Capital Showband's Paddy Cole learned a valuable lesson about drinking in moderation from promoter Albert Reynolds. After a show was cancelled in Muff, the band stopped off on the way back to Dublin in Reynolds' pub, The Longford Arms. The tee-total Reynolds was surprised to see Cole, who was strictly a stout man up to that point, knocking back brandy 'like sweet milk', as Cole later recalled.

'I didn't know you drank shorts,' said Reynolds.

'It's great stuff Albert,' Cole replied.

So Reynolds bought a large brandy for Cole. The musician arrived at his girlfriend's flat in Dublin around midnight literally unable to speak. The flat's occupants poured coffee into him until he was sober enough to prop up behind a wheel. The last stage of the process of getting sober involved 'driving around the city in my VW with all the windows open, trying to get a breath of fresh air'.

The advent of the ballrooms created a network of big venues across the country which meant promoters could tour international stars. Big names like Chubby Checker, Jim Reeves and Little Richard were lured to Ireland, with mixed success. Sometimes a global star would be faced with a half-empty hall because a showband was playing up the road. When the Beach Boys played the Adelphi in Dublin in 1967 their support act, The Freshmen, blew them off-stage playing an entire set of Beach Boys covers.

The showbands scheduled their year by the church calendar. They weren't allowed to play in Ireland for the forty days of Lent so they headed to Britain. When Pope John XXIII died in 1963 all the ballrooms shut as a mark of respect. Top promoter Albert Reynolds had booked Jim Reeves for two shows and had to cancel. Reeves kept his £650 fee.

The brown paper envelope was endemic to the showband circuit. In the mid-Seventies there was a falling-out between one star and his manager. The singer squealed to the taxman about his manager's loose compliance with the tax laws. The taxman was agog on hearing of the true amounts being generated, and undercover agents were dispatched to investigate the entire industry.

The swizz they uncovered worked like this. A band would draw 2,000 punters to a gig. The official receipts would show that 1,200 paid in. The door takings from the other 800 would be divvied up between the promoter and the band's manager. After the squealer squelt, tax officials began turning up at halls with clickers to do a headcount of the audience going in. A couple of top promoters fled the country rather than give satisfaction to the taxman

Around the same time, The Big 8's manager tried to rustle up some publicity by putting out a yarn that the band were thinking of buying a Vegas casino. The story got lots of column inches, as planned. What the manager didn't foresee was that by exaggerating the band's wealth, he'd attract keen interest from the Revenue.

Just because showband managers were raking it in didn't mean they were inclined to flush away money on frivolities like making records. The Capital Showband recorded several tracks in New York for release as singles in Ireland, but Dublin Airport customs officials demanded import duty on the master copies. Faced with a choice between stumping up the tax or scrapping the planned singles, the band's manager decided to keep the money.

In order to keep up with the latest hits, the bands had to rehearse new material on an almost daily basis. The bigger outfits fitted special record-players, with sprung suspension, in their coaches so they could mimic as they travelled. Lower down the food chain the musos would tune in to the Radio Luxembourg Top 20 on a Sunday night to get a gist of the newest hits. They'd rehearse them on Mondays, their day-off the road, and unveil them on Tuesday.

The Capital even did a tribute-band set called 'The Parade of the Showbands' during which they played cover versions of their Irish rivals doing cover versions of international hits. The more adventurous bands slipped in songs they'd written themselves. Bizarrely, the test of a good self-penned number was that the audience wouldn't know it was one of yours.

Showband culture has produced enough memorable utterances to fill a book. One star excused his sanction busting visits to Sun City during the apartheid era by explaining: 'The reason I went to South Africa is that when I was a young lad I used to collect silver paper and send it off to the black babies, and I always wondered what they did with it. So I went to South Africa to find out, and discovered that they make money with it. So I took it back.'

Joe Dolan once claimed: 'I'm very popular in Israel because of my big nose.' Dolan was also popular in 'alternative' territories such as South Africa and the Soviet Bloc. When Meath councillor Fergus Muldoon returned from a trip to communist Romania he reported that the people there knew very little about Ireland. 'They never heard of Dev or Willie Cosgrave,' he said, 'but they know all about Joe Dolan.'

Jim Tobin of The Firehouse once admitted: 'My voice comes out very flat on tape, but singing's a lot better than shovelling gravel for a living.' The even more humble Jim Conlan of The Royal confirmed his retirement saying: 'I quit showbiz because of my utter contempt for my own musical performance.' T.R. Dallas, who popularised the song 'O Lord It's Hard To Be Humble', once praised his mentor with the words: 'Donie Cassidy is the brainchild of my success.'

Memorably, showband Senator Paschal Mooney once quoted *Hamlet* something rotten to the Seanad, telling his colleagues: 'Like they said long ago in a story, something is wrong in the state of Holland.' Meanwhile, the owners of the Sound Of Music club in Glenamaddy slotted all visiting acts into one of just three categories: Country 'n' Western, Pop or Mad Pop.

Spotlight magazine was the in-house organ of the showbands. The Capitol's Paddy Cole recalled: 'If you didn't take ads in the magazine you didn't get write-ups. If you featured on the front cover you had to take so many ads.' When The Capital fell out with the people at *Spotlight* all mention of them was expunged from its pages. A reconciliation was effected for the financial sake of both parties (this involved a *Spotlight* hack writing a flattering piece on The Capital for one of the newspapers).

New Musical Gazette was published in Longford to promote the chain of ballrooms owned by Albert Reynolds, reducing the need to spend money with *Spotlight*. Several others appeared including *Starlight*. None of the showband publications were known for their rigorous musical criticism. Shay Healy did the horoscope for *Spotlight* – a task which involved cutting out the horoscopes from *Jackie* and rearranging them on the page each month, so that last issue's Aries became this issue's Taurus and so on.

Shay would never accept money for giving an act favourable coverage, but he would accept cash for writing press releases for bands. The press releases would then appear verbatim in *Spotlight* under an assumed name. He would buy English magazines such as *Screen Gems* and *Melody Maker*, pull out quotes from various Elvis interviews, stitch them together and recycle them under a headline such as 'ELVIS TALKS EXCLUSIVELY TO SHAY HEALY IN HIS GRACELAND MANSION'.

The magazine's agony aunt, 'Dear Mary', was one of Healy's male colleagues. His services were dispensed-with after a reader wrote in asking if unsightly red marks on his privates could be venereal disease. 'Mary' told him to relax, the weals were most likely just friction burns resulting from overly vigorous masturbation.

Writing in a 1964 issue of a magazine for housewives produced by the Spar supermarket chain, Jimmy Magee did a spot of crystal ball gazing. The pop picker wrote: 'I've no doubts Cliff Richard is here to stay. So too are Cilla Black, Elvis, The Beatles, Ray Charles and The Bachelors – and I'd like to think the Migel Five as well.'

The showbands were a bunch of merry pranksters. One evening The Firehouse, managed by Donie Cassidy, were driving to a gig when they passed a blazing house. The driver pulled over and the musicians dashed to the scene of the fire – to shoot some publicity photos. One elderly manager with a weak bladder kept a potty under his bed in Wynne's Hotel. One day a musician emptied a tin of

Andrews Liver Salts into the receptacle. When the manager received his usual call of nature in the middle of the night, the darkness exploded as the mixture snapped, crackled and popped all over the floor. A doctor had to treat the manager for shock.

Other stunts were in more dubious taste. It wasn't unknown for bands to force the cancellation of shows by rivals by phoning hoax bomb warnings to the venue. As they drove home from gigs at the crack of dawn, the members of at least one band would keep an eye out for early risers cycling on deserted country roads. They'd overtake the cyclist, and a couple of bends later they'd stop the van. One of the musicians would kneel by the roadside and another would produce a starting pistol and – just as the cyclist arrived on the scene – would 'shoot' his victim in the head, execution style. Then turning towards the horrified cyclist, one of them would shout: 'He's seen us – get him!'

That 'joke' was retired after the whole showband scene reached a tragic turning point in July, 1975. The Miami showband were nearing the border on their way back south after a gig. They were flagged down by a man in uniform, flashing a light. They presumed him to be a British soldier. They stopped the van and 'soldiers' lined them up facing away from their van with their hands on their heads. Two of these 'soldiers' made like they were searching the back of the van. In fact, they were planting a bomb which was intended to go off further down the road. In addition to killing the band the explosion would provide 'proof' of Loyalist claims that southern show-bands were a front for smuggling Republican arms into the North. This in turn would make all southern show-bands 'legitimate targets'.

Except the bomb went off when the disguised Loyalists were planting it, killing two of them. The others opened fire on the musicians with machine guns, killing three and critically wounding one. Another survived by playing dead and then escaping in the confusion. The Miami massacre sounded the death-knell of the showband era.

The Superstars were launched in 1975, and were pretty typical of how the showband scene had evolved away from the ballrooms which defined its 'classic' period. They'd play cabaret venues and hotels rather than the ballrooms, as their maturing fan-base no longer had the stamina to dance for five hours. Former Capital mainman Paddy Cole was the Superstars' leader. Twink would take care of the 'women's songs' as she put it. The band would play chart hits of the day, a bit of jazz, and a lot of country. Their drummer would perform current comedy hits like *The Trail Of The Lonesome Pine* and *King Of The Cops*.

Twink summed it up: 'We were liked because we filled a void at the time. We weren't quite as *avant-garde* as the sort of Chips-type band who were the best there was.' (Fronted by Linda Martin, Chips did Eurovision-type covers of the Bay City Rollers, Linda Ronstadt, Elton John and so on.)

Men would write to Twink saying: 'Would you come down if I sent you the train fare?' Her friend Maxi got one letter saying: 'I've been a great fan of yours for many years, though not of your singing. I read somewhere that you like tall, skinny men. I'm a tall, skinny man and if you'd like to meet me please sing the Everly Brothers' *Let It Be Me* the next time you're playing town.' (In fact it was Twink who liked tall, skinny men.)

After one TV appearance Maxi's girl band Sheeba received a letter from a fan: 'I've got a big farm. I'd like to marry the one in the middle. Are you interested?'

The cabaret scene which superseded the ballrooms was popularly known as the rubber chicken circuit after its staple diet. Paddy Cole later observed: 'That's when I learned what showbusiness is all about. It's not about getting a standing ovation in The Capitol, when they would have cheered even if we played *Ba Ba Black Sheep*. Showbusiness is about going out on your own and trying to entertain people while they are eating . . . This was a new challenge.'

Twink reported squabbles over the type of material The Superstars should be performing. She wanted to sing 'quality' material like *Evergreen* and *Pearl's A Singer*. Band leader Paddy Cole agreed to *Evergreen*, partly because it had a nice flute solo which would showcase his talents. But generally, his approach was: 'Twink, it's too fuckin' sophisticated. The punters won't understand it.'

Twink eventually decided to get out. She went up-market, into panto. As the showband scene wound down many musos invested in pubs. Paddy Cole and his wife decided to introduce pub grub. This was truly *avant-garde*. Mrs Cole held advisory meetings in an attempt to persuade other publicans that serving food was the way of the future. It was all too much for one bar owner to get his head around. He demanded: 'And where am I meant to get parsley in the West of Ireland?'

Mrs Cole put exotic fare like prawns and duck on her menu but the diners wouldn't touch it. One customer ordered a plaice for his main course. After he'd finished it, Mrs Cole asked if he'd like a dessert. He replied that he'd already had dessert. But, she told him, she hadn't served it yet. The 'dessert' the man had eaten was the bowl of tartar sauce served with his fish.

By the end of the Seventies the showband scene was dead. Ironically, Ireland's favourite act of the day was

Germany's James Last whose populous orchestra was essentially a suped-up showband with extra beards and tuxedos. Last used to lead from the front, whipping audiences into a frenzy with his baton. This gave rise to the last of the great showband jokes.

Q: What's the difference between the James Last Orchestra and a bull?

A: A bull has the horns out front and the asshole at the back.

NO MAN OF SPIRIT WOULD HAVE DONE OTHERWISE

The Case Of The Chattel Wife.

Who? The boss of Roches Stores. A German married couple.
When? June 1972.
What? Werner Braun said his wife had been 'debauched'.
Where? Under the ancient law of Criminal Conversation.
Why? It was as if his 'thoroughbred mare or cow' had gone.

The scandal unfolded in Dublin's High Court. It heaped disrepute on the doorstep of Roches Stores, part of what we are. Yet there was something disconcertingly un-Irish about the whole affair. For one thing, native wisdom had it that you didn't wash your dirty bloomers in public. But Werner Braun was a German sophisticate with no pressing regard for the pieties of small-town Ireland.

It was June, 1972. The man in the dock was Stanley Roche. The fortysomething Roches Stores director was charged with 'debauching' Mrs Heide Braun at various locations in Cork, Limerick, Dublin and Germany. Werner Braun maintained that his wife and Roche had flouted the arcane law of Criminal Conversation and that he was entitled to his pound of flesh. Roche admitted the affair with Heide Braun, but pleaded that her husband had suffered neither loss nor damage.

As the salacious facts of the case emerged, the newspapers were sent into a tizzy. They decided that discretion was the better part of candour. The dowdiest of headlines were employed as fig leaves to camouflage the indecent courtroom exposures: 'GERMAN BORN AGENT SUES CORK DIRECTOR', 'HUSBAND'S ACTION FOR DAMAGES AGAINST BUSINESS-MAN'.

Werner seemed to have an unanswerable case. He was an 'outraged' husband whose pretty young wife had been swept off her feet by the tycoon yachtsman of Roches Stores. The court heard that Stanley Roche had 'set up in style' with Heide Braun. 'He lived with her and called her Mrs Roche and she had borne him a child.' Heide had been unfaithful to Werner at intervals over their ten-year marriage but he'd always found it in his heart to forgive her.

Werner smelled a faint whiff of rat after Heide began working for Roche as a decorating consultant in the summer of 1970. Roche had given Heide an Austin Mini car as a Christmas present. Later he trumped this with a sporty Triumph because the Mini, according to Werner, 'would not be good enough for the places she had to go' on business. Werner often didn't know where his wife was. When asked, she'd usually fob him off with 'here and there'.

Werner Braun learned of his wife's affair with the Roches Stores man through an anonymous Christmas card late in 1970. The missive suggested that Werner was a 'pimp'. It added that Roches Stores stocked the best turkeys around. The card featured Santa Claus and another figure sitting in a car. In court, Heide said she didn't think the cartoon referred to the car Roche had given her as a Christmas present. The illustration probably represented her husband driving in Stanley Roche's Jaguar, as he was sometimes wont to do.

Tipped off by the anonymous missive, Werner con-fronted his wife's lover. Nonsense, retorted Roche, they were just good friends. He personally wanted to come clean with Werner, but Heide insisted otherwise, 'for the children'. At the start of 1971, Heide left Ireland to consider her future. Upon her return she arranged to meet her husband and children on Valentine's Day at the Imperial Hotel in Cork.

The *Irish Independent* shrank from scandalising its readers with the full sordid details of this encounter. The *Independent* reported that Werner 'struck her because the meeting was held in the room she had in the hotel – the physical evidence of the intercourse she was having with Roche'. That was it, clear as mud.

The *Times* flirted with titillation for the sake of clarity. It revealed that Werner 'went to the hotel where his wife had a room booked. In the room he found contraceptives and a pornographic book.' Heide arrived and they quarrelled. Werner explained himself in court: 'I told her I would not tolerate this, that she was behaving as Stanley Roche's whore.' Then he belted her one. Werner's counsel 'said that no man of spirit would have done otherwise'.

Werner's chivalric image was soon in tatters. Heide told the court that their relationship had not been an exclusive one. Mrs Braun was asked: 'How many women do you claim that your husband criminally knew?' 'Approximately five,' she answered. One of those women was a young Dutch national named Anne Dobbe. Ms Dobbe told the court that on one occasion she was watching television and sipping sherry with the Brauns. When the married couple retired to bed, Ms Dobbe took her glass and followed them. According to the *Irish Independent*: 'It all developed in a way she could not remember the details of, and they all undressed and went to sleep.' In fact, the court heard that they didn't just sleep. Ms Dobbe had sex with Werner. It was 'enjoyable', she recalled. Heide was asked whether she'd minded this indiscretion on her husband's part. 'Not very much,' she replied.

Mrs Mareoline Tenino had been Werner's typist. Her husband was a business partner of his. She told the court how Braun had dispatched her husband on an errand one morning. Left alone with Mareoline, Werner 'suddenly started feeling her clothes and asked her to go to bed with him'. No way, she told him. She reported his conduct to his wife. Heide responded that, in future, she'd make sure Mareoline wasn't left alone with Werner. Later in the court proceedings, the same clothes-feeling incident was mentioned, but with the tantalising addition that Werner had 'done his performance with his trousers down'. The reports didn't elaborate.

Heide said she'd wanted to divorce Werner from early in the marriage. He'd beaten her. He'd cheated on her. He'd recently told her that he enjoyed having sex with other women and that 'he preferred this to emotional involvement'. But the presence of young children had put divorce on the back-burner. She'd also feared that her own infidelities – of which Werner was well aware – might stand between her and custody of the kids.

Heide didn't agree with the prosecution that she had disgraced her husband. Werner's counsel tried again, asking: 'You don't think it is a disgrace that he should be known in Cork or written about as a pimp?' His disgrace was his own fault, she replied. Would she apologise for disgracing him? No, she would not.

Stanley Roche explained that Heide was originally a friend of his wife, Cary. The pair had become involved when Cary was abroad in Spain. His marriage had been a 'working relationship' and had recently ended in separation. He and Heide now lived together. They had an infant child. Asked if his behaviour had made Werner Braun a pimp in the eyes of all Cork, Roche said: 'I don't recognise it.'

Justice Butler told the jury they must view the evidence coldly and dispassionately. It had been admitted, the judge said, that a wrong had been done to Werner Braun. His wife had been seduced and kept from him. The judge decreed that Braun was entitled to damages.

Criminal Conversation, Justice Butler explained, had been abolished in England in 1857 but it remained a right to be availed of under Irish law. The judge pointed out, as reported by the *Irish Independent*, that: 'In this country a wife was regarded as a chattel, just as a thoroughbred mare or cow, and the jury was concerned merely with compensating Mr Braun for the value of the loss of his wife and the damages to his feelings.'

After ninety minutes of deliberation the jury assessed that Stanley Roche should be penalised to the tune of £12,000 for causing hurt and damage to Werner Braun. They'd heard that Braun was a philandering wife-beater but the judge's directions were clear, Heide was his chattel and his loss must be made good. The award was hefty, the price of a four-bedroom house in 1972. Wives leaving husbands – even bad wives leaving bad husbands – went against the cultural grain.

The public outcry barely registered a single decibel. A few days after the verdict, the *Irish Times* carried an editorial headed 'THE CHATTEL WIFE'. The article meekly suggested that in the light of the Criminal Conversation conviction: 'It might well be that our legislators will think the dignity of women and of marriage is impugned by its retention.' The leader-writer could allow only one – 'feeble' – justification for retaining Criminal Conversation on the statute books. He wrote: 'The only possible excuse for such an action is that it might tend to lessen the chances of violence. An injured husband uses the courts instead of a club.'

Labour deputies Conor Cruise O'Brien and Justin Keating took up the matter in the Dáil, to no avail. They wanted to know if Justice Minister Desmond O'Malley would repeal a law that deemed women to be their husbands' property. The Minister replied that, as far as he knew, the law didn't place married women in the position of chattels. He insisted that, if there were any remaining areas of legislative inequality, they could only be minimal. A decade later, the same Des O'Malley told a female interviewer from *Image* magazine: 'I hope you won't ask any silly questions like what's my favourite colour shirt.'

At the time of the Minister's reassurances to O'Brien and Keating, the average industrial wage for an Irish woman was half that of a man. Women were barred from apprenticeships and had restricted access to jury duty. In 1972, it was standard practice amongst banks and hire purchase firms to refuse a loan to a married woman unless her husband underwrote it, even if she was working. If a husband and wife shared a passport he could travel on it alone but she could only do so with his permission.

It could truly be said of the Ireland of the day that a woman's place was in the wrong.

ONLY A SHOWER OF WIFE-SWOPPING SODOMITES

Youth Defence Vs The Libbies.

Who? A determined group of anti-abortion campaigners.
When? 1992 onwards.
What? They wanted abortion made even more illegal.
Where? The streets, the pubs, the free-houses of Ireland.
Why? Because other anti-abortion campaigners were 'soft'.

They just couldn't let a sleeping dog lie, and in the end they got bitten. A 1986 referendum had made abortion illegal in Ireland, but Youth Defence wanted it made *more* illegal. Their Holy Grail was a new referendum to seal a hairline crack in the existing legislation.

Youth Defence entered the world kicking and screaming in early 1992. Ethic cleansing and no dithering was their avowed agenda. One activist (Dislikes: 'liberalisation', 'queers', 'Japs' – in 1992 anyway.) found words to match the heady mood of the organisation's first months. At an early social he raised the rafters of The Piper House pub with a cry of 'Tiocfaidh ár lá!' as his fellow Defenders basked in the warm glow of moral certitude and a few beers.

By the end of 1992 Youth Defence claimed 3,000 paid-up members, although the wrinkle-count at their rallies suggested a rampantly permissive 'young at heart' admission policy. Nevertheless, the movement did exude a cocksure zeal generally associated with those who are about to inherit the Earth. The elder SPUCers (members of the Society for the Protection of Unborn Children), it was widely felt, were running a 'soft' anti-abortion campaign. One veteran fuelled this view at a media-grooming event attended by Youth Defence delegates. 'Our first mistake was trying to sound reasonable,' announced SPUC's Phyllis Bowman. That would never be a problem for Youth Defence.

In the war against sexually-related sinfulness, aiming below the belt had a certain logical appeal. Fine Gael's Nuala Fennell was shaken by a vociferous anonymous late-night housecall. Unwilling to condemn this, Niamh Nic Mhathuna (Ambition: 'To get married and have thirteen kids.') noted: 'There wasn't such a big deal when the homosexuals picketed the Papal Nuncio's house, we didn't see the media then.'

Pro-Choice physician Dr Paddy Leahy and Student Union leader Maxine Brady were singled out for slanderous tongue-lashings in a 1992 interview. Asked if she was suggesting that Brady was in the pay of abortion clinics, Nic Mhathuna replied: 'She has a credit card, I don't know any other student who has one.' When contacted about this accusation, Maxine Brady could only laugh and reply: 'I used to have a credit card but I can't afford one anymore . . . These people are fanatics. At a debate in Trinity College Nic Mhathuna's mother went for me and called me a murderer – that is what you are dealing with.' Dr Leahy would not be an intractable problem. 'He's seventy-five years old and he will be dead soon,' remarked Nic Mhathuna's colleague Peter Scully in the same interview.

'Your job is to hijack the media,' was Phylis Bowman's advice to the Young Turks of the Catholic hard-right. They tried, bless 'em, but the media wouldn't play ball. Worse, there were shrill allegations that RTÉ had turned up the volume on Niamh during one studio interview in an attempt to make her 'sound hysterical'.

The streets of Dublin promised a fairer hearing. They'd gather of a Saturday afternoon – Niamh, Mick, Peter, Jody McDonagh (Motto: 'You have to be mental to join Youth Defence.') and little Bethany, the plastic foetus. Together with friends and supporters, they'd brandish harrowing photo-evidence in support of their case.

Squeamish gardaí would regularly order Youth Defenders to desist from their God-anointed mission. The heckles of 'pro-abortionist' shoppers were another irritant. Things came to a head in the summer of '92 when scuffles broke out on O'Connell Street during a 'Pro-Life' rally. Niamh Nic Mhathuna rubbished suggestions that 'minders wearing knuckle-dusters' attached to Youth Defence had been cruising for a bruising. 'They were our boyfriends and fathers and brothers,' she explained. 'We felt it would be a good idea to assist the gardaí in allowing us our democratic right to voice our opinion. God, if we only had the money to use hired muscle . . . It must cost a fortune.'

Pardon, Niamh?

Bad choice of words. She reiterated that not a penny raised from subscriptions, 'church collections, cake sales and sale-of-works' had been frittered away on heavies.

But there was more to Youth Defence than ill-tempered street politics. There was travel. One expedition to Longford yielded disappointing results. Instead of the expected strong turnout of local activists only three people turned up – half an hour late – two of them children. As they departed the town, the campaigners tried to leave some foetus pics with the proposed Chairman of their Longford affiliate. The local man reluctantly declined, explaining: 'Anywhere else but not my home town. People wouldn't accept it.'

Besides the travel there was karaoke, the perfect pick-me-up after a hard day's slog on the campaign trail. Undercover reporter Michael McCaughan left his bleeding heart liberalism at the hat-check and joined the conga line. He discovered that leading light Mick Haughey does a mean Jon Bon Jovi impression. He wept at Niamh Nic Mhathuna's stirring rendition of *Irish Ways And Irish Laws*. He joined in the chants: 'Uggy, uggy, uggy. Oi, Oi, Oi!' and 'Mac-ma-hoo-na, hey, Mac-ma-hoo!' (to the tune of Gary Glitter's *Rock'N'Roll Pt 2*). After the pub, it was back to a free house. The singing continued, the highlight being a rousing: '*Humpty Dumpty sat on a wall . . . Ooh-aah, up the Ra!*'

Alas, it was all to no avail. The referendum Youth Defence so craved finally came in 1995 and their side finished a close second. As the awful truth dawned, the mother of Youth Defence's Niamh couldn't contain her disappointment. The scene was the RDS count centre. The poor loser was Una Bean Mhic Mathuna.

'Ye're only a shower of wife-swapping sodomites,' she quipped.

'And you're only an old Bible basher,' responded a young man wearing a 'Yes To Divorce' badge.

'I don't give a shite about the Bible,' snapped the middle-aged mother-of-nine.

'You *do* give a shite about the Bible,' the man informed her.

'Shuddup you,' she explained.

'You're a lunatic,' he concluded.

Nearby, Una's daughter Niamh was stoical. She'd lost. 'But we really can't lose,' she reflected. 'Since everything we said would happen will happen now. We won't take any pleasure in that, but we did warn people.'

And how.

VAN MORRISON, I TAKE IT, ARE A GROUP

Ireland Vs Punk Rock.

Who? John Lydon AKA Johnny Rotten.
When? October 1980.
What? The former Sex Pistol was put behind bars.
Where? In Dublin's Mountjoy Jail.
Why? To protect Dublin's citizens from 'this sort of thing'.

S uch was the vile hum of Johnny Rotten's reputation that it lingered long after he'd taken an early bath from his Sex Pistols playing days. Its pungent stench got up noses even in Ireland's loftiest ivory towers. '*I am an antichrist*,' he'd brayed memorably on the way to selling an awful lot of t-shirts. '*I am an anarchist*,' he'd sneered. Its unlikely that many copies of that tune were worn out on the Law Library jukebox, but Official Ireland got the gist. By the time the two came face to face in October 1980, Johnny Rotten had become plain John Lydon, about as thoroughly as creaky, poisonous Windscale would soon become squeaky clean Sellafield. In the carry-on that followed, John Lydon fell victim to Johnny Rotten's success. The immortal words of Kenneth Williams' embattled Caesar captured his predicament: 'Infamy, infamy, they've all got it infamy!'

The Devil's music had been dragged through the Irish courts some months before. Abroad, The Boomtown Rats were regarded as a featherweight pop combo whose mouthy singer had blagged them onto the punk bandwagon. At home, by virtue of winning approval in Britain, they were installed as the authentic voice of Young Ireland. It was only five months since the Pope had wowed the daddies and mammies with his 'Yong peebol off Irelant, I luff hew' soundbite. Scruffy whinger Bob Geldof and his rat pack were clearly not the type of yong peebol the Pope was in luff with.

The Rats wanted to play an outdoor gig in Dublin's Leopardstown Racecourse. Objections were swiftly lodged. District Justice Frank Johnston nailed his starched colours to the mast. Refusing a licence, the judge said: 'I have to take into account the behaviour of fans at these concerts elsewhere. They have been sent to the Isle Of Wight and other places where there is nothing to break.' The judge's verdict met with dismay in BBC Television's Children's Department. They'd planned to fly a group of handicapped youngsters to the Dublin show as part of the *Jim'll Fix It* wish-fulfilment programme.

The case went to the Dublin Circuit Court. The yawning cultural chasm separating the two sides was laid bare by Peter Sutherland, counsel for the objectors. He quizzed a witness: 'Van Morrison, I take it, are a group?' The case was still undecided the day before the proposed concert, for which thousands of tickets had been sold. At this late stage the Rats' lawyers discovered that the 1890 Public Health Act didn't extend to Leopardstown, which was beyond the City limits. After all the rigmarole it turned out they didn't need a licence. They'd just wasted a needless week in court.

Word of the Rats' legal victory was conveyed to the media. The gig would go ahead as planned. The next day, with the concert only hours away, the objectors were back in court with three more hopeful showstoppers. The judge threw out the first two applications, but he found himself inclined to agree that there might be a 'stampede' if the Rats were allowed unleash their primal rhythms. The judge told the band's representatives that the concert could go ahead, but only if they raised a daunting two million pounds in insurance cover. They couldn't. The gig was off with mere hours to curtain-up. The judge expressed no fears that the last minute cancellation might spark a stampede of disenfranchised ticket-holders.

If The Boomtown Rats debacle was the phoney war, John Lydon brought the Irish judiciary eyeball to eyeball with the real thing. The former Sex Pistol arrived in Dublin in October 1980, with several members of his London-Irish family. His brother, Jimmy, had formed a band, 4" Be 2". They couldn't play, they couldn't sing, they looked awful. Their prospects of going a long way seemed to reside in passing the driving test for heavy goods vehicles. Jimmy Lydon seemed determined to prove that his famous brother didn't have the family monopoly on obnoxiousness.

Jimmy had lost an eye when two black persons attacked him with a bottle. They'd taken exception to the swastika he wore as a fashion accessory. It was put to him that the loss of an eye was a high price to pay for trying to wind people up. 'Nah,' he reasoned. 'If you're gonna get your head kicked in to wear what you want, then you're gonna get your head kicked in, 'cos you're not gonna stop wearing it, are you?' Growing up in London, Jimmy had suffered for his Irishness. He'd been taunted and assaulted. Sadly, he reckoned, racial disharmony in London was now worse than ever. He knew who was to blame as well. It was 'the Greeks and Pakis and Chinks'. 'We're overdone with them,' he griped. 'There's so much emigration.'

Jimmy Lydon's ramshackle band were to play Trinity College on the night of Friday, October 3rd. The former Johnny Rotten was expected to join them on stage. Around tea-time, the ex-Pistol was approached for an autograph by a fan on the street. The stranger offered to buy his hero a pint. The pair entered the Horse & Tram pub on Eden Quay. The publican, Eamonn Brady, refused to serve them. There was a skirmish. When the dust had settled, John Lydon had a court appointment pencilled in for the next morning, Saturday.

As far as the singer was concerned, it was a storm in a teacup. He went to the Trinity gig, which degenerated into an ugly brawl. Back at the hotel, John Lydon drank and talked football into the early hours with other members of the entourage. The next morning, he appeared before District Justice McCarthy. The judge fixed bail at £250 but then refused to accept that sum from the band's Irish co-ordinator, John Byrne, or from the 4" Be 2" manager, Jock McDonald. McDonald's father, a resident of the Dublin suburb of Coolock, was rushed to court to put up the money. The judge asked McDonald Senior if he knew Lydon's Dublin address. The Coolock man said he didn't. He'd only just got here. John Lydon was remanded to Mountjoy Jail. Preceding Lydon in the dock was a man who'd been arrested at the 4" Be 2" Trinity gig the previous night. He'd smuggled a hammer into the concert and applied it with force to somebody's head. The hammer-wielding thug walked out of court on a bond of £50. As the erstwhile Johnny Rotten was led to his cell, the inmates of Mountjoy paid rousing homage by singing a Sex Pistols rewrite entitled *Anarchy In Dublin*.

On Monday, John Lydon stood in front of District Justice Ó'hUadhaigh. Publicans Eamonn Brady and

Eamonn Leddy said in evidence that the defendant and his now vanished accomplice had been ejected for spitting and hurling obscenities. Brady said that he was pulled out onto the street by his tie. He claimed that Lydon kicked him twice. Leddy, referring to the accused repeatedly as 'Rotten', added that the men had called Brady 'an Irish pig' and a 'wanker'. Lydon denied using obscene language or spitting. He said that when Brady refused him a drink he'd simply asked why – was he black or something?

'Then,' Lydon continued, 'when I was walking out I got smashed on the back of the head. My response to the punch was to look around and then *that* happened.' Here, he indicated his bruised cheeks. Lydon's solicitor put it to barman Leddy that he'd 'completely over-reacted', thumping Lydon in the eye after going at him 'stripped for action'. Leddy denied it. He did, however, agree that he had forcefully punched Lydon in an unspecified part of his anatomy 'above the shoulder'.

Justice Ó'hUadhaigh dismissed Lydon's version of events. He launched into a speech, described by London's *New Musical Express* as a 'customary smug, highbrow sermon', outlining his duty to 'protect the citizens of the city' from 'this sort of thing'. Passing sentence, the judge lectured Lydon that there was 'a lot of indiscriminate violence in Dublin by people with drink and without drink taken, who went around looking for trouble'. He was tempted to give the defendant six months in jail. However, leniency got the better of him and he'd impose a sentence of just three months. The Irish representative of Virgin Records offered to put up bail while the case went to appeal. The judge refused. He eventually relented when the Virgin man produced a letter from his bank manager vouching that he was solvent. John Lydon was on the next available flight to London.

John Lydon's brief imprisonment allowed him, in his own mind at least, to become Johnny Rotten once more. Years later, when he came to write his autobiography, his brush with the Irish law had gained more embellishments than the *Book of Kells*. In his mature recollection, he'd been hauled off to a Garda station not once on the Friday of the brawl, but twice, just for good measure. His English lawyer's 'upper-class, twitty voice' had antagonised the judge. At one point, a brand-new BMW had been put-up as bail. Asked for an Irish address, he'd given that of his uncle in Cork. He recalled: 'They wouldn't accept that either, and went on a tirade about "damned kulchies", which is what Dubliners call people from the country.'

The warm welcome which had greeted him at Mountjoy frosted over in the chill mists of time. In Lydon's revised version of events, he was saved from a fate close to death at the hands of the prisoners only by the warders' callous decision to make an example of him. He'd been stripped naked, thrown in the exercise yard and hosed down. This convinced the other jailbirds that he must be okay. Then, as chance would have it, the prison's Saturday night movie happened to open with a performance by The Sex Pistols. At this point his fellow inmates finally recognised him. They were a tough bunch: 'IRA, UDA, psychopathic murderers, the lot.' Presumably the IRA and UDA men had hidden in the toilet cubicles when all paramilitary prisoners were removed from Mountjoy in the early Seventies.

The erstwhile prince of punk recalled that his cellmate was a jewel thief who'd been captured when a brick he'd thrown at a window bounced back and knocked him unconscious. Lydon's sleep was disturbed when: 'In the middle of the night, two warders decided to come in and

beat me with truncheons. You know the way they do:
"Your blanket isn't straight!"' The protests of the other
prisoners saved him. But he felt uneasy. Neither the IRA
nor the UDA knew what to make of him. 'I'd lost both
ways because of my Irish name and my English accent,'
he explained.

'I learned to be vicious pretty quick in that environment,' he wrote. He'd have had to learn very quickly
indeed, since he was only there for two days. No, scratch
that: 'I was locked up for four days – felt like four years . . .
My father flew into Ireland from London the day I was
released from prison . . . My father's hotel room was
searched by the police for IRA weapons and fugitives.'
Hmmm . . .

And finally to the appeal against the three-month jail
sentence. Despite the actual facts of the matter, Lydon
recalls returning to court the day after his release on bail.
'The years were going by in front of me. Five. Ten.
Fifteen. I was scared.' The case before Lydon's involved a
'gypsy woman' charged with stealing a watch. She got
three months. The gypsy pointed out in court that she was
entitled to a state-provided transistor radio for her cell. She
asked the judge to double her sentence on the sound
reasoning that six months behind bars must be worth a
television to her. Lydon had dumped his twitty-voiced
English lawyer for an Irish one this time. This was a
shrewd move: 'He said to the judge, "Hello sir! How are
you doing? I'll see you later on. We'll have a game of golf."
Those were the first words out of the guy's mouth.'

Ripping yarns. Rotten memory.

WE HAVE BEEN COMMITTING NATIONAL HARI-KIRI FOR GENERATIONS

Archbishop McQuaid Vs Yugoslavia.

Who? The Catholic Archbishop of Dublin.
When? October 1955.
What? The Archbishop wanted a match cancelled.
Where? Dalymount Park, Dublin.
Why? The FAI had arranged it without consulting him.

John Charles McQuaid was rarely drunk on power, but he was seldom sober. The Archbishop was used to getting things his own way, but on an October day in 1955 over twenty thousand people turned out to let Ireland's most powerful cleric know that he was over the limit.

Throughout the middle decades of the Twentieth Century, politicians of all hues genuflected before Dublin's Catholic Archbishop as a matter of course. In time, McQuaid began topping up his social quota with a secret habit. Perennial Taoiseach Eamon de Valera organised the after-hours sessions. McQuaid was given a codename, 'A B', and a free hand to run a red pen over social legislation before it reached the democratic institutions of the state. Another De Valera, Vivion, witnessed the Archbishop's vision for a better Ireland at the squinty end of its range.

Vivion de Valera was made a director of the *Irish Press* while still a student at Blackrock College, one of McQuaid's personal fiefdoms. One day, the young de Valera was summoned to the cleric's room. There, McQuaid produced a pile of cuttings which he'd snipped out of the *Irish Press*. They were mostly front page adverts for Clery's department store. The Archbishop wanted the adverts stopped. The offending items were line-drawings of women, illustrating the armour-plated underwear of the day. McQuaid gravely informed de Valera that – with the use of a magnifying glass – it was possible to make out the shape of a lady's, eh, you know, rude bits.

Between attending to the spiritual and political running of the country, Archbishop McQuaid didn't have much time for sports. And certainly not foreign games like soccer. Because of this, His Grace didn't learn about a visit by the Yugoslav national team until a few days before the scheduled Dalymount Park kick-off. It was 1955 and the Cold War was threatening to deepen into an Ice Age.

The friendly match was set for Wednesday, October 19th. With precisely one week to go, the Department of Justice phoned the Football Association of Ireland. The FAI were informed that they'd need permission to bring the Eastern Bloc players into the country. The Association replied in astonishment that they'd never needed permission before. Visiting teams had always made their own travel arrangements. The Department wasn't interested in what happened before. The FAI would have to supply the names of the travelling party so they could be checked against a government blacklist.

More bad news was conveyed privately to the FAI. The President of Ireland, Seán T O'Kelly, would be absenting himself from the match. The next to withdraw was the Army Number One Band, despite the fact that sheet music of the Yugoslav national anthem had been specially flown to Dublin for their convenience.

As all this was happening the Archbishop's Chancellor contacted the FAI. He informed the Association's secretary that the Archbishop 'had heard with regret that the match had been arranged'. The Chancellor, Father O'Regan, said it was a pity that the FAI hadn't had the courtesy to obtain the views of the Archbishop on the proposed game. It was the Archbishop's hope that, even at this late stage, the match would be abandoned. Three years earlier, in 1952, the FAI *had* gone cap in hand to Archbishop McQuaid seeking his go-ahead to play a Yugoslav selection. On that occasion, the Archbishop had told them he wasn't pushed either way. As the day got nearer, however, he'd suggested that the FAI should consider scratching the fixture if they 'could get out of it discreetly'.

Three years later, on the Saturday before match day, the FAI convened a meeting to discuss the escalating hostilities or, strictly speaking, to discuss discussing them. The Association's Vice-Chairman, Mr L Cleary, proposed that there should be no debate on the matter. Just get on with the game, he said. District Justice O'Riain seconded the motion. 'The less discussion the better,' he advised. Chairman Prole argued that, 'as lovers of freedom', the FAI should open the matter for discussion. The Munster delegate, Mr Sheridan, pointed out in their favour that most Yugoslavs were Catholics.

A vote was taken. The match would go ahead. To cancel now would ruin Ireland's good name in world football. The Leinster delegate, Brian O'Clery, wanted it on the record that if the FAI had known of any government or ecclesiastical opposition to the fixture beforehand, they would never have arranged it. He added that it would be a sorry day for Ireland when visiting players were asked their politics or religion. The only vote in favour of abandonment came from the Army delegate. The FAI decided to send the Archbishop a letter as it was agreed he was owed an explanation.

Having decided to proceed with the match, the FAI were now obliged to promise the Justice Department that they'd pay the cost of repatriating any Yugoslav player who overstayed his visa period in Ireland. They also had to withstand a concerted attack by the forces of Catholicism roused by the Archbishop's call to arms. The guilds of Regnum Christi said that it was a sorry day for Ireland, and so on. The Supreme Secretary of the Knights of Columbanus complained that the FAI's decision was 'regrettable'. Radio Éireann's chief soccer commentator, Philip Greene, withdrew himself from the game in accordance with the Archbishop's wishes.

A body calling itself the Catholic Association for International Relations sent an open letter to the Yugoslav footballers. It warned: 'You will, no doubt, be cordially greeted by the thousands of followers of the sport who gather at Dalymount Park . . . You will hardly guess by the demeanour of the crowd, that the great bulk of the Irish people are rather unhappy about your visit.'

Another group, The League of the Kingship of Christ, issued a statement pointing out that all people are brothers in the mystical Body of Christ: 'But, at the same time, we must distinguish between the state controlled Yugo-Slav soccer team, which represents a tyrannous regime of persecution, and the human persons who are members of that team.' The League's point was that Ireland must be prepared to welcome, with open arms, any player who had the common decency to defect to the West. Would-be asylum-seekers must not be obstructed by 'the amazing and absurd guarantee which has been forced on the

Football Association of Ireland by our Department of Justice'.

Radio Éireann still couldn't say whether they'd be covering the match. The station's Director, Mr Goram, was abroad. In Rome, as it happened. By the time the Yugoslav party arrived in Dublin on the Monday night, the national broadcasting service had finally thrown in its lot with the Archbishop. The station released a curt statement: 'Radio Éireann announces that it is not now broadcasting the commentary on the association football match between Ireland and Yugo-Slavia on Wednesday, 19th instant.'

The visitors were met at Dublin Airport by an FAI delegation, some protesters, and a cordon of uniformed and plainclothes gardaí doing a tight man-marking job. A dismayed Yugoslav spokesman said the team had travelled to five continents and had never come across such a protest. A reporter explained that the cause of the fuss was the imprisonment of Cardinal Stepinac, an innocent cleric whose only crime was to undermine the Yugoslav state. 'We completely ignore it,' replied the soccer man.

Uncertainty surrounding the game mounted. There were rumours that several members of the Irish team had 'cried off'. Transport FC, the footballing wing of the bus and rail service, were boycotting all functions held in the Yugoslavs' honour. The non-footballing branch of the company, however, confirmed that normal services to and from Dalymount Park would be provided. The Chairman of Dundalk FC announced he would be boycotting the communists.

The matter reached the Waterford Board of Public Assistance in Dungarvan. There, a Mr Curran proposed a strong protest against the FAI for inviting the Yugoslavs.

According to one report: 'There was a long silence following Mr Curran's statement.' This was eventually broken by a Mr Fitzpatrick who said: 'I don't feel that it is our business to do anything about that matter here today.' The motion of censure against the FAI was seconded by the Mayor of Waterford.

The Yugoslav envoy in London expressed himself dismayed by the situation. Ambassador Velebit said: 'It is regrettable that the Archbishop of the Catholic Church in Dublin has used the friendly meeting of the football representations of Yugoslavia and the Republic of Ireland as an occasion for a campaign of intolerance.'

Meanwhile, the moral tussle had spilled onto the letters pages of the national press. One writer wanted to know whether the FAI had done background checks on the Yugoslav players to make 'certain that none of the mass-murderers are amongst those with whom they propose to break bread as guests'.

There were small pockets of away support. One correspondent pointed out with evident bemusement that, less than a month previously, a team of Russian scientists were 'wined and dined' by the President and Taoiseach. The writer couldn't recall a single anti-communist protest, 'and certainly not from any of the people or organisations that are now kicking up a rumpus'. The vital difference, of course, was the intervention of an Archbishop.

On the day before the game, the Republic's coach, Shelbourne's Dick Hearns, withdrew his services from the team. Asked why, he replied: 'I would rather not say.' The Yugoslavs trained on Tuesday under the watchful eye of a sizeable garda presence. Meanwhile, following the withdrawal of the Army Band, the FAI were scouring Dublin for a vinyl copy of the Yugoslav national anthem to

play over the Dalymount loudspeaker system. When all
else failed, a group of musicians were put in a recording
studio with the sheet-music sent from Yugoslavia. A special
disc of the visitors' national anthem was pressed-up in
time for the game.

And still the condemnations mounted. Commandant W
J Brennan-Whitmore urged the scrapping of the game on
grounds of cultural purity, saying: 'Since the game of
soccer is an alien mode, it is part and parcel of the alien
facade behind which we have been committing national
hari-kiri for generations.' Sean Brady TD simply wanted
to know: 'Would it be asking too much of Dublin workers
to deny themselves the pleasure of witnessing a good
soccer match as an act of respect for, and sympathy with,
the brave, distinguished prisoners of Yugoslavia?'

In a word, yes. In the face of the Episcopal ban, nearly
22,000 people converged on Dalymount Park to see
Ireland take on the much-fancied Communists. The Irish
players were on £30 a man, win or lose. It was speculated
that the visitors would get £25 each if they won, nothing
if they lost. There were other differences between the two
sides. The Republic team had been designed by a
committee of five selectors, some of whom didn't see the
point of attending Ireland's away matches. In contrast, the
Yugoslavs favoured the new fangled Continental system of
having a single manager who took a professional interest
in the team.

The Yugoslavs took the field to loud cheers. The
visitors' national anthem was accorded due respect.
There was a huge roar of approval when the loudspeaker
informed the crowd that, 'The teams will field as
announced on your programmes'. The Irish trainer apart,
there had been none of the feared defections. The sum

total of protest consisted of a lone individual parading a Papal flag outside the ground. Just before kick-off, Yugoslav officials politely requested that their national flag be turned the right way up as a mark of respect. The incident was as close as the Irish got to causing an upset on the day.

The cultured Yugoslavs knew too much for Ireland's hoofers. The home team stuck to their match plan of kicking the ball hopefully in the general direction of the opponents' goal. This forced the visitors to fall back on the old tactic of pinpoint passing, close control and fancy footwork. The Yugoslavs unsportingly disguised their centre forward in a No 8 jersey, bamboozling the home defence brought up on the convention that centre forwards always wore No 11. The subterfuge was a great success and the interloper helped himself to a hat-trick. The Yugoslavs eventually romped home 4–1 winners.

Posterity doesn't record whether Archbishop McQuaid was sick as a parrot.

EVERY NAME UNDER THE SUN

Stephen Roche Vs Roberto Visentini.

> Who? A young Irish upstart and an Italian cycling champ.
> When? The summer of 1987.
> What? Roche had the temerity to take on his team leader.
> Where? During the Giro Italia on Visentini's home turf.
> Why? Because Roche believed his time had come.

The mid-Eighties were the best of times for Irish cycling. Teak-hard Sean Kelly was the undisputed world Number One, his superhuman prowess in the saddle already legend. By 1985 Stephen Roche had manoeuvred stealthily into Kelly's slipstream, actually pipping the Waterford man for third place in that year's Tour De France. Roche's 1986 season was disrupted by injury, but he did enough to show he could breathe down the necks of the world's best. As the 1987 circuit slipped into gear, Roche felt that the force was with him.

'You've got to accept that you're either going to be a super champion or a normal rider,' he said before the season began. 'If you can't win races, you have to put yourself at the service of other riders, be a team member and help your team leader.' Roche had a team leader, Roberto Visentini. '*If* you can't win races' he'd said. It was to become a big, big 'if'.

The crunch came during the fifteenth stage of the 1987 Giro Italia, cycling's most prestigious ordeal after the Tour De France. Carrera teammates Roche and Visentini had swapped the lead for most of the previous fortnight, with

Roche shading it. Then Roche came to grief in a Stage 10 pile-up, leaving him stiff and sore. Visentini took full advantage in the Stage 13 time trial. Back in Ireland, where cycling was strictly for kids and postmen, the newspaper headline was small and short: 'VISENTINI TROUNCES ROCHE'. 'My behind was killing me,' moaned the Dubliner at the stage finish. He was now nearly three minutes adrift of his associate, a potential aeon in top class cycling. 'I can still come back,' he said defiantly.

Few believed him. It wasn't just that Roche was several tenderised hues of black and blue. Visentini was the defending Giro champion, while the Irishman had never won a major race. In addition, Roche was shackled by protocol. As the junior partner in the Carrera team, his primary function was to protect and serve. Besides, Visentini was the local hero. His impending victory would be good PR for the sport.

What happened next rocked the cycling world. Staking his professional future on the line, Roche stormed through Stage 15 like a man with a hornet's nest clenched between his buttocks. This was not in the team script. Visentini had drained himself recapturing the lead from Roche. He needed a rest. But now, instead of enjoying a restorative cruise from Lido Di Jesolo to Sappada, the Italian was forced into a lung-bursting pursuit of his runaway sidekick. At the end of the tough mountain stage Roche was race leader again. Visentini languished in seventh place, a spent force. Oh how they booed as the Irishman accepted his victor's garland.

With one inspired piece of riding, Stephen Roche had become Italy's public enemy number one. The Italian press screamed 'betrayal!' The Italian public turned out in huge numbers for Stage 16 to harass and harangue the usurper. 'I was scared,' he later confessed. 'It was very, very frightening in the mountains. People were trying to get me. I had a police motorbike on either side on the hills, pushing people back for me to come through. Visentini was behind me and everyone was pushing him up the hills and they were spitting at me. They used to fill their cheeks with wine and rice and spit it at me as I passed.'

When he reached the stage finish, Roche addressed a hostile Italian media. Visibly upset, he pleaded: 'I did nothing wrong on Saturday. For two weeks now I've been racing for Roberto. I am not a calculating man. I'm a professional who does a job to the full. If it goes on like this, maybe tomorrow somebody will punch me in the eye and I'll have to go to hospital.'

As luck would have it, atrocious weather and heavy security kept the vengeful locals at bay the next day. But now, ominously for Roche, the Giro course was winding into Visentini's backyard. Quaking on the inside, he brazened it out. Visentini's challenge had exploded. The hopes of the Italian Carrera team now rested with him. He urged reason. 'The team must win the Giro,' he said. 'There mustn't be any arguments. I think there are only two people I have to watch out for now.' The two riders Roche had in mind didn't include Roberto Visentini. But Visentini begged to differ.

Visentini's vendetta was now in full torrent. 'He cried out to everybody that I'd gone out to ruin his Tour,' said Roche. The Carrera team officials were inclined to side with their jilted Number One. Speculation was rife that Roche would be sacked at the Giro's end, leaving him without a team for the Big One, the upcoming Tour De France. The Irishman was left to stew by his employers, who compounded his isolation by slapping a media ban on him. Roche later revealed: 'For ten days I had breakfast in my room, bodyguards to take me down to the start and a police escort throughout the race.'

Hopelessly adrift, Visentini tumbled out of the Giro, injuring his arm in the process. As the Italian's martyrdom amplified, so did hatred of Roche. At the close of the penultimate stage, a large crowd closed in on the leader, marooning him from his police escort. At this point the story's love-interest made a most timely entrance. There, in the madding crowd, he espied Lydia, his wife. 'Everyone was jumping on me and poking me and calling me every name under the sun,' Roche related. 'And I turned around and I saw Lydia there and I was so delighted and so upset at the same time, because I wanted her to see me with everyone loving me, rather than seeing everyone hating me. But that saved my Tour Of Italy because I was on the verge of blowing a piston. That night we had a meal and a few words and the next morning I was unbelievable – it was like starting the Tour fresh.'

Stephen Roche proved himself a worthy champion of the Giro Italia by winning the final time trial in style. The imperious manner of his ultimate victory demanded respect. The *Gazetta Dello Sport* relented. 'We can now call him Stefano,' stated the newspaper. 'The crowd has adopted him.' Roberto Visentini was less forgiving. Even as Roche was accepting his garlands, the vanquished champion was wagging a bandaged finger on live TV.

Visentini very publicly dissolved his partnership with Stephen Roche that same day. His vaguely sinister final word on the matter was: 'The really important thing is that where I race, he doesn't. Otherwise something really serious could happen.' Carrera's millionaire boss agonised over the nasty rupture in his team. The following day he announced that Stephen Roche would be leading Carrera in the 1987 Tour De France.

When the Dubliner coasted into Paris to claim cycling's greatest prize, a jubilant ITV commentator hailed the achievement of: 'Stephen Roche, the only British or Irish cyclist to win the Tour de France.' Taoiseach Charles Haughey arrived on the scene to claim the victory for Ireland. A beaming Haughey told a reporter: 'The scene here is the greatest experience of my life!'

Haughey was later asked: 'Wasn't that claim a bit excessive?'

He replied: 'What I said was that it was the greatest experience of my life on the Champs Élysées.'

For Roach, his elevation to national hero brought mixed blessings. A year after his *annus mirabilis*, being recognised everywhere he went was becoming a bit tyresome. 'You end up being hassled by people talking about bicycles all the time,' he explained. 'That's why I stay at home a lot.'

WHO WILL MIND THEIR CHILDREN IF THEY ARE ELECTED?

The CCCP Vs The CPP.

Who? A Christian party. An even more Christian party.
When? In the run-up to the 1991 local elections.
What? The CPP was slammed for not being Christian enough.
Where? In thirteen constituencies.
Why? The CCCP disapproved of the CPP's women candidates.

April 26th 1991, the Feast Of Our Lady Of Good Counsel, was to be a red letter day in the annals of Irish politics. The nativity of the Christian Principles Party marked a new departure back to a brighter future. Local elections were just two months away and the CPP were piously eyeing up thirteen seats. The infant party's manifesto embraced measures to preserve the environment, the health services and Ireland's neutrality. They would staunchly foster Christian social teachings, 'maintain the Constitution of Ireland' and oppose 'Anti-Christian' legislation in any guise.

All of the CPP's candidates were first-timers, but what they lacked in electioneering *nous* they made up for with catchy slogans. Seán Clerkin, for instance, ran in North Dublin under a banner of JOBS FOR YOUTH – NOT CONDOMS. His personal CV outlined his commitment to women's rights, the lower paid, the Irish language and Gaelic Games. Clerkin's testament even suggested he'd converted out of political expediency. It said: 'Now he is an enthusiastic supporter of Jack's Irish Soccer Team.'

The CPP's campaign drew early support from the hitherto unknown figure of Gloinn Mac Tire. In a letter to party headquarters, Mac Tire rejoiced in a trinity of felicitous signs, namely the fall of Marxism, the Pope's latest social encyclical, *Centesimus Annus*, and the foundation of the Christian Principles Party. Mac Tire wrote: '*Centesimus Annus*, not condoms for children, is the true spirit of Ireland . . . We need not face the cross-channel tragedy of separated spouses remarrying, nor see our children pregnant before we can protect them from sex education.'

Mac Tire suggested that the CPP had a leading role to play in reinventing an Ireland 'of Saints and Scholars'. To achieve this, he insisted: 'We must all unite, although we need not, of course, become Unitarians. I would suggest the title CCCP – the Co-ordinating Committee for Christianity in Politics. These initials were, of course, also used by the Soviet Marxists, and their use in this new positive sense would be a rich irony for all atheists. Am I unrealistic to be so optimistic? I think not. Many would have thought Christ unrealistic though, in His own words, they would have known not what they thought.'

The letter closed with an oblique reference to 'some trusted cross-channel colleagues . . . who have a not insubstantial amount of money which could be ploughed into such a worthy venture. Neither they nor I would seek (nor, indeed, want) any personal publicity or public position – we are content that our deeds will be judged by Another. Please let us know what you think.'

The Christian Principles Party were not the only ones circulated with a letter from Gloinn Mac Tire. Copies were posted to members of the Catholic Hierarchy, the Oireachtas and beyond. Bishop Jeremiah Newman of Limerick sent back his best wishes but stressed he didn't 'get directly involved in politics'. Nor did the Archbishop of Dublin, who suggested that Mac Tire contact the Knights of Columbanus. The Cathaoirleach of the Seanad, Sean Doherty, responded that 'what you propose is certainly an interesting idea'. The Vatican wrote back to say that the Holy Father had been appraised of the situation.

The telltale signs were there, although no-one appeared to spot them, that Gloinn Mac Tire said more than his prayers. The clues were present in the writer's cracked logic, in the CCCP acronym, in a dig at Pope Leo XIII for 'supporting the British in Ireland' and in the gibberish put into the mouth of Jesus Christ. On the other hand, Gloinn Mac Tire's correspondents had no way of knowing that his moniker was a pidgin-Irish translation of 'Glenn Wolfe'. The name had been plucked from the Guinness Book Of Records where Wolfe held pride of place as the World's Most Divorced Man.

Gloinn Mac Tire was the brainchild of Dubliner Michael Nugent, and one that had clearly been touched by the hand of God. Five years earlier, in 1986, Nugent had flirted with the paparazzi when he threw his hat into the ring for the vacant position of Republic Of Ireland football supremo. The graphic designer offered to manage the team part-time on a government job creation scheme. The manager's salary saved by the FAI, he mooted, could be 'ploughed into the upgrading of Dalymount Park'. In the final reckoning, Jack Charlton emerged as the Association's surprise choice for the post.

If the FAI job application was a transparent caper, Nugent's invention of Gloinn Mac Tire was a prank

requiring considerably more guile. He now found himself
ducking and weaving in a surreal Twilight Zone where
reality and parody co-habit. With three weeks to go to the
local elections, Mac Tire received a hand-written letter
from the Christian Principles Party. It said: 'Our printing
costs to date are over £2,500. A sample leaflet for
the Cabra Electoral Area candidate for the Dublin
Corporation is also enclosed for your information. Our
funds are now running low and any help financially from
you and/or your friends would be much appreciated.'

Mac Tire's response to the CPP was sent out on the
newly devised headed stationary of the CCCP. The
umbrella group's logo featured a shattered hammer and
sickle lying at the feet of Holy Ireland, having been smote
by a crucifix in a clenched fist. The letterhead echoed Sean
Clerkin's election literature. 'MARRIAGE, NOT SEX', it
proclaimed, 'JOBS, NOT CONDOMS'. The officers of
the CCCP were listed as: 'Uachtaran: G Mac Tire.
Cathaoirleach: E O'Ceallaigh.' Eoin O'Ceallaigh was the
nom-de-plume of Arthur Mathews. Through his regular
soapbox column in a Dublin magazine, the fictitious crank
barked out routine denunciations of trades unions, abstract
art, young people, the British, Sinead O'Connor, bearded
intellectuals and modern life in general.

Without actually mentioning money, the CCCP
response gently ruled out any possibility of a cash
contribution to the CPP's election fund. It explained:
'While we hope you do well in the local elections, we must
point out some areas in which we see you (no doubt
unintentionally) drifting towards liberalism. Firstly, your
proposal for compensation for the stay-at-home wife
implies, does it not, that such a role is a chore, for which
compensation is necessary, rather than a joy and the

rightful role of woman. The use of the term 'stay-at-home' wife also implies that there are other wives who do not stay at home. While this is clearly the case *de facto*, it is dangerous to reinforce the concept with such careless phrases. This brings us to a more fundamentally worrying point – that several of your candidates appear to *be* women. Who will mind their children if they are elected?'

Mac Tire closed the subject by saying that the CCCP would encourage electoral support for the CPP's male candidates, but: 'cannot fully endorse your party at this point in time. We hope you understand our position on this delicate but fundamental point.' He signed off with an attack on an Irish women's magazine, writing that 'decent citizens should not be exposed to such organs'. The suppression of women's magazines, said the CCCP, would help to 'revive the morally healthy climate of the 1950s'.

The CCCP took its campaign to the letters pages of the national newspapers, who obligingly made space for the gobbledygook: 'From Symeon, later Peter, of Bethsaida, thrice the Master's denier yet also the rock on which his Bride was built . . . the Good News has not faltered in the trials of two millennia under the stewardship of near fourteen score Popes.' And so on.

A body called the Community Standards Association wrote to the CCCP requesting a meeting 'because of your objectives which coincide with ours, and because we belong to an umbrella organisation – COSC – which has been in existence and you appear to be duplicating it'. Since Gloinn Mac Tire and Eoin O'Ceallaigh didn't exist, a meeting was problematic. Instead, their creators pressed ahead with their most ambitious project yet. The first issue of *Majority Ethos*, the official organ of the CCCP, was published in July 1991 after the elections.

Beneath the headline '3,000 DUBLINERS VOTE FOR OUR LORD', the front page of *Majority Ethos* carried a detailed analysis of the recent local election results. The lead story applauded the 'near election' of the CPP's Sean Clerkin and Dominic Noonan as sending a 'clear message' of warning to the mainstream parties. 'Predictably,' said *Majority Ethos*, 'the impact of the Christian parties was even greater than expected.

'In particular Clerkin and Noonan, with their combined mandate of 2,182 votes, would have outpolled such established liberal figures as outgoing Lord Mayor Michael Donnelly (only 1,958) and Fine Gael's Jim Mitchell (a mere 1,164). In fact, even taken individually, either Clerkin or Noonan would have overwhelmed both the well known Galway Socialist and friend of Marxist Nicaragua Michael 'D' Higgins, and the English Protestant Shane Ross.' *Majority Ethos* calculated that the combined votes of all the Christian party candidates in Dublin would have swamped the 'meagre' total which elected socialist Jim Kemmy in Limerick. These 'quirks of quotas and boundaries', declared the publication, constituted a 'clear distortion of the wishes of the electorate'.

The election coverage continued inside the magazine. Gloinn Mac Tire launched an attack on the Christian Principles Party in an article purporting to call for 'greater unity between the new Christian political groups'. The CPP's women candidates, he argued, had cost the party crucial votes just as the CCCP had said they would. The clue for Eight Across in the *Majority Ethos* crossword was: 'Amount of Workers Party members facing eternal retribution (3).' The solution: 'ALL'.

Its work done, the CCCP went the way of its Soviet namesake, but its mischievous spirit lived on. Gloinn Mac

Tire was reincarnated three years later as John Mackay, 'author' of 'Dear John', a best-selling volume of bogus letters and genuine replies. Eoin O'Ceallaigh reverted to the name of Arthur Mathews and found acclaim as the co-creator of 'Fr. Ted'.

GOD SAVE IRELAND FROM INTELLECTUALS

Oliver J Flanagan Vs The Late 20th Century.

Who? The Fine Gael TD and one-time Defence Minister.
When? 1943–1987.
What? He raged against Jews, intellectuals, lounge bars.
Where? In the Dáil and in his constituency of Laois/Offaly.
Why? Because he was pledged to uphold 'the law of God'.

It was a kindness that Oliver J Flanagan expired before Irish politics was finally wrested from his kind by the spin doctors. No amount of political cosmetic surgery could have prettified his bristly red neck, nor would he have submitted to it. Oliver J is justly remembered for the startling revelation that: 'There was no sex in Ireland before television.' But there was more to the man than that. Much more . . .

The *piece-de-resistance* of Oliver J Flanagan's early election strategy was a sandwich-board bearing the legend 'HERE COMES OLIVER' on the front and 'THERE GOES FLANAGAN' on the back. It was crude but effective. He was elected to the Dáil by the voters of Laois/Offaly in 1943. He once reflected: 'To be a politician is perhaps the greatest calling after the Church.' He devoted his long Dáil career to keeping Ireland firmly anchored in 1943. And to sorting jobs for the boys. Boasting that he'd 'put hundreds into jobs', he explained: 'I have always believed in working for the people and helping a friend to secure a position in life.'

Oliver J wasted no time in making a splodge on the national political canvas. One of his first actions as a TD, in 1943, was to call for stern emergency measures 'directed against the Jews, who crucified Our Saviour nineteen hundred years ago and who are crucifying us every day in the week'. Throwing his lot in with the Third Reich, he continued: 'There is one thing that Germany did, and that was to rout the Jews out of their country. Until we rout the Jews out of this country, it does not matter what orders you make. Where the bees are there is honey, and where the Jews are there is money.'

Ireland successfully clung to 1943 for twenty years or so. But as the Sixties progressed, the old certainties began to hurtle away at a pace that Oliver J found disquieting. His unswerving adherence to 'high standards of decency' left him increasingly isolated in a Dáil swamped with Fianna Fáil's mohair proto-yuppies and the pinko swots infiltrating his beloved Fine Gael. Oliver J held no truck with excessive book learning. In 1967, concerned to protect young minds, he laid down his objections to the new Intermediate Certificate English curriculum.

He complained to Education Minister Donagh O'Malley that Frank O'Connor's *Guests Of The Nation* and Sean O'Faolain's *The Trout* contained 'language which might be expected in a low-class pitch and toss school'. O'Malley replied that only people of 'very delicate sensibility' would find the contents objectionable. This wasn't good enough for Oliver J who managed to have the issue listed for a late night debate slot reserved for 'urgent' matters.

In the Dáil chamber he quoted from *Guests Of The Nation*. One line really riled him: 'The capitalists pay the priests to tell us about the next world so that you won't

notice what the bastards are up to in this.' This, he
charged, was not the proper stuff to be teaching children,
many of whom were perhaps preparing for a religious
vocation. He objected to the words 'bleeding' and
'bastards', raising sniggers from the government benches.

This sort of language might be acceptable to Fianna
Fáil, he charged, but responsible parents would not stand
for it. He cited other taboo expressions in the text such as
'poor bugger' and 'Ah, for Christ's sake'. There was worse,
though. O'Faolain's *The Trout* was 'most suggestive'. He
read aloud: *'Her pyjamas were very short so that when she splashed
water it wet her ankles. She peered into the tunnel. Something alive
rustled inside there. She raced in, and up and down she raced, and
flurried and cried aloud, "Oh, gosh, I can't find it," and then at last
she did. Kneeling down in the damp she put her hand into the slimy
hole. When the body lashed they were both mad with fright. But she
gripped him and shoved him into the sewer and raced, with her teeth
ground, out to the other end of the tunnel and down the steep paths to
the river's edge.'*

The Minister asked if Deputy Flanagan had read the
story in its entirety. 'Very suggestive,' replied Oliver J,
without answering.

The Minister closed the 'urgent' late night debate with
the cryptic comment: 'If the mentality of Deputy
Flanagan is like that of the unfortunate girl who went into
the tunnel to catch a trout and not to catch anything else,
may the Lord have mercy on us all.'

The Seventies brought a fresh threat to the endangered
world order of 1943 – the fear that artificial contraception
might be legalised. Condoms were more evil than bad
housing, and bad housing was pretty dangerous. Oliver
J fervently held that: 'Bad housing is fertile soil for com-
munism and every other sort of -ism. Fertile soil

for lawlessness, fertile soil for every kind of juvenile delinquency.'

Deputy Flanagan pointed out that every vote against the condom 'is a vote against filth and dirt . . . Coupled with the chaotic drinking we have, the singing bars, lounge bars, the side shows and all-night shows, the availability of condoms will, in my opinion, add more serious conse- quences to those already there. You do not quench a fire by sprinkling it with petrol.'

In 1971 the *Sunday Independent* had the temerity to label Oliver J as 'the prime idiot' of Leinster House, because of his entrenched conservatism and the profound stupidity of some of his views. This criticism stung the Deputy into arguably his most inspired litany of sustained drivel. It was delivered to a Fine Gael meeting in Mountmellick.

He set out by launching an attack on the 'Johnny-come- latelys' in Leinster House who wanted to legalise contra- ceptives. With the Jews seemingly forgotten about, he contended that artificial contraception constituted 'the most serious challenge to this nation in a century'. He stated: 'The people who are behind the demand for a change in the law have not been elected by the mass of the people, and it is doubtful if they ever would, and the country must realise that they are new in public life and do not even know their way around Leinster House.

'The Irish people should give serious thought to what the intellectuals of our Parliament have in store for them. The demand for a change in the law in this regard is called for by professors, journalists, economists, the doctors of everything and of nothing. They regard themselves as having a monopoly of brains, ability and intelligence. They pride themselves with knowing all things for all men, but when it comes to the real essentials of life they are the most ignorant bunch you could imagine, as with all their intelligence they display great ignorance in relation to the law of God. While some of them profess to be Catholics they openly treat the teachings of Pope Paul VI with contempt, and laugh, sneer and jeer to try to belittle the advice and guidance given by the bishops of this country on a matter in which they have spoken for the good of the nation. God save Ireland from intellectuals.'

Allowing himself a little pat on the back, he continued: 'It is as well for the Irish people that there are in high places, a few poor ignorant men in public life, looked down on by the intellectual know-alls, but who are not afraid to stand up in defence of the law of God in a Christian country.'

He denounced calls by the *Irish Times* and *Sunday Independent* 'for calm discussion' on the question of contraception. There was no scope for *any* discussion on that issue. In Oliver J's version of democracy, Catholic legislators had a duty to submit to the guidance of the Catholic hierarchy. Anyone who wasn't with him was agin him. And agin God.

He asked of the *Irish Times* and *Sunday Independent*: 'Do they accept the law of God? Do they accept the teachings of the Pope? Do they ignore and scoff at the advice and guidance of the bishops of Ireland, who have advised as to what is for the common good of this nation . . . I would like this clearly answered and none of the "silly-billy" talk about calm discussion on a matter of so vital concern. Now is the time to talk, loud and clear and in strong tones, not when it's too late and the laws are passed and the permissive society have achieved the law of the jungle in preference to the law of God . . . No leading articles or "prime idiot" titles will prevent me as a Catholic deputy from standing four square against all and every odds in defence of the law of God.'

He wasn't finished yet: 'A computer must be fed with truth and correct material in order to produce correct results, and so it is with our conscience . . . In Ireland today conscience can be stretched very far and is used as excuses for all things.' His party colleague Garrett Fitzgerald was guilty of stretching conscience too far, he said. He noted that Deputy Fitzgerald had made a speech on the topic of contraception with 'no reference to the law of God'. Deputy Fitzgerald was an intellectual, the dirtiest word in Oliver J's vocabulary.

He blustered down the home straight. 'The handful of intellectuals demanding this change can do untold damage to all future generations . . . I am convinced that there are outside forces at work and using these intellectuals to undermine Christianity and the law of God in Ireland.'

So to the punchline. 'Let us hope and trust that there are sufficient proud and ignorant people left in this country to stand up to the intellectuals who are out to destroy faith and fatherland and to replace the law of God and the law of the land with the law of the jungle. There is no such thing as a liberal Catholic . . . and the sooner our people realise this to be a fact, the better for success and good luck to fall upon our country.'

Oliver J Flanagan couldn't abide stretched consciences in the realm of sexual morality, but he could be surprisingly permissive in areas of direct consequence to the voters of Laois/Offaly. Farmers who were unable to get their heads around the concept of paying tax, for example, had his sympathy. He once explained that: 'Tax evasion might be a sin but tax avoidance is not. And how do you know the difference? D'ya see, if you don't know the difference, how could it be a mortal sin?'

In his later years, Oliver J Flanagan would make regular visits to his own graveside in St Joseph's Cemetery. 'One can look around the headstones,' he explained, 'and think, all problems solved.'

Unless God turned out to be Jewish.

WHITE SHOES, WIND JAMMERS, THE HAIR ALL FIXED

Chris Cary Brings Glamour To Ireland.

Who? Chris Cary AKA Spangles Muldoon AKA the Bossa Nova.
When? He was the kingpin of Ireland's 1980's radio pirates.
What? After leaving Ireland, he reached for Murdoch's Sky.
Where? In Britain, where he ended up breaking out of jail.
Why? He'd been imprisoned for a £30 million fraud.

'Chris Cary treats the Irish the way I'd treat the blacks.' That condemnation was issued by 'Captain' Eamonn Cooke, the wicked godfather – he was jailed for child sex abuse in 2003 – of Dublin's radio underground. Happily, Cooke never got to run a cotton plantation. Cary, on the other hand, ruled Ireland's first super-pirate with an iron fist, a sharp tongue and a brass neck.

Englishman Chris Cary – Spangles 'The Goon' Muldoon to his listeners – began buccaneering in the Swinging Sixties with the legendary seaborne pirate, Radio Caroline. His next port of call was the infant home-entertainment sector where he had a hand in pioneering the first TV video game (two lines and a dot that went blip, blip and vaguely resembled tennis). Considerably enriched, Cary took the post of station manager with Radio Luxembourg. He then moved into pocket calculators and prototype personal computers. Inventor Clive Sinclair claimed that Cary plagiarised his work. They sued each other. Sinclair won, except in the lucrative US jurisdiction.

Chris Cary arrived in Ireland in 1980 determined to shake up a dull broadcasting scene and make a packet. He set up Sunshine Radio with Robbie Dale – teething troubles included Captain Cooke chopping down their aerial – but the pair quickly split because Dale insisted on having some talk content. Loud, brash and in-your-face, Radio Nova was created in the image of its maker. When it launched in 1981, Cary boasted that Nova would be 'the McDonalds of radio'. Complacent, tame and meek, the existing stations were blown away in the battle for listeners and advertising revenue. In less than a year, Nova had more listeners than RTÉ Radio 2 (now 2FM).

The Bossa Nova prided himself on his reputation as a tyrant. Asked what he did for amusement, Cary replied: 'I have a row.' One employee observed: 'He treats people like toys in a game.' Cary docked a day's pay from one deejay, who protested that he'd only missed his shift because he was in Britain on station business. Cary's staff worked in constant fear of being fired on a whim. This was known as 'Van Halening', a reference to Cary's dismissal of one DJ because the jock's spoken introduction to Van Halen's *Jump* was 'too long'.

Having said that, some of the station's deejays provided compelling evidence that Cary's instinct to curb their chatter was spot-on. In June 1983 Nova's John Laurence told his listeners: 'This is the birthday of George Orwell, who predicted the end of the world in 1984. Was Orwell right? Let's stick around another year and find out.'

From 1981 to 1986 Nova coined it big time. A self-proclaimed union-bashing Thatcherite, Cary espoused the conspicuous consumption of the age. He acknowledged that his staff regarded him as something of 'a cunt', but he was proud of what he'd done for them. He boasted:

'There are guys working in this building that have nice cars, white shoes, the wind jammers, the hair is all fixed. When they first came here they arrived on bikes, the hair was all unfixed.'

Chris Cary flew the coop from Nova in 1986. He blamed the despised National Union of Journalists for the closure – the union had picketed the station ever since he summarily sacked fourteen staffers in 1984. In an affidavit to the High Court, one of the sacked staff, newsreader Ken Hammond, said that Cary had threatened to smash his face in if he continued to picket the building.

In fact the real reason that Cary left Ireland was because his business partner had called in the receiver. The partner had paid £60,000 for a quarter of Nova. Or so he'd thought. In fact, the company he'd bought into owned just a few fittings and 80,000 bumper stickers. Any equipment of value was being leased by Nova from an English company. The highly unusual lease arrangement said that the more the station earned, the more it paid in leasing fees. The owner of the leasing company was – surprise, surprise – Chris Cary. Leaving his wife behind in Dublin, Cary settled into Surrey grandeur with his long-time girlfriend and his money.

Shortly before leaving his creditors high and dry, Cary ruminated on his options if Nova went under. 'I'll go and learn about TV,' he said. And so he did. He learned how to mass produce illegal Sky decoder cards and how to flog them for up to £450 a go. Naturally, BSkyB took umbrage and called in the law. Sensing he was about to have his collar felt, Cary liquidated his assets and moved into rented accommodation. In 1998 he pleaded guilty to defrauding BSkyB of up to £30 million. If he was expecting a light rap on the knuckles he was to be sorely

disappointed. He got the maximum four years imprisonment allowable.

After five months in jail, Cary's bid to have his sentence
appealed was turned down. Ten days later he told staff at
Ford Open Prison that he was going to fetch some
compost from the prison farm. On the roadway beside the
farm a white Peugeot pulled up and he made good his
escape. British police speculated that Cary had holed up in
Spain and that there was little prospect of his capture. But,
it was reported, Sky's owner Rupert Murdoch was not
going to give up so easily on the man who had taken him
for £30 million. Private detectives hired by Sky tracked
Cary to New Zealand. He was bundled back to Britain to
serve out his full term in a high-security prison.

Cary had a stroke in jail and was left partially paralysed.
After being released in 2001 he set up home on the Isle of
Man. Late in 2003 he announced on his website that he
intended applying for a licence to start a new Dublin
station, together with a radio training academy to nurture
local talent.

FLUKY WEATHER IN DUBLIN BAY

The Tailteann Games Are Born Again.

Who? The scattered children of the Gael.
When? 1924, 1928, 1932.
What? The ancient Aonach Tailteann festival was revived.
Where? In and around Dublin, with Croke Park the crucible.
Why? To unite the people through an 'Irish race Olympic'.

The early weeks of 1922. The infant Free State was battered and battle-weary, but it was also a time for optimism and application. There was much to do. The Shannon had to be damned to provide jobs and electricity. National piety levels were soaring but there was still a whole outside world that needed to be kept-out through more and better censorship. A 100 percent Irish-speaking nation was still several years away.

But the years of strife since 1916 had sundered families and communities. There was a lot of bad blood circulating. What was needed was a national pick-me-up, something to make a divided people feel like one big happy family once again. And so it was decided to revive the ancient Tailteann Games.

The two dates most commonly given for the start of the original Aonach Tailteann are more than a millennium apart – 1829 BC and 632 BC. Tradition has it that the first Olympic Games took place in 776 BC. Held at the royal site of Tara over nine days, the Tailteann Games featured daytime competitions in horsemanship, athletics, swimming, spear-throwing, hurling and chariot-racing. The evenings were devoted to music, drama, art, singing, oratory, storytelling and dancing. Ireland's High King would present the champions with jewelled ornaments and rings of gold.

In the words of the *Irish Independent*, the reborn national games would represent 'a racial re-union for the scattered children of the Gael'. In the Dáil in February 1922, JJ Walsh submitted a programme of events for the first modern 'Irish race Olympic' to take place in August of that year. The lengthy list of events included rowing, motor-boating, motor-cycle racing, yacht racing, step dancing and band competitions.

JJ Walsh proudly declared: 'It will be seen at once that the foregoing is at least twice as comprehensive as anything hitherto attempted in foreign countries.' On another occasion that year, TDs debated the provision of £10,000 for the upgrading of Croke Park to host the Games. When one deputy questioned giving a big lump of state money to a private organisation, the same JJ Walsh defended the grant, pointing out: 'The GAA, as all of you know, suffered very severely during the last three or four years . . . mainly through the fact that its members had been the principal contributors in the fight against England.'

Unfortunately, the games that were to bring together the Irish race in friendly competition in August 1922 had to be scrapped when niggling rivalries and resentments erupted into a full-scale Civil War in June of that year. The inaugural modern tournament was postponed until 1924.

As it transpired, the delay proved a boon because 1924 was Olympic year and the home games were able to piggy-back on the bigger event, promoting themselves as a warm-up tournament for Irish and international competitors bound for the Paris Olympics. However, when the official souvenir programme of the Games was published some weeks in advance, one TD urged the Dáil's finance committee to 'withdraw this book from circulation – it is un-Irish'.

Deputy Cahill told his colleagues: 'Turning to page 163, we find under "General Information" a list of the principal churches. The first page is devoted to the Episcopalian Church. Now the vast majority of the people of this country are Catholics, and yet we find the list of Catholic churches relegated to a secondary position, and dismissed with a total of seven. What impression will this create in the mind of visitors to the Aonach?' He also objected that the booklet contained: 'Not one word about the signatories to the Proclamation of Easter Week, 1916.' He was furious to see the Royal Hospital, Kilmainham described as 'the Chelsea of Ireland', and he took exception to the fact that, on page 181, a short guide to the Phoenix Park had picked out the polo and cricket grounds as places of interest.

As the opening ceremony neared, Dublin's streets got a lick of paint and rosettes of blue and gold bunting. With the Games underway, Croke Park played host to a festival of gymnastics, archery, hurling, handball, Gaelic football and chess. Plays and poems with a Gaelic theme were performed and awarded. There were Irish dancing competitions, an air display, a mass-choir rendition of a specially commissioned 'Ode' and the mandatory star turn from John 'Count' McCormack.

Ambitious and well-intentioned though they were, the 1924 Tailteann Games fell some way short of racially reuniting the Irish people. Republican heavyweights from the losing side in the Civil War boycotted the ceremonies. Large swathes of rural Ireland ignored the fuss in Dublin.

Right in the middle of the games, there was a strike by
30,000 municipal workers. Protesters marched the
spruced-up streets with placards saying 'We Want Work,
Not Paint And Decorations' and 'We Want Flour, Not
Flowers'. For polite society, the highpoint of the games was
a banquet in Dublin Castle. The strikers engineered a
power cut and the lights went out on the grand occasion.

The next Tailteann Games, in 1928, again managed to
attract a strong contingent of top athletes by closely
shadowing the Amsterdam Olympics of that summer.
Four years later, however, the Aonach Tailteann struggled
to make an impact, coming just days after the biggest thing
to hit Ireland since Daniel O'Connell's monster meetings
of a century earlier. The 1932 Eucharistic Congress was a
religious orgy of, eh, Biblical proportions. Churches stayed
open all night, serving communion to endless shuffling
lines of devotees. The influx of Catholic holymen from
around the world gave the city what passed for a clerical
freakshow – the Sioux priest with his feather head-dress;
the Indian Bishop of Kottayam; the black Archbishop of
Galilee with his flowing white beard. Other jolly sights
included a troop of Dutch Catholic Girl Guides greeting
the Cardinal Legate with a fascist salute. The Congress
ended with a million faithful marching to O'Connell Street
for a final Benediction. The march had a strict pecking
order. Led by a vanguard of 60,000 men, it incorporated
'cardinals, archbishops, bishops . . . judges, foreign ministers
. . . National University representatives . . .'. And, bringing
up the rear . . . 'women'.

With the country basking in the spiritual afterglow of
successfully staging the greatest show on Earth, that year's
Tailteann Games had a tough act to follow. Worse, the
1932 Olympics were happening 6,000 miles away in Los

Angeles, so the Tailteann's international dimension this time was largely imaginary. Most of the team events in this 'feast of manly competition' were contested between 'England', 'Ireland', 'Scotland' and 'Wales'. It was all highly notional, like schoolboys playing 3-and-in will 'be' Manchester United or Sligo Town or Brazil.

As before, just about any non-Brit activity happening on the island was given a 'Guaranteed Irish' tag and claimed for the cause – motor racing in the Phoenix Park, golf, bowling, clay-pigeon shooting, Irish dancing in the Mansion House. Only one marching band entered the Junior Class contest, so no prize could be given, but when 'South Africa' and 'Great Britain' drew their hurling match at Croke Park, the Committee decided they both should have trophies. The boxing was a washout and the yachting regatta fell victim to 'FLUKY WEATHER IN DUBLIN BAY' according to the *Irish Times*.

As the Games petered out, the Dáil began debating the future of Irish sport. Fianna Fáil had just come to power and they planned an 'entertainment tax' on all sporting events. Only one body was to be exempt – the GAA. Fianna Fáil's Deputy Gibbon told the Dáil that this was only fair on the grounds that: 'Association (football) is tainted with professionalism, while rugby suffers from a superiority complex.'

With the superiority complex out of fashion in Irish sport, Ireland's race Olympics had sadly run their course.

ASK THE MEDICAL MEN TO SLEEP WITH A GIRL WHO HAS AIDS

No condoms – that was the deal.

Who? Father Michael Kennedy.
When? September 1995.
What? The world's media camped outside an Irish church.
Where? The seaside town of Dungarvan, Co Waterford.
Why? An 'Angel of Death' terrorised the Sunny South East.

It was early September 1995 and the media silly season was having an Indian summer in the seaside town of Dungarvan, Co Waterford. Camera crews from RTÉ, Sky News, the BBC and TV networks across the globe jostled with their print counterparts for a good picture, a snappy soundbite and a decent B&B for the night. This normally serene hamlet of the Sunny South East had been visited by mass hysteria. Sunday mass hysteria.

It all began on the Black Sabbath when Father Michael Kennedy unleashed a homily that no-one present would ever forget. The priest informed his congregation that a young woman, recently returned from London, was deliberately infecting young men in the town with the Aids virus. The unidentified hussy, it emerged, had offered sex to all comers, on one condition – no condoms. 'That was the deal,' stated Father Kennedy. Up to eighty of her conquests, from as far afield as Youghal and Clonmel, could be carrying the HIV infection.

A *Cork Examiner* reporter at the mass broke off from his contemplations and scribbled down some notes.

By Sunday evening the town was consumed with fear and loathing. By Monday all of Waterford – not to mention Youghal and Clonmel – had its knickers in a twist. By Tuesday Dungarvan's faceless 'Aids Avenger' AKA 'The Angel Of Death' was national front-page news. By Wednesday the world's media were camped on Father Kennedy's church steps. By now, though, the Doubting Thomases were starting to butt in. 'But this, but that…' said the medical experts, pointing out that an entire data-bank of statistics flew in the face of the priest's tale.

When it was put to him that all the known evidence contradicted his claims, the cleric retorted: 'Ask the medical men to sleep with a girl who has full blown Aids and they can come up with an answer themselves.' Hardly scientific, or rational even, but it made good copy. Father Kennedy insisted that he held his sensational information in strictest confidence and wouldn't be divulging it to either the gardaí or the South Eastern Health Board.

He assured the doubters that one local youth had come to him fearing he had contracted the virus, and when he got himself tested it turned out his fears were well founded. Four friends of the unfortunate young man had also told him they were similarly afflicted. He insisted: 'I went out to one of them this morning and saw the certificate proving he was HIV positive. He and his family are adamant that the others have certificates also confirming they are HIV positive. These four and their families have also told me they are HIV positive and I believe them.'

By Thursday, the people of Dungarvan were already tiring of being the centre of attention. On Friday a member of the Southern Health Board called for Father Kennedy to face prosecution if he didn't pass on potentially life-saving details to the authorities. The priest then claimed that the woman in question had gone to England to die. He did, however, invite journalists to interview a man who'd been infected. By now, though, there was a widespread suspicion that this was a priest who said more than his prayers. Dungarvan's notoriety as the world's deadliest seaside resort lasted little more than a week. But what a week …

It was never likely that Father Michael Kennedy was going to disappear below the horizon forever. Long before the Aids Angel swept through Dungarvan he had shown a shine for the limelight, initially finding recognition as an accomplished inter-county hurler. Back in 1974 he'd been elected to Birr Urban District Council as a Sinn Féin representative, topping the poll. A distant relation of US President John F Kennedy, he'd had a cameo role in the glitzy 1993 wedding of Aids foundation activist Courtney Kennedy and Guildford Four fit-up victim Paul Hill.

Some observers would have viewed the priest's next two re-emergences as manifestations of the infamous Kennedy curse which has dogged the family ever since the assassination of JFK.

In November of 1998 Father Kennedy released a prepared statement apologising for stepping grievously out of line the previous December. To be more precise, the priest had stepped out in front of a car being driven by retired factory manager Tim McCarthy. The elderly motorist made the mistake of tooting his horn at the cleric. Father Kennedy's rather unchristian response was to storm up to the driver's window and punch the eighty-one-year-old repeatedly in the face. Adding insult to injury – according to witnesses – the holy man's parting words were: 'I hope you die without a priest.'

The assault didn't go to court, with Tim McCarthy explaining: 'I am not a vengeful man.' Father Kennedy agreed to pay an undisclosed sum of money in compensation to his parishioner. The Bishop of Waterford and Lismore took pains to emphasise that the payment hadn't come from church funds. The media were once again very interested in talking to Father Kennedy, but his short statement told them: 'I am of the opinion that any further comment on the matter will serve no useful purpose.'

The following year, 1999, Father Kennedy was in the news again, this time officiating at the society funeral of John F Kennedy Jnr and his wife Carolyn, following the young couple's untimely death in a mysterious plane crash.

CATHOLICS INTERFERING IN ULSTER SINCE 1641

The IRA's 'Best Recruiting Sergeant'.

Who? Ian Richard Kyle Paisley AKA Doctor No.
When? 1926 – present.
What? Aged 23, a 'vision' told him to fight 'Papishes'.
Where? 'Ulster', the Vatican, European Parliament.
Why? To stop the Pope sending secret messages to the IRA.

'O father, we can see the great pan-nationalist conspiracy, with the Pope at its head, sending his secret messages to the IRA.' The speaker was Ian Paisley, keeping his flock on their toes in 1993 with a message that hadn't changed since 1973 or 1953. Pedalling a winning formula of hatred and paranoia, Paisley forged a wildly successful career, a political party and a wealthy church.

Ian Richard Kyle Paisley was written off as a spent force more than once over the decades, but his staying power confounded and dismayed his detractors. Outside Stormont Castle in 1998 as the Good Friday power-sharing deal loomed large, he resembled a knackered Canute huffing hot air at Unionist politicians who were nominally on his own side. Five years later, his Democratic Unionist Party was reborn as the biggest electoral force in Northern Ireland.

Born in 1926, the son of a Baptist minister, Ian Paisley began developing what's been described as his 'cabaret' style of fire and brimstone preaching at the age of sixteen.

He was ordained a minister in 1946 and three years later had a 'vision' that he'd been 'anointed with the power of God' to defend His chosen people from all-comers. In the late Fifties he began to make the world sit up and take notice. Or, in the case of some non-chosen types, duck down and take cover. In 1957 Paisley advised a rally of Protestants in Belfast that 'Papishes' were invading their turf. He told the mob: 'Number 425 Shankhill Road, do you know who is living there? Pope's men, that's who.' The crowd set off down the Shankhill Road on a spree, putting in windows and enthusiastically setting the world to rights.

The pattern was set. Northern Secretary James Prior branded Paisley 'a man who thrives on the violent scene'. Another Northern Secretary, William Whitelaw, noted his 'unrivalled skills at undermining the plans of others. He can effectively destroy and obstruct but he has never seemed able to act constructively.' Maurice Hayes, a long-time acquaintance, wrote: 'He very often filled the atmosphere with an inflammable vapour that other people could and did ignite.'

Paisley quickly became a figure of fear and loathing amongst Northern Ireland's Catholics. They'd been long used to institutionalised discrimination in a one-party police state, but Paisley's inflammatory rhetoric heightened the risk of spontaneous combustion. In the Paisleyite viewpoint, Catholicism isn't so much a spiritual condition as a contagious disease. In 1969 Paisley put the civil rights grievances of Nationalists in a nutshell for British Minister Jim Callaghan. He told Callaghan: 'The incidence of unemployment and shortage of houses can be attributed exclusively to the papal population. These people breed like rabbits and multiply like vermin.'

In 1958, a Catholic priest suggested that Paisley's naked bigotry wasn't conducive to Christian fellowship. Big Ian's

witty rebuff: 'We know your church to be the mother of
harlots and the abominations of the Earth. Go back to
your priestly intolerance, back to your beads, holy water,
holy smoke and stink and remember we are the sons of
the martyrs whom your church butchered.' He followed
up in 1959 with a blistering attack on the Queen Mum, of
all people, for visiting the Vatican. Grandma Windsor's
audience with the Pope was a clear case of 'spiritual
fornication and adultery with the Antichrist'. Worse, he
predicted that the curse of a vengeful God would fall on
England as a result of this treachery. By way of proof, he
cited the fact that the Queen of Brazil had met the Pontiff
and next thing she'd given birth to a deformed baby.
When Pope John XXIII died in 1963 Paisley led a furious
protest against the flying of the Union Jack at half-mast at
Belfast City Hall. Two years previously he'd called upon
Protestant employers to sack Catholic staff and replace
them with needy Protestants.

In 1977 he claimed that Catholic churches were
doubling as arsenals for the IRA. When he broke bread
with the brutal Philippines' dictator Ferdinand Marcos, the
two men discovered they had something in common. One
of Marcos' newspapers proclaimed that he and Paisley
were at one in denouncing Catholic troublemakers for
using their churches 'as a flag to cover up an army of
conspirators and violators'. On another occasion he
claimed that a theological conference in Belgium was a
flimsy pretext for a sordid gangbang fertility rite. Irish
Primate Cathal Daly, he contended, was: 'The little
serpent-like Cardinal with the skin of a snake on his face.'

Paisley took exception to the fact that, as he put it: 'The
Catholics have been interfering in Ulster affairs since
1641.' He devoted his life to putting the meddlers back in

their place. In 1959 he and a band of yahoos broke up a meeting of Catholics being addressed by a prominent ecclesiastic. In 1962 he travelled to the Vatican to deliver a rant in person. His most infamous set-piece came in 1988 when he was removed from the European Parliament while screaming 'Antichrist!' at the visiting John Paul II. This level of political debate wasn't improved by the Catholic Cardinal Tomas O'Fiach who asserted: 'Ninety percent of bigotry is to be found amongst Protestants.'

An MEP of long standing, Paisley once described the European Union as 'a beast ridden by the harlot Catholic Church', but he reserved some of his strongest venom for Protestant clerics deemed to be soft on Popery. For him, ecumenism is a dirty word, an appeasement with the Devil.

Paisley was never big on appeasement. The Democratic Unionist Party (DUP) was founded in 1971 as a harder-line alternative to the Ulster Unionist Party (UUP) which had ruled the state like a private members' club since partition. Mirroring Big Ian's personality, the DUP set out its stall as a rejectionist party and found a wellspring of support amongst working-class Loyalists neglected by the plumy-voiced gents of the UUP. Given Paisley's persistently shameful use of language, the use of the word 'Democratic' in the party's name rates as just a minor misdemeanour. The DUP was never structured to implement rank-and-file initiatives. It has always been ruled from the top down. Some academics have gone the whole hog and described the party's structure as 'fascist'. As early as 1966, the Northern Ireland Prime Minister, Terence O'Neill, saw in Paisley's scheming 'a parallel in the rise of the Nazis to power'.

When three IRA members were shot dead in Gibraltar in 1988 Paisley quipped: 'I hope this is not an isolated incident.' He was jailed more than once for leading

unlawful assemblies, but his relationship with the Loyalist
men of violence has always been ambiguous. His comments about resisting Southern interference 'to the death'
are legion. Pressed on the methods of this resistance,
however, Paisley's standard fallback line was always that
he'd abide by the democratic will of the people. For the
record, he once warned: 'We are not prepared to stand
idly by and be murdered in our beds.'

Paisley made alliances with masked men when it suited
him to do so. In 1974, he co-operated with the paramilitary UDA to stage the Loyalist workers' strike which
scuttled the North's first attempt at power-sharing. Just a
year later he denounced the self-same UDA as murderers
engaged in atrocities 'just as heinous and hellish as those of
the IRA'. A further two years down the road he was back
in cahoots with the masked men to orchestrate another
stoppage.

Many times he called for the formation of a Protestant
'third force' to tackle the IRA. In 1986, he assembled 4,000
men for a march through the village of Hillsborough in the
dead of night to protest against the Anglo-Irish Agreement
struck up between the British and Irish governments.
Paisley's DUP and the rival UUP were united against the
accord. Jim Molyneux of the UUP articulated broad pan-
unionist sentiment when he complained: 'Why shouldn't
the Pakistan Government look for an Anglo-Pakistan
Agreement to look after the Pakis in Bradford?'

On another occasion a group of reporters were taken to
a hillside in darkness to encounter a militia of 500 men.
Each man brandished a piece of paper, a gun certificate.
Paisley warned: 'I will take full responsibility for anything
these men do. We will stop at nothing.' In 1993, he
claimed that the IRA were plotting his death. However,

back in the Seventies a Protestant minister asked the IRA chief Daithi ÓConaill whether Paisley's life was in danger. According to the cleric: 'Ó Conaill simply told me, "There's no way we would kill Ian Paisley. Paisley is the best recruiting sergeant we've got".' The IRA man observed that whenever Paisley made one of his inflammatory speeches 'a chill goes down the spine of every Catholic in West Belfast, and after that we have no trouble getting volunteers, safe houses and money'.

Money is one commodity that Ian Paisley has never wanted for. For over two decades he was entitled to duel salaries as an MP and MEP. The Free Presbyterian Church he founded in 1951 is now a multi-million pound concern with dozens of outlets globally. It's understood that Paisley, through his church, controls significant tracts of property in Canada, the US and Ireland. The bookshelves in the foyers of his churches are well stocked with volumes of the Reverend's teachings. Tape recordings of his firebrand sermons find a steady market amongst the faithful, along with CDs showcasing the hot Gospel stylings of his party colleague, the Reverend William McCrea. 'I am British through and through,' McCrea once declared. 'When I hear Paddy jokes I laugh at them.'

Legend has it that Paisley initially filled the coffers of his church by insisting on 'silent collections' which dispensed with the noise, inconvenience and plain smallness of small change. While this claim is of doubtful provenance, it fits the popular image of a supercharged demagogue demanding the last drop from his flock. One man with an unhappy experience of Paisleyite collection methods was Andy Pollack, the religious affairs writer and co-author of a book on the preacher. Pollock was present at a Paisley rally in 1986 when he was asked to contribute to the collection

being taken up. In all conscience he felt he couldn't. So
some particularly ardent followers knocked lumps out of
Pollack within a few yards of the big man up on his
podium.

The Free Presbyterian Church will outlast its charismatic
founder. Substantial grants from the North's Department
of the Environment in the 1970s and 1980s helped the
Free Presbyterians to expand their operations at roughly
twice the rate of their presumably unfree co-religionists.
Branches in North America, Australia, Britain, Africa and
the despised Republic are flourishing.

At the beginning of 2004, the year he turned 78, Ian
Paisley announced that he would not stand again for his
European Parliament seat. With a UK general election
due in 2005, speculation mounted about the future
leadership of a party that was always an extension of its
founder's personality. The question arose once before, but
only fleetingly. In 1977 Paisley attempted to organise a
general Loyalist stoppage along the lines of the 1974
Ulster Worker's Council strike which had sunk the
Sunningdale power-sharing agreement. Paisley pledged
he'd withdraw from public life if the planned protest
failed, which it duly did. Undaunted, he simply declared
the action a success and carried on regardless.

The last word on Ian Paisley goes to the late journalist
James Cameron, who remarked: 'Mr Paisley has never had
a good word to say about anyone other than himself and
Jesus Christ, whom he refers to as His Maker – a rather
poor testimonial.'

WHO DOES THAT FUCKING NIGGER THINK HE IS!?!

The moments that blemish a nation's sporting soul.

Who? Ireland's politically incorrect sporting stars.
When? 1930s, 1970s, 1980s.
What? Irish rugby, hockey, football, cycling, plus lots more.
Where? Nazi Germany. Apartheid Africa. Pinochet's Chile.
Why? Because playing with evil regimes makes them *less* evil.

During the years when right-thinking folk everywhere supported a sporting and cultural blockade on South Africa's dastardly Apartheid regime, many stars of Irish sport were tripping over each other in an unseemly scramble to get out to the land of the rand.

The rugby fraternity remained firm friends with the sporting wing of the white supremacist junta throughout most of the Apartheid years. Apologists for this canoodling parroted the deeply offensive, not to say moronic, fiction that rugby tours against all-white teams actually helped *promote* racial integration in South Africa. The tours went ahead against the wishes of the many Irish people who believed it was an obscenity to be playing rugby in the world's most avowedly racist state – not to mention against the wishes of others, most of them GAA hardliners, who believed it was an obscenity to be playing rugby at all.

In 1970 the whites-only Springboks came to Lansdowne Road and 10,000 people assembled outside to protest. Sadly, the gesture was somewhat undermined by the fact that there were three times that number of alickadoos cheering on the South Africans inside. The occasion reached its immortal nadir when protest organiser Kadir Asmal, an exile from Apartheid, was marshalling his anti-racist troops. As Asmal pushed through the ranks of his own placard-brandishers, one of them exclaimed loudly: 'Who does that fucking nigger think he is?'

Rugby's stick-fighting cousin, hockey, also failed to cover itself in glory in its dealings with 'white-is-right' South Africa. The Irish Hockey Union packed off two sanction-busting tours to that country in the seventies. When pressure finally told on the official body in the following decade, a bunch of top players got around the problem by touring South Africa in 1985, as the Irish Emeralds and The Shamrocks.

Cycling colossus Sean Kelly was another who seemingly had no moral qualms about offering his sporting services to the world's ugliest regime. A decade earlier, Kelly took the art of subterfuge a degree further than the jolly-hockeysticks mob. In 1975 Kelly, with sidekicks Pat and Kieron McQuaid, raced in South Africa under false identities as part of a makey-uppy 'British' team. The three amigos were rumbled by a genuine British photo-grapher who smelled a rat. The *Daily Mail* exposed the impostors. The punishment meted out by the Irish Cycling Federation was a seven month ban which was duly reduced to six months, four of which spanned cycling's off-season, handily enough. The International Olympic Committee handed down a more meaningful penalty, banning the three Irishmen from competing in the Olympics for life and denying Kelly his very real chance of a medal at the 1976 Games in Montreal.

Even the Beautiful Game has given rise to moments when Irish sporting dignity has looked either skimpy, threadbare or crumpled down around the ankles. Starved of proper funding, the very first football team to represent post-independence Ireland turned out to play the fancied Bulgarians in a makeshift strip of blue and black. Green shamrocks sown onto their shirts gave the only small clue to their Irishness. The venue was Paris, the occasion the 1924 Olympics.

The Irish squad virtually had to hitch a ride to the Games because JJ Keane, the head of the Irish Olympic Council, was a rabid GAA man who was dead set against the very idea of Ireland being represented abroad at soccer. Starved of funds by the Olympic Council, the FAI was forced to scrape together its fare to Paris as best it could. The newspaper, *Sport*, complained: 'The fund was disgracefully supported, not only by the sporting community but by those from whom not only a response was expected, but due.' According to legend, the rough passage to Paris wasn't made any smoother when French customs discovered that one of the Irish players, Ernie Crawford, was carrying a gun in his luggage. It was for peace of mind, he told them.

A valiant team performance ensured the trip wasn't a complete shambles. In their first fixture as the representatives of an independent state, the Irish players beat Bulgaria 1–0. The joy was short-lived, as they went out to the Dutch in the next round. Robert Murphy, the vice-president of the FAI, was a poor looser. He muttered: 'What makes the defeat so unpalatable was the patent inferiority of the Dutch team.'

Eleven years later, in 1935, an Irish XI turned out to play Germany in Dortmund and came back with a team photo that isn't on prominent display in the boardroom of the FAI's Merrion Square headquarters. It featured the

Irish visitors lined up and giving their hosts a Nazi salute.
When the Germans arrived in Dublin for the return tie
in 1936, a swastika-decorated coach was laid on to meet
them at the airport. Ireland beat the master race 5–2 and
the Dalymount Park crowd cheered the vanquished team
off the pitch with massed Nazi salutes.

The FAI scored an appalling own goal in 1974 when
the Association dispatched a squad to play in Brazil,
Uruguay and Chile. The blood had barely dried on
General Pinochet's murderous coup and many sporting
nations were taking pains to give the newborn Chilean
dictatorship a wide berth. The USSR had even opted to
forfeit a place in the 1974 World Cup Finals rather than
turn-up for the second leg of their qualification play-off
against Chile, leaving the South Americans to go to West
Germany by default.

The Irish association, however, seemed determined that
sport and politics should not mix. The boys in green
trooped onto the pitch of the Nacional Stadium, which
Pinochet had recently used as an abattoir for his political
enemies. The Irish emerged with a 2–1 victory but the
episode left a blemish on the nation's soul.

WE HAVE OUR OWN PEOPLE GOING TO AMERICA

Grandpa Simpson Rakes Up The Past.

Who? Father John Creagh. Lord Mayor Stephen Coughlan.
When? 1904, surprisingly reprised in 1970.
What? An orchestrated campaign to do down the Jews.
Where? The Colooney Street district of Limerick.
Why? The message was: 'Go back to Russia!'

In an episode of *The Simpsons* entitled *Homer The Vigilante*, the venerable Abe boasts that he ran the Irish out of Springfield in 1904. An Irishman pipes-up: 'And a fine job you did too.'

Grandpa Simpson's line was a knowing reference to the infamous Limerick pogrom of 1904, which resulted in the flight of that city's Jewish population. (Strictly speaking, 'pogrom' is arguably too strong a word for what took place in Limerick, as in its original sense it specifically referred to the organised extermination of Jews in Russia.) The sporadically violent persecution and boycott which was orchestrated in Limerick was led by a firebrand Redemptorist priest, Father John Creagh.

In the two decades before the events in Limerick, Ireland's tiny Jewish community had doubled to around 3,000 as new arrivals fled a fresh outbreak of virulent anti-semitism sweeping Russia. By 1904, Limerick had a Jewish population of around 150, most of them living in and around Colooney Street (now Wolfe Tone Street).

On January 11, 1904, in a thunderous sermon, Creagh lashed out at the dwellers of the nearby enclave. He told the faithful that Limerick's working classes were lowering themselves 'to become the slaves of Jew usurers'. They were entering into loan agreements with the 'rapacious Jews' even though they knew that those same Jews were the ones who had crucified Christ. He warned his flock that there were 'no greater enemies of the Catholic Church than the Jews'. Creagh urged an economic boycott of the small community. As the inflamed Mass-goers passed down Colooney Street, they jeered and threatened their neighbours.

The next day, the local rabbi wrote to land reformer Michael Davitt. The worried rabbi informed Davitt that the real reason behind Creagh's attack was that he'd been put up to it by local shopkeepers who resented increased competition from Jewish peddlers. The following Sunday, the priest renewed his incitement during mass. He said that while he wasn't advocating the use of physical force against the Jews, he still wanted the good Catholics of Limerick to 'keep away from them and let them go to whatever country they came from'. That night there were a number of ugly incidents in the Jewish quarter.

The boycott took hold under Creagh's watchful eye. Before 1904 was out, the priest had opened a bank, a shop and the Workman's Industrial Association in his efforts to force out the city's Jews. The boycott had the broad backing of Limerick Corporation, which convened a special meeting to call for the release of a stone-throwing youth jailed for injuring a Jew. One councillor with a blind spot for irony, complained about Jews coming into Ireland when: 'We have our own people walking the streets in their thousands and going to America to seek a livelihood.'

James Joyce first walked out with his future wife Nora Barnacle on June 16, 1904, and that date provided the backdrop for *Ulysses*. The super-humane anti-hero of the book is Leopold Bloom, a Jew, who lives in a Dublin of matter-of-fact anti-semitism. The character who opens the epic is stately, plump Buck Mulligan, a paper-thin caricature of Oliver St John Gogarty, who would go on to win a bronze medal for poetry at the 1924 Paris Olympics. Gogarty's naked anti-semitism dismayed and disgusted Joyce. In one issue of the *United Irishman* newspaper Gogarty wrote: 'I can smell a Jew, though, and in Ireland there's something rotten.'

Ireland's record of accepting Jewish refugees from the Nazi terror before and during World War II was perfectly captured in the infamous refrain: 'We never let them in.' Official documents of the period show that the Irish authorities repeatedly trotted out two 'reasons' why Ireland couldn't do more to aid a people being mercilessly wiped out.

The first 'reason' was that Ireland was a poor country with chronic unemployment that couldn't even provide a living for those born here. While there may have been some merit in that, the second 'reason' had the ring of a sick joke. The argument ran that, while the Irish were by no stretch of the imagination an anti-semitic people, they'd almost certainly *become* anti-semitic if any more Jews were allowed to live amongst them.

The wounds caused by the Limerick pogrom were re-opened in bizarre circumstances by the city's Lord Mayor, Stephen Coughlan, in 1970. Credit unions offering competitive loans had mushroomed throughout Ireland during the 1960s, and the Mayor picked a convention of the Credit Union League to launch an astonishing defence of Father Creagh's 1904 campaign.

Branding the Jews 'extortioners' and 'bloodsuckers', Coughlan told the gathering: 'I remember an unfortunate woman was having a baby and in they came, getting their five shillings a week, ten shillings, seven-and-six, scourging her . . . they took the bed from under her. It is tragic for me as Mayor of Limerick to say this but it is true.'

He informed his gobsmacked audience: 'Father Creagh, in his courageous way, declared war on the Jews . . . At the time Father Creagh declared war on the extortionists he had the support of everybody in the city of Limerick.'

As the row blazed, Alderman Gerald Goldman of Cork Corporation pointed out: 'It is a legal fact that in 1904, as now, the law specifically prohibits the taking of a person's bed.'

Sixty-six years after Father Creagh's crusade, Limerick's Redemptorists didn't feel any need to reappraise their stance. 'There have been faults on both sides,' said a spokesman. He added: 'In fairness to Fr Creagh, it must be stated that, as he explained, in speaking as he did of the Jews he never intended that his words should be taken as encouraging personal attacks on the Jews.'

The Catholic Bishop of Limerick, Henry Murphy, regretted: 'the digging up of past skeletons . . . especially when there is an implication that we today are somehow to be held responsible for events that happened before most of us were born.'

In his final say on the matter, Mayor Coughlan expressed his unhappiness with his audience at the credit union conference for taking him up wrong. He insisted he'd 'only been drawing a parallel'.

In 1990 the good burghers of Limerick sought to make amends for past shortcomings by restoring the city's Jewish cemetery.

'THE GREATEST BLEEDING HEART RACKET IN THE WORLD'

The Irish Sweep That Swept The World.

Who? Joe McGrath. Richard Duggan. Spencer Freeman.
When? The Great Depression to the 1980s.
What? The Irish Hospital Sweepstakes.
Where? The outlaw super-lottery was a world-wide smash.
Why? It offered massive prizes attached to a good cause.

In December 1978, after a five month investigation, an RTÉ investigative team had the scoop of the year within their grasp. The team were in the port of Rotterdam, keeping vigil over a bulk container that, according to its documentation, contained dried milk powder bound for the United States. What the reporters knew was that, concealed in the cargo, there was six million dollars worth of contraband Irish Sweepstakes' tickets.

The mission had been a success. Now, there was nothing left to do but tip-off the Dutch authorities and film the bust to give the story its fitting dramatic ending. The crew contacted RTÉ headquarters back in Dublin to get the go-ahead. It never came. Montrose got a bad case of the jitters. The reporters were instructed to say nothing and come home. The smuggled consignment went through undetected. The TV programme that had consumed five months of time and resources was quietly shelved.

Five years earlier, in 1973, Joe MacAnthony of the *Sunday Independent* had had better luck in getting out a report on an operation branded 'the greatest bleeding heart racket in the world' by Canadian police. MacAnthony's luck didn't hold, though. He won a Journalist of the Year award for his report – which estimated that the Sweep owners had amassed a fortune of £100 million – then, shortly afterwards, found himself emigrating to Canada in search of work. The *Sunday Independent*'s editor, Conor O'Brien, lost his job and the title itself changed owners before long.

Six months after MacAnthony's exposé, a current affairs magazine was about to go to press with a follow-up investigation. The July 1973 issue of *Profile* was pulled by its publisher, Hugh McLoughlin. He rubbished his own organ's cover story as 'second-hand', adding: 'There's nothing illegal about the Sweep's activity in this country – it may be illegal abroad.'

Hospitals Trust Limited was a huge advertiser, which gave it substantial clout over a tame Irish media. The private owners of the Trust, which was set-up as supplementary funding for the health service, were generous with their political donations across party lines. One of the few politicians ever to be openly critical of the Sweepstake was Dr John O'Connell. In a 1976 Dáil debate, O'Connell told the House: 'I have been intimidated by people in the last few months in regard to the Hospitals Sweepstake telling me that unless I voted for [continued support for the Sweep] there would be serious repercussions. There is a smell about it. I have been intimidated by people – not in the House – that there would be serious repercussions if I did not vote for this Bill. I would be smeared in my constituency – this was conveyed to me just two weeks ago, last Sunday week – that I would be smeared in my constituency and everything done to get me out. I am not happy about the Hospitals Sweepstake. It has a smell about it. It has damaged our good name abroad.'

According to one published report, when the *Daily Express* in Britain was preparing a damning exposé, the late Paddy McGrath of the Sweep dissuaded the newspaper's owner, Lord Beaverbrook, by threatening to have him shot.

Paddy McGrath inherited his position and his massive fortune from his father, Big Joe McGrath, the motive force behind the fantastic global scam of the Irish Hospital Sweepstakes.

On a spring day in 1966, Big Joe McGrath drew the final breath of a long, extraordinary life. Still working in his eigthieth year, the former IRA man and Westminster MP collapsed at his desk in the Sweep's headquarters in Ballsbridge.

Government ministers, bishops and industrialists led the clamour to pay tribute. President de Valera saluted Big Joe's heroic deeds, his noble spirit and his good works. Spencer Freeman, the last of the Sweep's founding fathers, said of his late partner: 'He was a glutton for work.'

Big Joe McGrath was a glutton alright, but not just for work.

By the time of his death, McGrath had parlayed political pull into fabulous wealth. His empire embraced Waterford Glass, Donegal Carpets, a vast property portfolio, stud farms, stables and an imposing mansion in Cabinteely. McGrath owed his wealth to the Irish Hospital Sweepstakes, but his place in history was secured long before he embarked on that audacious swindle. Big Joe pops-up Zelig-like throughout the formative events of this State.

McGrath cut his teeth selling newspapers as a boy. In his teens he worked alongside the young Michael Collins in Craig Gardiner accountants. McGrath graduated to the ITGWU, administering the union's insurance schemes.

Big Joe became an acolyte of firebrand Labour leader Jim Larkin and was at Larkin's side during the bitter 1913 Lock Out when an alliance of big employers forced 20,000 Dublin families onto the breadline. McGrath later stood guard while James Connolly printed his inflammatory Workers' Republic manifesto on an illegal press in Liberty Hall.

McGrath's role in the Easter Rising landed him in a succession of English prisons. In 1917, Michael Collins brought him under the IRA's intelligence wing. In 1918, he was jailed again. By the time he walked free in 1919 he'd been elected a Sinn Féin MP. He refused to take his seat and sat in the outlawed first Dáil of 1919.

During the Treaty negotiations with the British which would plunge Ireland into Civil War, McGrath couriered messages between de Valera in Dublin and Collins in London. When the split came, he stuck tight by Collins. He was made Minister for Labour in the first Free State government.

In 1922, a bookmaker named Richard Duggan approached WT Cosgrave's government proposing to run a sweepstake lottery with the proceeds going to Dublin's Mater Hospital. Puritanism was the new black and several ministers were dead against sanctioning gambling to any end. Besides, Duggan had something of a shady reputation. Back in 1918 a German U-boat had sunk an Irish mailboat, *The Leinster*, which had been carrying racegoers to England. Five hundred people lost their lives. Duggan set-up a lottery to raise funds for the victims' families, but it was widely suspected that he was the main beneficiary of the moneys raised. After consulting with his Minister Joe McGrath, a sceptical WT Cosgrave decided that Duggan's offer to aid the Mater was too good to refuse.

The sweepstake was a hit. The Mater got its money but it was widely believed that Duggan, who by now had moved his HQ to Switzerland, had made another bundle. Inevitably, others wanted to get in on the act. An unedifying game of 'My Good Cause Is Better Than Your Good Cause' broke out between would-be sweep promoters.

The puritanical Justice Minister Kevin O'Higgins complained: 'The carpet in my office has been worn out by people whom I never suspected of being philantrophists.' One Labour TD warned: 'Ireland is to become an enlarged kind of Monte Carlo.' Future sweeps were banned, but those already licensed could go ahead and Duggan moved another windfall off-shore to Switzerland.

Meanwhile, Joe McGrath had other, weightier, matters on his mind. Trouble was brewing in the Free State Army, with rivalries emerging between officers who'd fought on opposite sides in the Civil War. McGrath had been instrumental in integrating former IRA fighters into the force.

In early 1924, the Cosgrave government announced that it was going to downsize the Army from 51,000 to 18,000. There would be no golden handshakes, no redundancy packages. Two senior officers were literally up-in-arms over the lay-offs. They absconded from their barracks with guns and ammunition and, acting 'on behalf of the IRA organisation', presented a list of demands.

In response, the government demanded unconditional surrender. McGrath argued for a middle path. He stormed out of a cabinet meeting threatening resignation. Hours later his home was raided by troops searching for the mutineers. McGrath was affronted at the suggestion that he was in on the mutiny.

Shortly after, troops surrounded a pub where the missing officers and 20 or 30 disenchanted soldiers were

up to no good. A siege developed. McGrath arrived on the
scene and persuaded the plotters to come out with their
hands up. They were given beer and spirits for their truck-
journey to jail.

Feeling that he'd been ill-used by his cabinet colleagues,
McGrath carried through his resignation.

After recharging his batteries, McGrath re-emerged in
a role that we'd recognise today as that of 'consultant'.

In 1925, the rural electrification scheme began. The
Shannon was to be dammed at Ardnacrusha and a big
power plant erected. The German firm Siemens won the
construction contract. But a spate of labour relations
disputes threatened to cripple the project, with hostilities
flaring between Irish labourers and their German technician
bosses. For the Irish, the work was punishing and morale was
low. Some took the drastic option of amputating a toe in a
staged accident, and using the compensation from their
employers to buy passage to America.

With his trades union credentials and his glossy political
pedigree, McGrath was acceptable to both sides as the
scheme's highly-paid 'fixer'. Ardnacrusha was up and
running by 1929 and McGrath was on the lookout for a
new wage packet, when his old acquaintance Richard
Duggan unveiled a cunning plan to revive the outlawed
sweepstakes business.

With McGrath bending the ears that mattered in
Leinster House, and the tainted Duggan keeping his head
down, the Sweep organisers managed to cut a suspiciously
sweet deal with the Irish authorities. The government not
only gave the Irish Hospital Sweepstakes its blessing, it
drew up – with McGrath's guidance – the most astonishing
piece of legislation inviting the new organisation to furnish
bogus accounts.

Sweepstakes were illegal in almost every country in the world. Duggan's idea was to make Ireland to gambling what Switzerland was to off-shore banking. It was argued that the benefits to Ireland's crumbling hospital system would balance any moral deficit in the set-up.

The legislation permitted the Sweep to publish accounts that excluded 'all commissions, prizes and other remuneration given in relation to the selling of the tickets'. In effect, this was a palm-greasers' charter, a licence to bribe whichever lawmen and officials needed to be bribed in big Irish-American markets like Britain, the US and Canada.

McGrath recruited old IRA comrades to fill the administrative posts in Ireland, and to create a distribution network abroad. The individual United States were categorised into 'Hostile', 'Neutral' and 'Non-Hostile' for smuggling purposes, with different methods employed according to category. In its secrecy, its subterfuge and its disregard for what it regarded as bad law, the Sweep would share many characteristics with the Republican movement.

Duggan and McGrath brought on board Spencer Freeman who was to become the Sweep's master publicist. Born in Swansea, he was bright and brave, an old-style adventurer. He had risen to the rank of British Army Captain in the First World War. In the heady early years of the Irish Hospital Sweepstakes, Freeman choreographed lavish spectacles for the thrice-yearly draws. These extravaganzas lifted the pall of drabness that hung over Ireland in the thirties. Each grand draw was An Event, sanctified by Dublin's Lord Mayor, the Police Chief, politicians, sporting heroes, motorised floats, Grecian maidens and processions of little blind boys. Newspapers and newsreels would carry the pageantry around the globe, a twinkle of stardust in the gloom of the Great Depression.

With their first Sweep in 1930 – where the holders of drawn tickets would see their fortunes rest on the outcome of the Manchester November Handicap – the intrepid trio struck a chord that chimed around the planet. The $2,000,000 prize fund – the biggest ever heard of – found claimants on four continents. From Athens to Anchorage newspapers splurged on the pageantry of the Dublin draw, on Glorious Devon's romp to victory, but most of all on the dream-come-true stories of everyday folk made rich beyond imagining.

Britain had produced forty of that first Sweep's 76 winners and the buzz proved contagious. From Orkney to Jersey the nation launched itself gleefully into the throes of Sweepmania. Cinema audiences lapped up the fairytale beginning, middle and ending with ravenous eyes. Newsreel films of the big draw were re-packaged with footage of the Manchester race, and then re-run again with shots of the prizewinners receiving their cheques. It was still November 1930 but already the scramble was on to procure tickets for the second Sweep. For millions of people the Aintree Grand National in March couldn't come soon enough.

Meanwhile, Dubliners marvelled at the deluge of hard currency pouring down on their cash-strapped former second city of Empire. Ticket applications for the second Sweep clogged the mail service. Overnight, the new enterprise had leapfrogged the Guinness Brewery to become the country's biggest cash turnover business. The Bank of Ireland had to recruit extra staff to cope with the haystacks of international banknotes choking the Sweep's coffers.

Sweepstake headquarters was also creaking under the bountiful harvest. Even the garden of the big Georgian building on Stephen's Green had to be pressed into service as an ad hoc sorting factory. McGrath erected a terrace of huts on the lawn to house 800 young women working long shifts to process the applications and counterfoils in good time for the Grand National. On smoggy spring evenings, scores of young men milled about on the broad footpath outside No 13 awaiting the release of their ladyfriends. McGrath joshed about building – 'an extra hut to accommodate the sweethearts' – but he already had his eyes on a palatial new headquarters across town in Ballsbridge.

Within eighteen more months the Irish Sweep would have over 4,000 women on the payroll, making it one of the biggest employers in the Irish State (the entire civil service numbered just 19,000). But there was another, secret, payroll. Out there somewhere was a shadow workforce that didn't show up on the books. These were the runners, the fixers, the political cronies, the officials who looked the other way, the postmen who redirected the mail arriving from Britain and America with bogus addresses (naturally, marking a letter 'Irish Sweep, Dublin, Ireland' invited confiscation by US or UK officials). Precisely what proportion of the Sweep's vast income was directly reinvested in bribery and corruption was known only to Joe McGrath and his partners. But it was substantial, and – thanks to the lovey-dovey deal struck with the Irish government – it could all be written off as legitimate business expenses.

The 1931 Aintree Grand National was set for Saturday, March 27. The gala draw would take place in Dublin three days earlier. As the twin deadline approached, the hype snowballed. The Sweep's promoters took out full-page adverts in British and Irish newspapers. 'WILL IT BE A MILLION?' the big-type tantalised, hoping to sway waverers. Yes, a million and the rest. The prize fund closed at a breathtaking £1,181,815 (nearly $6,000,000), triple that of the previous November's inaugural draw.

Advertising copywriters piggybacked the craze. One motor advert averred: 'You Don't Need To Be The Winner Of A £1,000,000 Sweep To Own An Austin Seven – £153.'

And something for the morning after: 'Let's Have A Consolation Draw – Let's Draw A Paddy Whiskey.'

Extra trains were laid on to accommodate the last minute dash of ticket-buyers arriving from Britain. Two-thirds of the tickets for the second draw were sold across the Irish Sea, where 2,600,000 people languished on the dole. For the British authorities this haemorrhage of hard cash from a crippled economy was a deplorable scandal. For the millions of Britons hellbent on having a flutter, the Sweep was a bewitching chink of light at the end of a long dark tunnel.

The morning of the big draw arrived. 'THE WORLD'S EYE'S ON DUBLIN TODAY' proclaimed the *Irish Times*, without fear of contradiction. The paper added that 'phone lines between Dublin and London will be almost entirely monopolised' by the events taking place in the Mansion House, official residence of the city's Lord Mayor. In anticipation of another global spread of winners, the promoters had a battalion of linguists on standby to cable congratulatory messages in Dutch, French, Italian, German, Spanish, Greek, Arabic and Chinese.

Once again, Spencer Freeman choreographed a lavish parade that lit up the drab streets of Dublin. Once again the great and the good lent the affair a veneer of respectability – the Lord Mayor, the Garda Commissioner, government ministers, sporting heroes – and the world's press chronicled the motorised floats, the weaving procession of clowns, acrobats and carnival figures. Conspicuous by their absence were the little blind boys who'd picked out the tickets for the inaugural draw. Their place on the platform would be taken this time by pretty nurses all in a row, a sexy image upgrade befitting the Sweep's new box-office primacy.

The parade snaked its way to the Mansion House. The dignitaries and reporters were ushered inside for champagne and canapés, while the heaving crowds outside made do with a loudspeaker feed and wrapped sandwiches. Up on the stage the big steel drums gleamed like a row of miniature submarines in dry-dock. Inside the capsules were three-and-a-half million tickets. The drawing of the tickets took place military style – the drums rotating, the nurses plucking and showing with synchronised smiles, the exercise repeated again and again. As the names were matched with horses the details were wired to newsrooms in London, New York, Rome, where special editions would hit the streets while the Dublin bubbly still fizzed.

The Sweep worked like this – tickets were distributed, in books of twelve, from the Sweep's Dublin HQ to agents around the globe. The agent returned the cash for ten tickets, the other two being the agent's commission to sell or keep. The Sweep was a two-tier raffle. At the grand draws in Dublin the wheat was separated from the chaff. At one draw, the nurses, working in shifts, drew 7,200 tickets by hand from the giant drums. Each drawn ticket would be matched with a horse running in a big English race. The Grand National and the Epsom Derby were regularly used because of their newsworthiness, which translated into piggyback free publicity for the Sweep.

The draw before the 1931 Grand National draw reduced the three-and-a-half million tickets in the drums down to a few dozen. Only a handful of individuals and syndicates remained in the reckoning, and they were now plunged headfirst into 72 hours of frenzy before the Moment Of Truth, the race itself. Every newspaper wanted a posed photo, some background and a quotable quote. Neighbours and well-wishers laid siege. Long lost relations came out of the woodwork. For the ticket-holders this was limbo in a goldfish-bowl. They were celebrities but not *real* celebrities, not the finished article. They were each on the cusp of incredible riches, but most of them would end up with a consolation prize of around £1,200. Of itself, it was a handsome enough sum. Set alongside what might be, it was a pittance.

The race favourite for the 1931 Grand National was Easter Hero. The ticket that had drawn Easter Hero belonged to Bob Berkley, a colliery weighman from County Durham in England. Several hundred miles south, in the London suburb of Battersea, a middle-aged Italian café owner called Emilio Scala had drawn another of the fancied runners, Grakle. Across the Atlantic, in the American town of Buffalo, a factory mechanic called Clayton Woods had the ticket for Gregalach.

Bob Berkley, Emilio Scala, Clayton Woods and the others who had drawn fancied runners found themselves tracked down and hemmed-in by bookmakers. The bookmakers were desperate for a share of the hot race tickets and were prepared to offer big money. From the outset, the bookies had identified the Sweep as an effective way of laying-off bets. Bookies hate it when favourites win because it costs them a big payout. If a bookie could buy a share in the ticket holding the race favourite, he could more or less cover himself against taking losses on the race. If the favourite won, the bookie could afford to be down on his book bets thanks to the astronomical return from his winning Sweep ticket. And if the favourite failed to win, then the bookie should be okay on his book bets anyway.

From the moment their names came out of the drum in Dublin, ticket holders were put under immense pressure to sell off part of their potential fortune. First in line to buy shares in fancied tickets were the owners of the Irish Sweep themselves. The practice of buying up their own prizes from nervous punters was known as 'plucking the chickens'. The Sweep organisers were always one step ahead of the bookmakers who wanted a piece of the action since they knew who the 'chickens' were before even the chickens themselves knew.

Spencer Freeman's brother Sydney cut quite a dash in the New York of the thirties. Holding court in the Ritz Carlton hotel, Sydney would track down the holders of promising tickets and make them an offer they could rarely refuse. On one visit, Sydney arrived with a million dollars and made over 300 deals, buying into the entire field of runners bar the 100–1 shots. Sydney was merely a commissioned agent of the Sweep's three real earners, but when the British tax authorities caught up with him in the late Thirties he was able to suggest a settlement of £250,000, a fantastic sum at the time.

Only the very brave, or the very foolhardy, could resist the safety net the bookmakers could provide. Clayton Woods and his five-strong Buffalo syndicate were offered $50,000 for a half-share in Gregalach. The decision had to be made fast, the race was just two days away. If they refused the bookies' offer and Gregalach failed to perform, they'd be left with a mere $6,000 split five ways. After an all-night confab Woods and his companions made the momentous decision to keep the whole ticket. To friend and foe alike this was sheer madness. They'd spurned cast-iron financial security for an all-or-nothing punt on the world's most unpredictable horse race, the English Grand National.

Bob Berkley was more pragmatic. The colliery worker travelled down to London, signed away a share of his ticket for £13,000 – an elegant sufficiency for a lifetime of comfort back in 1931 – and celebrated by taking in a show at the Palladium. Emilio Scala was also persuaded to hedge his bets by the bookies. The accordion-toting family man had emigrated from Italy thirty years earlier hoping to make his fortune. The day before the Grand National he finally pocketed the jackpot of his dreams, selling three-quarters of his ticket for the princely sum of £10,500.

Emilio Scala didn't go to Aintree to watch the Grand National. With his windfall secure in the bank, he shut-up Scala's Ice Cream Parlour on Battersea Park Road and spent race-day sharing a picnic with forty members of his family. He didn't see Grakle, backed at 100–6, gobble-up the formidable Aintree course to come home in a record time of 9 minutes 32.8 seconds. Grakle had won the Grand National, but the name that resonated around the world that evening belonged to Emilio Scala, winner of the greatest cash prize ever heard of: £354,724.

Emilio Scala was celebrated and envied from pole to pole. His name immediately became a byword for glamour and riches, for the little guy coming out on top. Even grubby old Battersea, hitherto known for its power

station and its dogs' home, achieved glamour by association and became 'The Scala Suburb'. The Scala
Cinema subsequently became a well-known Battersea
landmark. One of Britain's top dance bands of the 1930s
and 1940s was the Primo Scala – the name was a cheeky
amalgam of Italian boxing champ Primo Carnera and the
world's luckiest guy, Emilio Scala.

Within days of his hitting the jackpot, the world's press
were speculating that Scala's luck had deserted him in
record time. 'UNEASY LIES THE HEAD THAT WON
THE IRISH SWEEP' trumpeted one headline. Two
cousins from Soho were claiming partnership in Scala's
monster win. Hairdressers Antonio Epicella and Matteo
Constantino claimed that the winning ticket was part of
a pool of 61 held between themselves and Scala. 'He was
almost like one of the family,' muttered one of the claimants,
revealing that they'd be going to court to get satisfaction.

So, instead of arriving in Ireland in triumph to collect
the world's most famous cheque, Emilio Scala landed in
Dublin to fight a court case that might be the ruin of him.
But Scala didn't simply face losing one third of his fortune
to Epicella and another third to Constantino. Before the
race he'd sold three-quarters of the winning ticket to a
bookie – an unauthorised act, said the hairdressers –
meaning that his entitlement would be £99,000, not the
full pot of £354,000. If the Dublin court decided against
him, Scala might have to find £236,000, which he didn't
have, just to square things with the hairdressers. Both sides
settled in for a protracted court battle.

But Emilio Scala didn't have a monopoly on unwanted
melodrama. Across the Atlantic the holders of the second
prize, the Buffalo Five, were reluctant stars in a pot-boiler
of their own.

Clayton C Woods was earning $50 a week as a
mechanic in the Fisher car assembly plant in Buffalo
when, the previous January, an acquaintance came to him
trying to offload the last two Sweeps tickets left in a book.
The price was $5 the pair. Woods took the tickets 'to help
him out', but then found himself short of money for lunch
and tobacco. Woods' wife gave him a dollar from money
she'd been saving for a summer dress, in exchange for a
fifth share in the investment. Woods' brother Kenneth
offered a dollar for another fifth share, and Woods'
brothers-in-law, Elmer and Clarence Batt, also pitched in
a dollar each. The five were now equal shareholders in the
brace of tickets.

One of the tickets drew a horse for the Grand National,
Gregalach. In a scene that was replicated in workplaces
around the world the day after the Dublin draw to match
horses with tickets, the Fisher factory ground to a virtual
standstill as Woods' workmates discussed his chances.
Woods' employers weren't best pleased. 'So the foreman
came over,' Woods later recalled. 'And he said, "Clayton,
you can beat it out of here. You're fired".' When he got
home, Woods found a bookies' agent waiting for him with
the offer of $50,000 – twenty years' wages – for a half-
share of his ticket on Gregalach. With the decision made
to reject the offer, the Woods and the Batts hid themselves
away and awaited their fate.

On March 27, Clayton Woods was guest of honour at
the office of the *Buffalo Evening News*. There, he watched
the AP ticker-tape machine stutter out the result of the
English Grand National. Grakle the winner. Second,
Gregalach. Woods watched in numbed disbelief as the
compositor set up an eight-column headline: 'WOODS
WINS $886,630'. From that moment on, things would

never be the same for the Woods and Batts. They complained of sleepless nights. They pored over travel brochures. Clayton decided on a trip to France: 'I was there in 1918 and it wasn't much fun. This time I'm going to make whoopee.' Clayton's wife wanted a bigger home with a modern kitchen. Kenneth and Elmer wanted to see the world, but first they were going to buy farms for their families and ponies for their children.

But the US government had other plans for the quintet's money. Unlike its British counterpart, the US Revenue was determined to take a hefty cut of the winnings. Brazening it out, Clayton said that if the government wanted more than 25% he'd move to Canada. There was worse to come. Buffalo's city fathers informed the five that under an old law all lottery winnings could be confiscated and used for poor relief. By now, the Revenue had completed their calculations – they wanted more than half the syndicate's winnings.

The lifestyle of the rich and famous was rapidly losing its lustre for the Buffalo Five. They were snowed under with begging letters, petitions, hard-luck stories, charity appeals and investment offers. They couldn't walk the streets without attracting an entourage. Clayton's boss from the factory called on him to offer his congratulations. He found Woods fretful. 'I told him I just couldn't loaf,' said the new tycoon, 'and I would be back at work before long.'

It all got too much. The Woods and the Batts made good on their word and fled Buffalo for Canada, holing up in deep forest where they were safe from prowling reporters, taxmen, beggars and estate agents. After three weeks in exile the five were lured home with assurances that the Buffalo authorities and the US Revenue would cut them a fair deal.

Meanwhile, back in Dublin, Emilio Scala walked out of the High Court a happy man having seen off the challenge of Antonio Epicella and Matteo Constantino. Now he would take that trip he'd dreamed about for thirty years – back to his home village of Isoladel Liri. But the trip turned into a wake when his mother died from the strain of 'too much happiness'. Worse, the Mafia pursued him back to London seeking a contribution to their cause. Somewhat taken aback by the monster they'd created, McGrath & Co decided that in future they'd scale down the size of the prizes and spread the wealth across a greater number of winners.

After the Scala phenomenon, all Britain was awash with Sweepstake tickets despite the fact that their importation was banned. To the unending embarrassment of the authorities, policemen frequently turned up on the lists of winners published in the newspapers. There were redder faces too. In one instance the Mayor of Rye in Sussex was listed as a member of a winning Freemasons' syndicate. Just days before his lucky strike, the Mayor, acting in his capacity as local Magistrate, had fined a businessman for his role in propagating the Sweep.

Unable to stop people betting on the Sweep, the tormented British government brought in legislation that barred them from finding out about it from the newspapers or wireless. The publicity blackout had some limited success, although the Sweep got around the radio ban by becoming the biggest advertiser with Radio Luxembourg, which broadcast into Britain. The smuggling continued apace.

Different countries responded to the financial drain of the Irish Sweep in different ways. Some, like Britain, firmed up their anti-lottery legislation. Others, like France,

Australia and Belgium, decided if you can't beat 'em, join 'em, and set up their own versions. But even as one territory pulled down the shutters, another opened its doors. As Britain took action to repel the Irish pirates, McGrath, Duggan and Freeman were plunging their fingers ever deeper into the biggest honeypot of them all, the USA.

The United States – the land of promise where millions came to make their fortune but where gambling was mostly illegal – was a ready-made market for an illicit flutter. And then there was the Irish factor. Of all the migrant groups in the States, the Irish maintained perhaps the closest links with the old country. Over a couple of generations, continental European settlers would adopt English as their first language, becoming cut off from their mother tongue and motherland. Not so the English-speaking Irish. From 1919, the IRA had organised a highly efficient collection network in the USA to channel home funds for the War of Independence. By the early 1930s the machine was still in place, albeit a little rusty.

The States and Canada were swamped with illicit tickets. At first, these arrived on a modest enough scale, often mailed in hollowed-out religious books. But as the years rolled on the scale and sophistication of the smuggling racket reached industrial proportions. The tickets arrived by land, by sea, by air. In 1948 in a swoop on a liner docking in New York, one million tickets were seized. As late as the 1970s Canadian police declared that only the Mafia had a bigger smuggling network.

In the States a white-collar sales network grew up. Beauty parlours and hair salons played a significant role in the distribution because many women who normally took a poor view of gambling were avid players. At one point the trial of two men accused of selling tickets had to be delayed for two days because a jury couldn't be found of twelve people uncontaminated by the Sweep's contagion.

The task of stemming the tide of tickets fell to the US Postmaster-General, but successive incumbents failed dismally in this duty. One Postmaster-General, an Irish-American named Jim Farley, went so far as to announce publicly that he didn't see much wrong with the Sweep. Suspicions that he'd been bought off were fuelled when, after his retirement, he became a regular visitor to Dublin where he was lavishly wined and dined by Big Joe McGrath. As with Britain before it, the USA slapped a publicity blackout on the Sweep, but word-of-mouth kept it thriving.

For over three decades the Irish Sweep organisation played a lucrative game of cat and mouse with the US authorities, with the cat suspiciously clawless and listless. Attorney General Robert Kennedy was amongst many who fulminated from time to time, but the palm-greaser's charter granted by the Irish government way back ensured that there was never a shortage of obliging blind eyes. On one occasion a gang set up a printing press in Canada to forge Irish Sweep tickets. If the forgers succeeded, the Sweep would suffer long-term damage to its credibility. A logical response from the US authorities might have been to sit back and let it happen. Instead, the FBI prevailed on Scotland Yard to ask the Mounties to crack down on the forgers. The Sweep's supposed persecutors had turned protectors.

On another occasion when a man was arrested in New York for selling Sweep tickets, the cops on station duty spent the whole night writing out receipts for each of the many confiscated tickets so that these receipts could go into the draw in lieu of the real ones so as not to deprive anyone of a chance to win.

In the early days of the Sweep's operations in America, the Mafia presented more opposition than the forces of law and order. One ripping yarn from the 1940s tells of how the Sweep saw off a challenge from the Mexican government. The story goes that the Mexicans tried to grab some of the Sweep's action by mounting a North American lottery. Shrewdly, McGrath placed adverts in the press announcing that the Sweepstakes would be pulling out of America because of administration problems. So the Mexicans enlisted McGrath, with his expertise in the field, to help them set-up. Big mistake. The Mexican Lotto was sabotaged by the Irish who ensured that lots of the money was diverted to Ireland, forcing the Mexicans to abandon the scheme.

The hospitals did less well out of the Sweep than the organisers and, unlike McGrath & Co, the hospitals had to pay government tax on their share of the vastly under-declared proceeds. The Sweep's contribution undoubtedly did make a difference to the Irish health system, even though only a fraction of the total filtered through. Indeed, by the mid-Thirties, flush with new money, the hospitals began engaging in a bizarre game of one-upmanship, building grandiose wings and installing state-of-the-art equipment that there was no call for. When Dr James Deeny took over as the State's Chief Medical Officer in 1944 he discovered that plans for a new children's hospital in Cherry Orchard included provision of a nine-hole golf course for the exclusive use of the consultants.

But as time rolled on the share going to the hospitals looked more and more like the afterthought it was. By the early Seventies a government official described the Sweep's contribution as 'insignificant'.

By then, the golden era of the Irish Sweep had passed. The arrival of the first US state lottery in New Hampshire in 1964 had signalled the beginning of the end. With the USA market shutting down state by state, the Sweep's promoters concentrated on Canada. It was to be their last refuge. The 'well oiled cash register' began to seize up and belated reports began to appear in the North American media about what a rotten scam it had been all along.

HER SHAPELY LITTLE BOTTOM ON A CHAIR IN STEPHEN'S GREEN

It's a man's, man's, man's, man's world.

Who? The uppity women of Ireland.
When? March to December 1981.
What? *Status* magazine – the voice of Irish feminism.
Where? At an advertising confab it was ritually torched.
Why? It didn't know its place and had no horoscopes.

In November 1981, *Status* magazine published a photograph of the 'Officers of the Cork Ladies Football Association'. The line-up featured John Aherne (President), Michael Lynch (Chairman), Christy Burke (Vice-Chairman), Dermot O'Donovan (P.R.O.) and Keith Browne (Financial Controller). There were two ladies in the picture, both of them charged with secretarial duties. The photo appeared under the banner: 'No Comment.'

Status had been launched the previous March with great fanfare. Over one thousand women, amongst them some very prominent figures, attended the birth at a conference in Dublin's Liberty Hall where they voted to approve a *Status* Women's Charter for social reform. Edited initially by Marian Finucane, *Status* had a twofold purpose: to champion the feminist cause in Ireland and to bring down the monthly overheads of its parent publication, *Magill*. The theory was that two titles coming out of the same building would be more cost-effective than one. The practise turned out to be a nasty shock for all involved.

Status got off to a flying start, with Issue 1 selling out in
days. The cover headlines on that first edition included,
'THE PILL: SAFE OR NOT?' and 'IS YOUR SON
SEXIST?'. In her first editorial, Marian Finucane targeted
a potential new audience for the feminist creed: 'There are
categories of women that have been somewhat ignored
both by the media and the women's movement. One of
these I would see as the thousands of women on our farms
in remote towns and villages.'

Issue 1 ran a state-of-the-nation review of the recent
gains made by women in relation to contraception,
property ownership rights and equal pay. The EEC had
ordered Ireland to write equal pay legislation into the
statute books by the closing day of 1975. The government
complied, but then did nothing to enact the laws which
would have entitled a woman to be paid the same as a
man for doing the same work. The Federated Union of
Employers raised furious objections to paying women
equally, claiming that the move would banjax the country.
The Fine Gael/Labour coalition announced it would
defer equal pay until the end of 1977, by which time the
electorate had decided to spare it the burdens of office.

For some commentators, the real problem wasn't
women wanting equal pay, it was women wanting to work
at all. As the debate raged, the Reverend Brother Vivien
Cassels observed: 'There is still a high percentage of
married women working for no valid reason, though they
realise that by doing so they are depriving many young
people from starting their careers in the civil service,
banking or teaching . . . These people are not willing to
forego the perks that a second salary can bring, like the trip
to the Costa Brava, that second car or that well-stocked
cocktail cabinet.'

To leaven the heavyweight mix of politics and polemics, *Status* had celebrities. Issue 1 asked some well-known men what they thought of women. The Reverend Ian Paisley was characteristically obliging, saying: 'You can leave me out of all this.' Previewing his role as lecherous Father Jack Hackett, Frank Kelly revealed: 'One of my earliest memories is falling in love with a couple of nuns in kindergarten.' Ireland's top sex symbol, Gay Byrne, gave the pithiest of replies: 'Sex is why I like women – that's all. Bitchiness is why I don't.' In a roles-reversed piece in Issue 2, Nuala O'Faolain admitted to having a crush on football's permed pinnacle of perfection, Kevin Keegan.

As the months went by, *Status* presented a relentlessly penetrating analysis of Irish life, but it was the read-it-and-weep pickings of the 'No Comment' section that threw the hostile environment of Ireland 1981 into starkest relief. Take the following extracts from a window display at Firstaff Personnel Consultants of Grafton Street in Dublin.

'Receptionist/Typist: Christmas decorating? Why not start with your reception area and employ a girl like Joan. Joan is 25, very attractive . . . Altogether a lovely girl and well suited to her choice of career.'

Continuing on a festive theme, another placement notice from the same firm advertised the merits of a Dictaphone Clerk/Typist: 'Deck the halls with bows of holly!!! How about decking your office with this lovely dolly??? Twenty years old, resident . . .'

An excerpt from the property section of the *Irish Independent* announced that 'a sophisticated computer system will render it immaterial whether the modern secretary puts her shapely little bottom on a chair in Stephen's Green, Sandyford or Santry'. Carrying on the theme, an advert for a new-fangled word-processor listed its advantages as doing '400 words per minute uninterrupted by boyfriends, broken nails or holidays'.

The Deaths column of the *Irish Times* noted the passing of one citizen, with the words: 'He is survived by his wife Bernadette, sons Brendan, Michael and Thomas, and three daughters.'

The upfront laddishness of *Business & Finance* warranted the attention of 'No Comment' more than once. For instance: 'We still await a successor to Ivor Kenny as Director General of the Irish Management Institute. We can reveal that a successor was chosen earlier this year and the candidate – a woman – accepted. Then, women being women, she changed her mind and said "no".'

Reporting on inflation, the same publication on a different occasion came up with the following commentary: 'Spirits led the drink increases at 80.8%. In the clothing sector women's panties went up 86.3% – but at least in that instance it was a case of what goes up must come down.'

Basking in the same spirit of the age, a periodical called *The Grocer* ran an advert for Zero Throwaway Panties. The ad featured a woman, who'd forgotten to put on her top, removing her briefs encouraged by the copywriter's elegant slogan: 'Get 'Em Off!'

In the early days of *Status*, the editorial staff agonised over what types of advertising the magazine could accept without selling-out its feminist principles. There was earnest debate over whether the wearing of perfume, make-up, frills and/or bows ought to be regarded as a woman's right to choose or as something intrinsically evil.

In the event, the agonising over advertising proved to be largely academic. The fashion and cosmetics manufacturers took one glance at *Status* and decided there was no way they'd be spending a penny of their ad budgets with a so-called women's magazine that didn't even have a horoscope. If the boycott of *Status* had stopped there, the publication might still have survived – after all, the magazine could offer other advertisers a substantial and desirable readership of educated, middle-class women. Instead, *Status* met with naked contempt from just about the whole of the male-run advertising industry. At a national conference of advertising executives in Tralee, a group of delegates rounded off an evening's networking by ceremonially setting fire to a copy of *Status*.

In December 1981, despite healthy sales, *Status* went to the wall.

THIS COULD BE OF MAJOR WORLD IMPORTANCE

'It wasn't about great singing at all.'

Who? GF Handel, Frank McNamara, Seamus Brennan.
When? December 1999.
What? The Irish public paid £700,000 to update *Messiah*.
Where? Dublin's RDS, RTÉ and 24 TV stations worldwide.
Why? It was more deserving than a Garda talent contest.

As the clock ran down on the second millennium of the Western calendar, the Irish government set aside £30 million of taxpayers' money and invited ideas for what to spend it on. One citizen suggested that Ireland could use: 'A Liberty-type statue of Jesus or Mary on Howth Head.' Another proposed: 'An artistic exhibition of used under-wear on Dublin's Ha'penny Bridge, featuring celebrity items and a booth for public donations.'

Both submissions were passed-over by the Millennium Committee, together with proposals for 'a national Garda talent competition with regional heats' and 'a national Garda pilgrimage to Lourdes'. However, the Minister for the Millennium, Seamus Brennan, found it in his heart to sign-off £700,000 for the upgrading of *Messiah*, which was premiered by Handel in Dublin in 1742. Minister Brennan had no doubts that the money would be well spent. Indeed, he went so far as to predict: 'This could be of major world importance.'

Of course, Handel's *Messiah* was already of major world importance, but it was very old and it dragged a bit in places. The gifted conductor Frank McNamara had a vision for streamlining the composition for the 21st Century. This vision involved soul divas and wailing guitars and snipping out a couple of the boring bits and bringing in Roger Daltry out of The Who. When Roger accepted the gig, he didn't know *Messiah* at all – 'I don't know the piece at all,' he confessed. 'What's it about?' – but he was sure that he'd quickly pick it up.

Frank's partners on the project dubbed *Messiah XXI* were John Kearns and Bernard Bennett, the two impresarios who'd scored a monster hit in 1996 with the *Faith Of Our Fathers* old-time-religion singsong. As *Messiah XXI* came closer to curtain-up, some people began talking telephone numbers and slipping the word *Riverdance* into conversations. These rising expectations were met with the rising doubts of those tapped for the £700,000.

Seamus Brennan got a roasting on Marian Finucane's radio show from listeners who wanted to know why £700,000 of their money was being put to use breeding, what one caller called, 'a cross between a rhinoceros and a racehorse'. And why, after relieving the public of all that money, were the promoters charging £29 and £39 for tickets to see it?

Minister Brennan replied that *XXI* would cost a hefty two million to stage. He went on to point out that he was 'no expert' on these things, and that it was all, admittedly, 'a bit of a risk'. But the good news was that the nation could enjoy the extravaganza on RTÉ television during Christmas week. Meanwhile, with just 53 hours to go before showtime, the imported star turns – Chaka Khan, Gladys Knight, Jeffrey Osborne and Daltry – gathered in Dublin for their very first rehearsal together.

The two performances of *Messiah XXI* were not an unqualified critical success. Terms employed by reviewers included: 'a pathetic production of breathtaking crassness', 'a corpulent mess', 'greedy showbiz travesty', 'a bit like inviting retired footballers to have a go at *Swan Lake*', 'there were only degrees of awfulness', 'butchered' and 'massacre'. The *coup de grâce* was delivered with the *Irish Times*' verdict that '*Messiah XXI* was as magical as a bucket of vomit'.

The same newspaper's Arts Editor, perhaps feeling that the 'vomit' remark was in dubious taste, rushed into print with a spirited defence of the production. She argued that the *real* problem the critics had with *Messiah XXI*, but which they failed to recognise, was that it was 'hard to categorise'. That, plus the fact that: 'We have a history of formal, private belief and we are in such shocked retreat from a Catholic system of values which we think has failed us that a religious message, emotionally delivered, is bound to have a rough time in the media.'

So there it was in plain language – *Messiah XXI* wasn't just shite.

If the Arts Editor was on extremely thin ice with that line of defence, she crashed beneath with the assertion: 'You have to give Frank McNamara credit for having the idea in the first place.' A legion of critics and a cross section of the public agreed that *Messiah XXI* brought credit on no-one. And as for McNamara having had the idea in the first place – a gospel makeover of Handel's work, entitled *Messiah: A Soulful Celebration*, had been in record stores across the United States since 1992.

In July 2002, the directors of *Messiah XXI* Productions – Kearns, Bennett and McNamara – broke the unfortunate news that the company would not be in a position to make the donation to charity which had been inserted into the terms of its £700,000 grant. The company had pledged to donate ten percent of any profits to Irish charities, up to a total of the given £700,000. The TV rights for the show had been sold to 24 countries, but *Messiah XXI* Productions had racked up accumulated losses of £129,801 on the project. Negotiations to sell the CD and video rights in the US had taken a turn for the worse when the likely buyer died.

But there was a happy ending of sorts when it emerged that Frank McNamara's artistry had not, after all, been wasted on revisiting Handel's meisterwerk. In addition to paying for the modernising of *Messiah*, the £700,000 of taxpayers' money had helped restore the original spirit of the piece, just as Handel would have wanted it. The nation learned this in November 2003 when Marian Finucane looked back over the millennium project with her studio guest, Frank McNamara.

Marian asked: 'Did you get a lot of attack over it?'

Frank replied: 'No, no. Just one of the newspapers, really, that was it. Everybody who was there came up to me and loved it and I still get letters about it from people who found it a very emotional experience.'

He then revealed: 'The funny thing was, at the first performance of it when Handel put it on in London, he didn't employ singers at all. He employed actors to 'sing', because he didn't want the message to be disguised in the coloratura of the sopranos or whatever. He wanted the message to come across, and for him it was a piece of evangelism and it wasn't about great singing at all.'

Phew!

THERE'S A BIG FELLOW CALLED SALVADOR

Fr Michael Cleary Vs Religious Orthodoxy.

Who? The Bingo/Mod/Late Late/Singing Priest.
When? 1960s–1990s.
What? Early on he'd hoped to be 'found out and thrown out'.
Where? Of the Catholic priesthood.
Why? 'Because it meant giving up football and girls.'

Whether his life is viewed as tragedy or travesty, religious orthodoxy was irrefutably never Fr Michael Cleary's strong point. From the very beginning of his vocation he was a square peg in a round collar. Before he entered Clonliffe seminary, the 'Mod Priest' in the making instructed his Earthly father not to throw out his civvy clothes – just in case.

Young Michael felt that destiny had big things in store for him. He was going to make a difference. But how? 'By a process of elimination,' he later recalled. 'I came to the horrifying conclusion of the priesthood. I didn't want it because it meant giving up football and girls, and I was very interested in both.' He blamed the church's screening process for failing him. 'I actually went in hoping I'd be found out and thrown out and I'd satisfy my conscience,' he admitted. 'But I wasn't found out.'

Once inside, Fr Mick gradually discovered that being a priest didn't necessarily mean having to give up football or girls. Or, for that matter, gambling or fibbing or cursing.

Giving up was not in his make-up, especially when it came to cigarettes.

In 1974, he was diagnosed with throat cancer. A serious operation was augmented with a course of painful radio-iodine treatment. His doctors gave him three years to live, ten if he was very lucky. He kept on smoking. Sixteen years later he marked National No Smoking Day 1990 with an unrepentantly bullish article entitled, 'WHY I'M DEFINITELY NOT GIVING UP CIGARETTES THIS LENT'.

Traditional Christian teaching has it that Lent is about self-sacrifice. Fr Michael tailored this to his own ends, deciding that: 'Lenten exercises should be aimed at making us easier to live with, rather than more difficult.' He backed this up with a short parable: 'Some time ago I flew to Bristol. I was almost two hours on the plane and I discovered that Aer Lingus had introduced an experimental total ban on smoking on the route . . . Locked in a small plane up in the clouds, unable to smoke for such a period, I experienced real panic for the first time in my life. The kind hostess offered me a glass of brandy which I declined.'

The offer of the brandy led the fuming cleric to deduce that: 'Apparently, I could get plastered drunk and become a nuisance and a danger, or I could pop pills or shoot heroin, but I could not smoke.' He further added that: 'If even one seat had been reserved for smoking I might not have needed a cigarette at all.' He cautioned: 'We must beware of ending up like Howard Hughes – a multi-millionaire who died from malnutrition in his pollution-free, sanitised and homogenised penthouse.'

Unlike his relationship with the demon weed, when it came to Catholic doctrine Father Mick could take it or leave it. He had no problem with the notion of married clergy, women priests or homosexual relationships between consenting adults. On the other hand he toed the Vatican line on contraception, claiming it rendered the sex act 'as meaningless as a handshake'. Michael Cleary had quite a hang-up about meaningless sex, once bemoaning the fact that: 'Anyone can get a girl to go to bed with him now because far too many girls make sex so readily available now – there's no need for anyone to rape.' Father Mick was a bundle of contradictions. Or, as the blurb on the back of his housekeeper's memoir put it: 'Michael Cleary was a man of many parts.'

One of his parts in particular saw a lot of action. Phylis Hamilton was unexpectedly introduced to it when she was 'a confused troubled kid' of seventeen. He was twice her age and in a position of trust and responsibility. With skilful manoeuvring it became a missionary position. He told Phylis they were man and wife. It was okay to play house together, but it had to be their little secret. Fr Mick practised what he preached about artificial contraception, and the union was blessed with two children.

Michael Cleary never contemplated quitting the priesthood for family life. He was a slave to the spotlight and his Roman collar was the crucial difference between amateur night at Butlin's Mosney and star billing at the Albert Hall. As 'The Bingo Priest' he claimed the dubious distinction of introducing cinema bingo to Ireland. Having paid his dues, he gradually worked his way up the bill, becoming 'The Mod Priest', '*The Late Late Show* Priest' and, finally, 'The Singing Priest'. 'I was third in his list of priorities,' acknowledged Phylis. 'The priesthood came first, then his performing and I was last.' She saw that their double life was like one of his poker games – he got off on the thrill of the bluff, the risk of exposure. The higher the stakes the greater the buzz.

And if damnation shadowed him, salvation was always at hand. Unhinged by the throes of advanced penile dementia, he christened his member Salvador, meaning 'salvation'. On one occasion he wrote to Phylis: 'There's a big fellow called Salvador here and he's coming to Ireland soon. He'll stay in "Ballyer". I told him you would look after him well – he's looking forward to that. He's an excitable guy but I think you'll enjoy him.'

Frisky Salvador contributed to a broader picture of devoted domesticity. On another occasion Michael wrote: 'Believe it or not, I am washing my teeth every day for you. Sounds silly, I know, but it's like something for love. I do it for you and it's a time for thinking for you . . . Skippy is a bit lost, Barbie is still chasing the cars and Salvador is driving me mad since you left. He misses you terribly.'

Michael Cleary played by his own rules and reached the finish line ahead of the pursuit. He'd put one over on us. He'd made off without apology or explanation. Our loss. Phylis had once caught him in bed with another woman. He talked his way out of it. 'All through his life he had a way of explaining things to make them seem normal,' Phylis wrote. His explanation? It was the woman's fault.

Nothing was ever Fr Mick's fault – his womanising, his compulsive smoking, his son's juvenile delinquency, his ending up in the priesthood. He swapped the orthodox clerical life of denial for a life *in* denial.

At the close of her bittersweet tome, Phylis remarks that journalist Paul Williams was 'the ideal candidate to help me write a book on my life because he had almost completed another book on the criminal, the General. I was flabber-gasted at the coincidence.'

Amen.